LEGENDARY LOCALS

OF

# BURLINGTON

## VERMONT

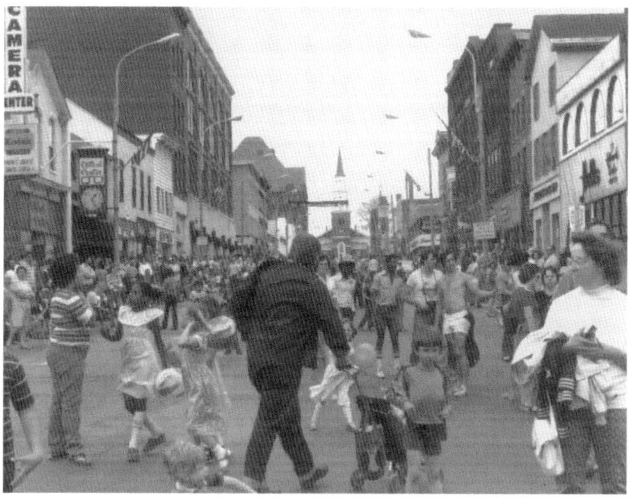

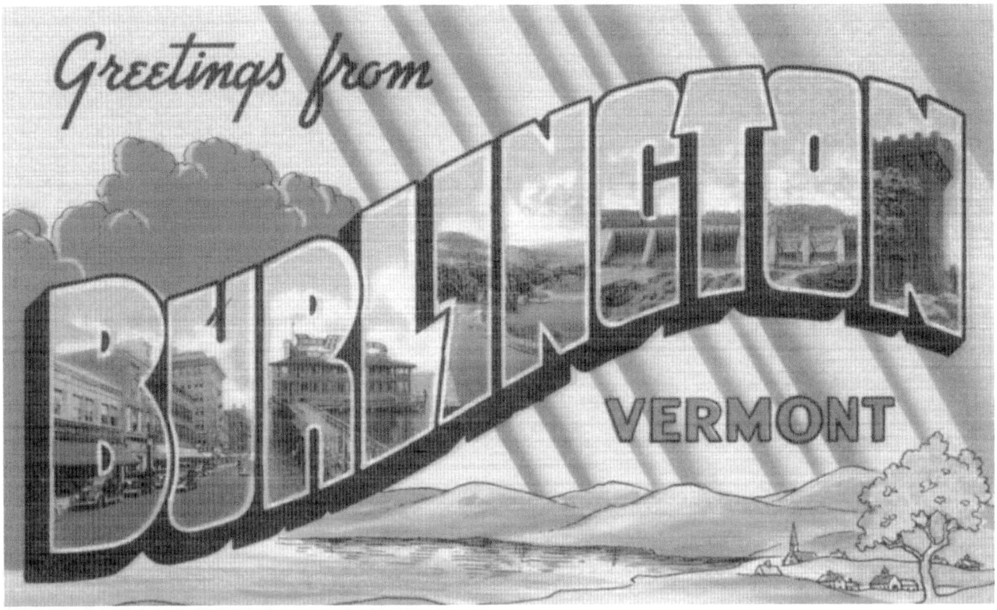


**Page 1:** Church Street
Several years before the creation of a pedestrian mall turned Burlington's main street into a model for cities around the country, Church Street was closed to traffic for a parade in the summer of 1979, and it seemed like the whole town was there! (Photograph by the author.)

**Page 2:** Greetings from Burlington
This Burlington postcard from the 1930s includes a view of the intersection of Church and Main Streets; the original Burlington boathouse on the city's waterfront (rebuilt by the city's parks and recreation department in 1988); one of the power dams on the Winooski River; and the Ethan Allen Memorial Tower (see page 14). (Courtesy of Fletcher Free Library.)

LEGENDARY LOCALS

OF

# BURLINGTON

## VERMONT

ROBERT J. RESNIK

LEGENDARY LOCALS

ISBN 978-1-4671-0066-3

Legendary Locals is an imprint of Arcadia Publishing
Charleston, South Carolina

Printed in the United States of America

Library of Congress Control Number: 2012950197

For all general information, please contact Arcadia Publishing:
Telephone 843-853-2070
Fax 843-853-0044
E-mail sales@arcadiapublishing.com
For customer service and orders:
Toll-Free 1-888-313-2665

Visit us on the Internet at www.arcadiapublishing.com

**Dedication**
*This book is respectfully dedicated to all the other local legends of Burlington who could not be included here due to limitations of time and space.*

**On the Front Cover:** Clockwise from top left:
Bernie Sanders, US senator (Courtesy of Matt Thorsen; see page 115); Nectar Rorris, restaurateur, with "Big" Joe Burrell, musician (Courtesy of Matt Thorsen; see pages 54 and 90); Bonnie Acker, artist and gardener (Courtesy of the Fletcher Free Library; see page 101); Merle Glasston, baseball player (Courtesy of the Glasston family; see page 96); Richard Haupt, musician (Courtesy of Matt Thorsen; see page 124); Elaine Greenfield, pianist (Courtesy of Matt Thorsen; see page 86); Rev. T.A. Hopkins, educator (Courtesy of the Fletcher Free Library, page 31); Rev. Roger Anthony "Yolanda" Mapes, drag queen (Courtesy of Yolanda; see page 121); Val Carter, radio personality (Courtesy of Hall Communications and Val Carter's family; see page 20).

**On the Back Cover:** From left to right:
Jon Fishman, Trey Anastasio, Mike Gordon, and Paige McConnell, musicians (Photograph by Danny Clinch, courtesy of Phish, Inc; see page 83); Ben Cohen and Jerry Greenfield, ice cream mavens (Courtesy of Ben & Jerry; see page 61).

# CONTENTS

# ACKNOWLEDGMENTS

There are many people to thank for helping out in the creation of this book. I would like to give special thanks to Burlington photographer Matt Thorsen and to the wise and wonderful staff of the Special Collections Archives at the University of Vermont, both major sources for the images used in this book. Thanks also to Lauren-Glenn Davitian of CCTV, Burlington artist Nora Ostrander, and Janie Cohen from UVM's Fleming Museum for help and support. At the risk of sounding self-serving, I would also like to mention the many wonderful resources at the Fletcher Free Library, Burlington's public library and my longtime workplace, where I never cease to be amazed at the wealth of information waiting to be found in its stacks. Thanks also to the many generous people who have supplied pictures of family and friends and who have provided information about them. The images and information have enriched this book. Finally, and most importantly, I would like to acknowledge the work of generations of dedicated local historians and librarians, including Lilian Baker Carlisle, David Blow, Connell Gallagher, Tom Bassett, Vince Feeney, Ralph Nading Hill, Paul Carnahan, Jeff Potash, and Aaron Goldberg. These largely unsung heroes have spent thousands of hours researching and organizing historical facts about Burlington and have paved the way for amateurs like me.

# INTRODUCTION

Behind the door of an impressive Victorian bank vault in the basement of Burlington's public library rests a framed document, yellowed with age, and dated June 7, 1763. This document, which begins with a greeting from King George III, grants permission for Benning Wentworth, the colonial governor of New Hampshire, to grant a township, surveyed and described this way: "Beginning at the southerly or south-westerly side of French or Onion River so-called at the mouth of said river thence running up by said River until it comes to a place that is Ten Miles upon a strait line from the mouth of the river aforesaid then runs upon a line perpendicular the aforesaid ten mile line southerly so far as that a Line to Lake Champlain parallel to this Ten Mile line aforesaid wills within the line of the shores of the said Lake contain six miles square. And that the same be, and Hereby is incorporated into a Township by the name of Burlington."

The appearance of the place-name Burlington, the date, and the names of the original grantees on the document are among the few solid facts known about the founding of the future Queen City of Vermont. For starters, there are differing opinions about how Burlington got its name. Some think that it was named after Edward Burling, a wealthy New Yorker and the grantee of the town of Colchester, and from whom Ira and Ethan Allen purchased some of the 300,000 acres that they obtained along the banks of the Winooski River, Burlington's northern border. Another possibility is that the town was named by Wentworth to honor Richard Boyle, the Third Earl of Burlington. Regardless of who it was named after, Burlington was founded at one of the most beautiful locations in the area, a sloping hill with a panoramic western view of the high peaks of the Adirondacks across the broadest part of Lake Champlain—a spot seemingly custom-made for viewing glorious mountain sunsets. From the top of Burlington's hill, there was also a broad outlook east toward Mount Mansfield, Camel's Hump, Mount Ellen, and Mount Abraham, four of the highest peaks of the Green Mountains. Novelist William Dean Howells, standing with a friend on the shore of the Bay of Naples while serving as an American consul to Venice during Abraham Lincoln's presidency, famously remarked that he considered only one scene in the world more beautiful than the one upon which they were gazing—Lake Champlain and the Adirondacks as seen from Burlington.

Brothers Ira, Zimri, Heman, and Ethan Allen and other early settlers did not choose the site for the scenery, though. It was the fertile Winooski River Valley, the potential for waterpower at the great falls of the Winooski, and access to easy travel via Lake Champlain that made the spot so attractive. Following the American Revolution and the War of 1812, Burlington grew steadily and became a gateway city for trade in Vermont and the Adirondacks of northern New York. In the 1820s, the Erie Canal and the Champlain Canal made it possible for lumber and other products to be shipped to New York City and through the Great Lakes. The completion of the Chambly Canal on the Richelieu River in 1843 opened up access to the St. Lawrence Seaway. By 1849, the Central Vermont Railroad had also reached Burlington from points south, and by 1860 Burlington was connected to Montreal and other Canadian destinations by rail. During the late 19th and early 20th centuries, Burlington was one of the country's busiest lumber ports. Lumber and railroad barons prospered. The wealth that poured into the city during its shipping heyday can still be seen in the opulent Victorian homes that survive in what is now known as Burlington's "hill section."

Burlington continued to prosper as a manufacturing center until the 1940s, but by the 1960s, the city's boom was largely over. Passenger train service to Burlington had ceased in 1953, and shipping by water had also nearly vanished. With a few notable exceptions, including the Blodgett Oven Company and a General Electric manufacturing facility, many of the buildings along Burlington's waterfront were either empty or underused, clusters of fuel storage tanks cluttered up stretches of the lakefront, and the Pine

Street Barge Canal, a busy waterway in the 19th century, was found to contain 40 years worth of coal tar waste, a by-product of a long-shuttered gas plant. The canal was declared a dangerous toxic waste site by the Environmental Protection Agency.

Happily, this is far from the end of the story. The 1970s and 1980s saw the beginning of an artistic and cultural renaissance in Burlington that is still in full swing. Church Street's pedestrian mall was dedicated in 1981, and the Flynn Center for the Performing Arts opened in 1982. Work on the railroad right-of-way that was to become the Burlington Bike Path, a major step in the reclamation and restoration of the city's waterfront, was begun in 1973 and completed with the help of state and federal funding in 1986. A workable containment solution was developed for the polluted Pine Street Barge Canal, and many of the postindustrial buildings along Burlington's south end waterfront were renovated into desirable office space, art galleries, and some of the coffee shops described later in this book.

It is not a secret that Burlington is an extraordinary place. The Queen City (now home to about 42,000 residents) is regularly featured on "best of" lists of all sorts: No. 1 on *Men's Health* magazine's list of "Best Place to Raise a Family in the USA" (2012); *Men's Health*'s "Best City for Men in the USA" (2012); *Forbes* magazine's list of "America's best downtowns" (in both 2011 and 2012); *Outside* magazine's list of "Top 10 Cities for Outdoor Recreation" (2011); No. 1 on the "Top Ten Small Cities" ranking in 2010 as determined by the Gallup-Healthways Well-Being Index; and *Forbes* magazine's "Prettiest Town in America" (2010).

Burlington is a constant winner for many more reasons than beautiful location, clean air, and prize-winning sunsets. The city's waterfront bike path, one of the first recreational bikeways in the country, is now connected, via a bike ferry, with bike routes in the Champlain Islands, making it possible to travel all the way to Montreal. Burlington's Discover Jazz Festival, the Vermont City Marathon, First Night Burlington, Burlington's Independence Day Celebration, and the South End Art Hop are just a few of the annual events that draw thousands of residents and visitors to the Queen City.

Burlington's most valuable resource, however, is its residents. This book will introduce you to some special ones.

# CHAPTER ONE

# People and Their Places and Things

It may seem strange that a book about some of Burlington's notable people would begin with a chapter describing, among other things, a Victorian library, a haunted college dormitory, a pedestrian street, and two creatures, one fake and one fabled. The subjects in this chapter (with the exception of the Lake Champlain monster!) were created by or are closely related to a "legendary local" and would be immediately recognizable to almost everyone in the Burlington community. Some of these places and things are so much a part of Burlington that it would not feel like "home" without them.

The Church Street Marketplace is a prime example. When Burlington's main shopping thoroughfare (named for the early-19th-century Unitarian church that stands at the head of the street) was turned into a landscaped pedestrian mall in 1981, thanks to the vision of local architect Bill Truex, the result was a new image for the city's center.

Others who have been responsible for building something that has become a true Burlington landmark include Frederick Billings, a native Vermonter and president of the Northern Pacific Railroad who built the beautiful Billings Library on the UVM campus in 1885; John H. Converse, a UVM graduate and another 19th-century railroad baron who is responsible for Converse Hall, one of the most singular dormitories and creepiest buildings in Burlington; Mayor William Van Patten, who is responsible for the construction of the Ethan Allen Memorial Tower on an overlook that was part of Ethan Allen's farmstead; and Louis de Goesbriand, the first bishop of Vermont and the driving force behind the building of the Cathedral of the Immaculate Conception, New England's first cathedral church, completed in 1867.

Two iconic creatures of Burlington are also well-known celebrities. The first is the life-sized fiberglass head of a black rhinoceros installed by local metalsmith Steve Conant to appear as if "she" is crashing through the second story of Conant's Metal & Light showroom on Pine Street. The second is Champ, the much-loved and always elusive monster of Lake Champlain, first encountered, so the legend goes, by Samuel de Champlain himself. Champ also serves as the mascot of the Lake Monsters baseball team. We're quite sure that the mascot is not real, but no one seems to have made up their minds about the lake monster!

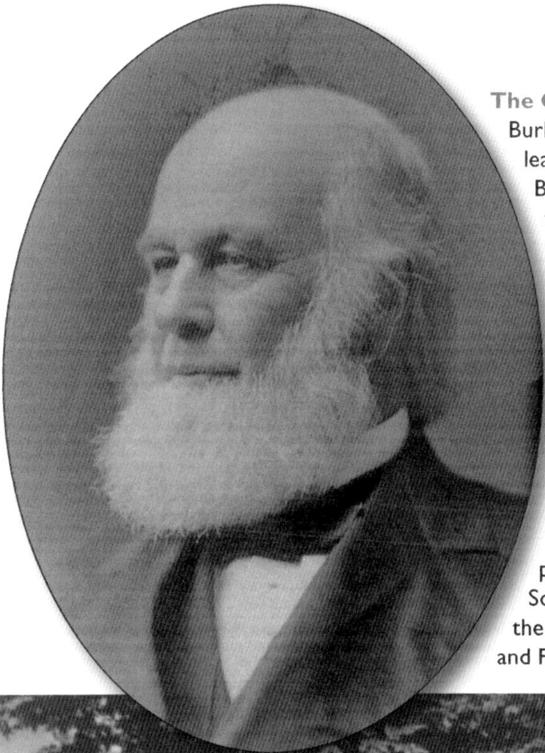

## The Queen City

Burlington was known as the "Queen City" of Vermont at least as far back as 1848, when the telegraph first arrived in Burlington and the people of Troy, New York, addressed their congratulations to "people of the Queen City." The title really took hold, though, in June 1865, when the City of Burlington's first mayor, Albert L. Catlin (left), stated in one of his early speeches, "We represent a young city, which may in time be known and distinguished as the Queen City of New England." In the 1950s, long before a law was passed banning billboards in Vermont, multiple versions of the welcome sign in the photograph below were displayed at Burlington's borders. Many remember a "Welcome to the Queen City" sign on the Burlington side of the bridge between Winooski and Burlington, but the billboard shown in this photograph was located next to Williston Road at the South Burlington entrance to the city. (Left, courtesy of the City of Burlington; below, courtesy of Richard Hawkins and Fisk family.)

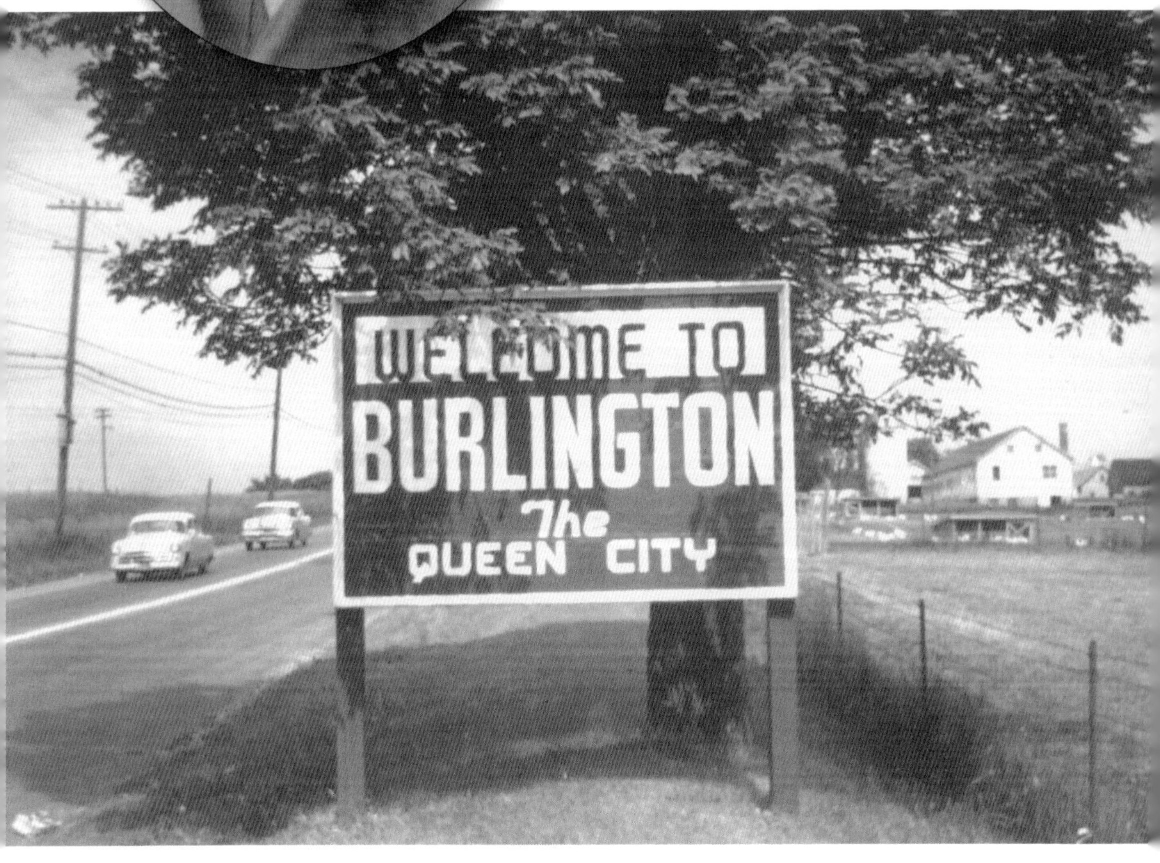

**John Converse**

Railroad executive John H. Converse (1840–1910) was born in Burlington and graduated from the University of Vermont in 1861. Converse worked in Burlington for a few years before moving to Chicago, but he always remembered his alma mater. Converse's contributions to the school included an endowment to found its department of economics and the design and construction of Converse Hall, a dormitory that resembles an old castle and that is considered one of the most haunted buildings in Burlington. According to legend, the hall was the home of "Henry," an overworked and lonely medical student who hung himself in the attic in the 1920s. There have been reports of mysterious footsteps and other mischief within the building ever since. (Left, illustration by Nora Ostrander; below, courtesy of Special Collections, University of Vermont Libraries.)

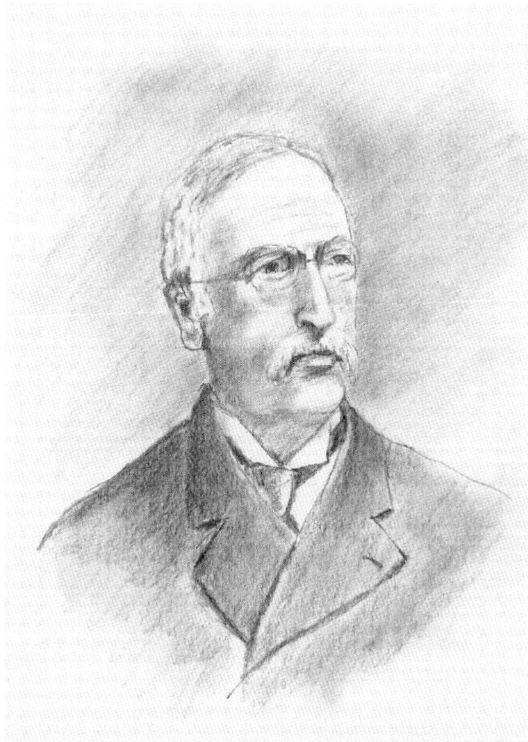

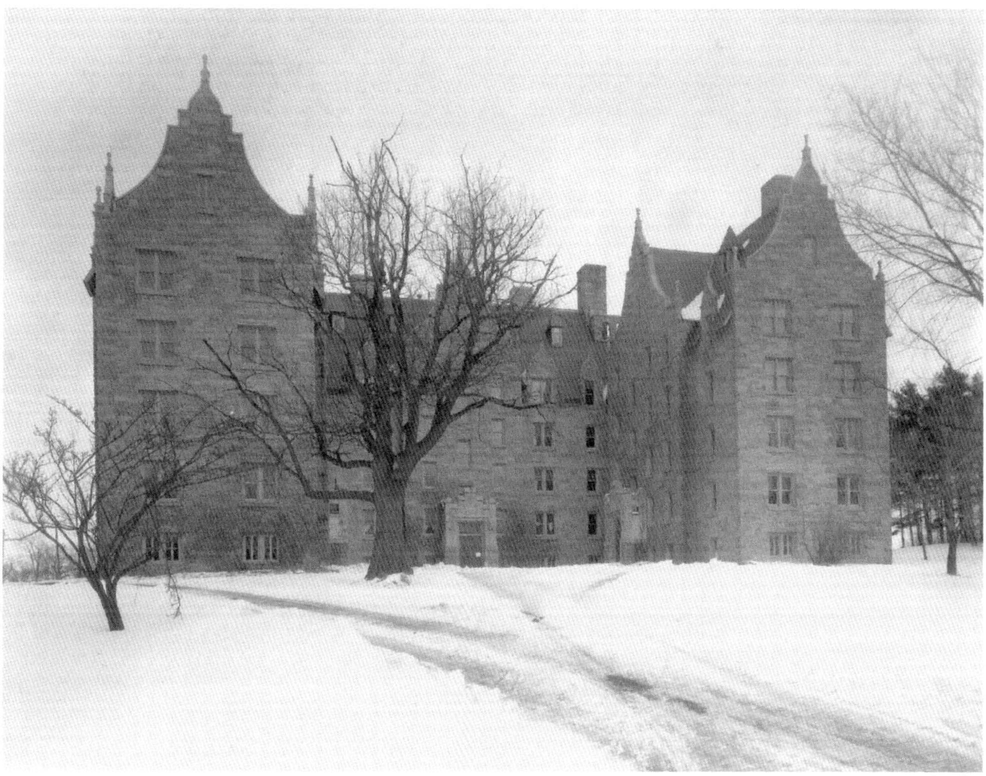

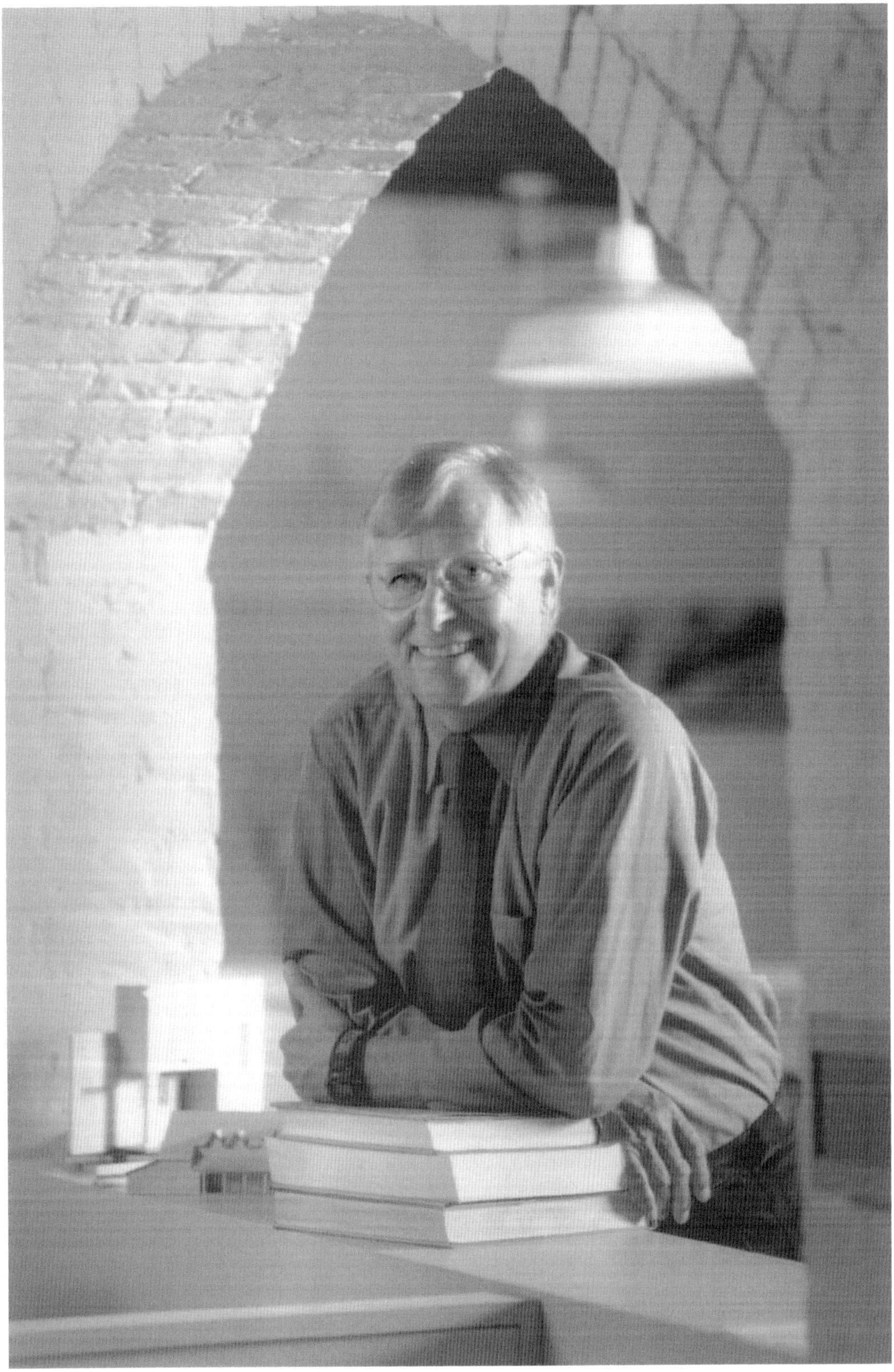

**Bill Truex's Big Improvement** (OPPOSITE PAGE)
The Church Street Marketplace, the pedestrian mall that is now a hallmark of downtown Burlington, was the brainchild of local architect Bill Truex. After two visits to Copenhagen, Denmark, in the early 1960s, Truex was struck by the positive changes that resulted when the city established a "car-free zone" in the center of town. In 1970, while serving as the chair of Burlington's planning commission, Truex requested permission from Pat Robins, the chair of the street commission, to close Church Street to traffic on the day of Burlington's annual sidewalk sale. Truex arranged to landscape the four blocks of Church Street with borrowed plants. Park benches and sculptures were brought in for the day, and concrete culverts were temporarily installed to serve as play spaces for children. The experiment was a popular success, and the following year, Truex and Robins convinced Church Street merchants to agree to another street closing, this time for a full week to host a crafts festival. After nearly a decade of planning challenges, including the design (once again by Bill Truex) of a downtown parking garage to replace the lost parking spaces on Church Street, and the launching of the newly coined Church Street Marketplace Commission to oversee the project, two blocks of pedestrian-only streets and four blocks of landscaping opened in September 1981. The "car-free" section of Church Street was expanded to four blocks in 1989. (Photograph by Susan Teare; courtesy of TruexCullins Architecture and Interior Design.)

**Church Street Marketplace**
The Church Street Marketplace is now famous for live music, outdoor dining, and a wide selection of vendor carts selling everything from gourmet cheeseburgers to jewelry. Along with pedestrian malls in downtown Boulder, Colorado, and Kalamazoo, Michigan, Burlington's Church Street Marketplace was one of the first of its kind in the United States. (Photograph by the author.)

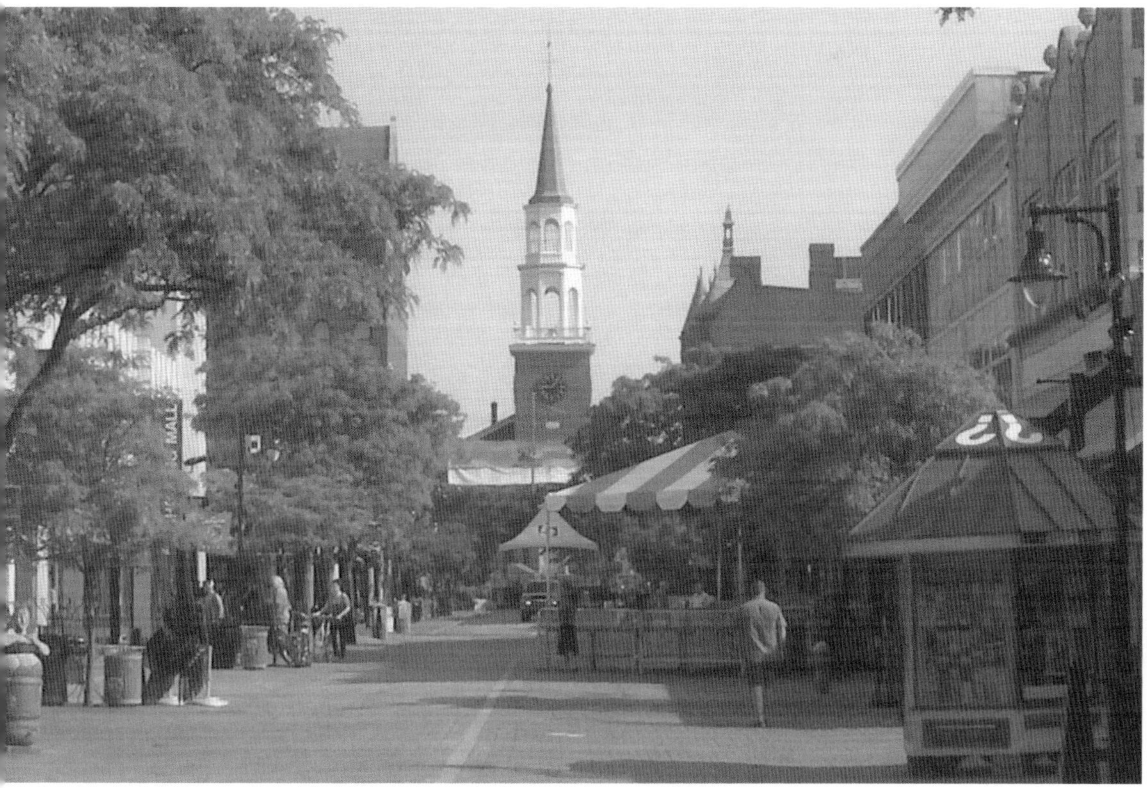

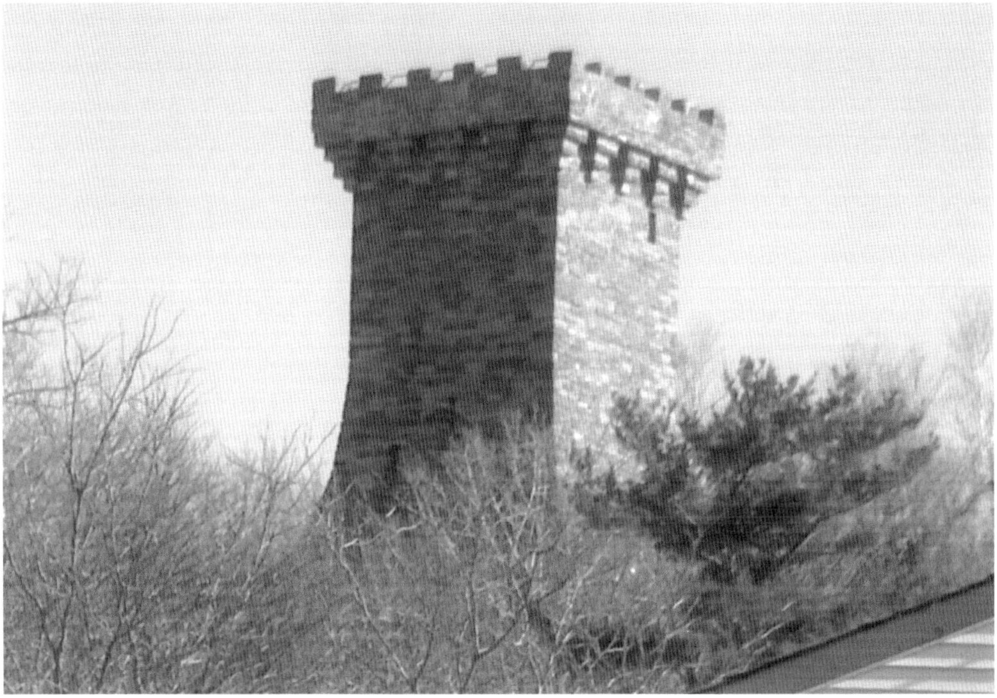

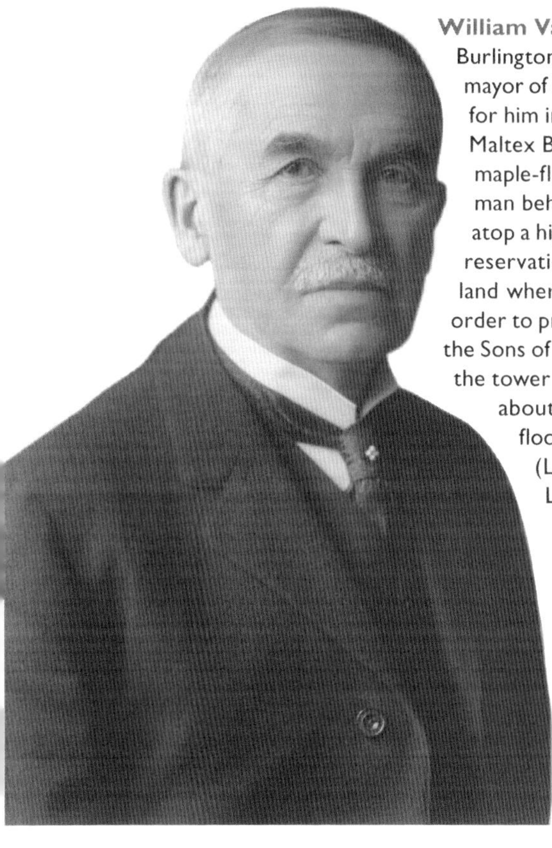

## William Van Patten

Burlington businessman William Van Patten, who served as the 13th mayor of Burlington during the years 1894–1896, has a street named for him in the city's north end. Van Patten was responsible for the Maltex Building on Pine Street, the place where Maypo, a popular maple-flavored oatmeal, was invented and produced. He is also the man behind the Ethan Allen tower, an impressive brick structure atop a high rock outcropping in Ethan Allen Park, a lovely forested reservation in Burlington's north end. Van Patten purchased the land where the tower would eventually sit in 1902 for $20,000 in order to preserve the area as a future park. He then gave the land to the Sons of the American Revolution on the condition that they build the tower and construct a road leading to Ethan Allen's farmhouse, about a half-mile away in the Intervale, the Winooski River floodplain. The tower still offers one of the best views in town. (Left, courtesy of Special Collections, University of Vermont Libraries; above, photograph by the author.)

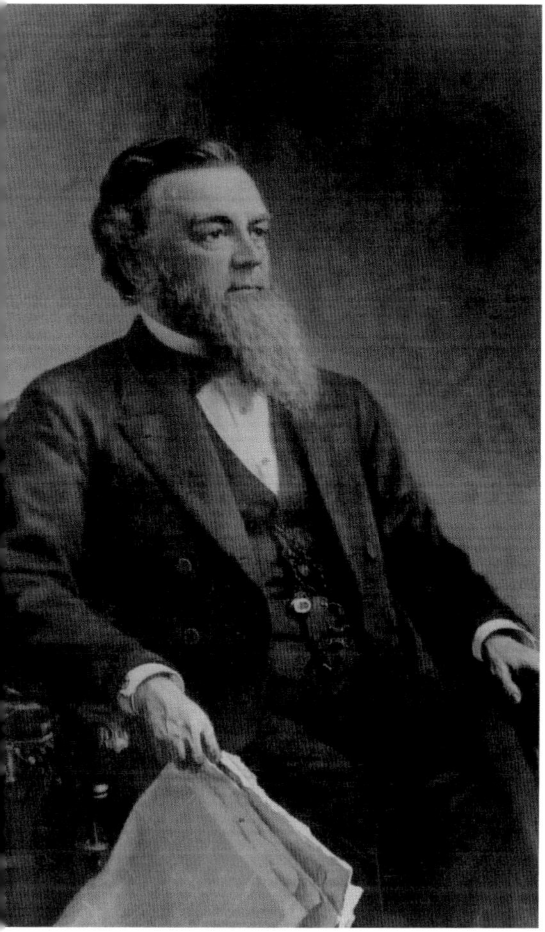

**Frederick Billings and His Library**
Frederick H. Billings (1823–1890), a UVM graduate and president of the Northern Pacific Railroad, purchased the library of Vermonter George Perkins Marsh, one of the country's first conservationists, as a gift to his alma mater. To house this collection, Billings hired architect Henry H. Richardson, now recognized along with Louis Sullivan, Frank Gehry, and Frank Lloyd Wright as one of the greatest American architects, to design a library building. The Billings Library, possibly Burlington's most beautiful building, was erected on the eastern edge of the University of Vermont green between 1883 and 1886. The library is a classic example of "Richardson Romanesque," a style originated by and named after Richardson that features picturesque rooflines, semicircular arches supported on clusters of squat columns, and round arches over clusters of windows on massive walls. Since the early 1960s, the Billings structure has served as UVM's student center and as a popular study space. As of 2012, fundraising has enabled the University's Special Collections library to move back into the building, allowing the Victorian structure to serve the purpose that Frederick Billings and H.H. Richardson originally intended. (Left, courtesy of Special Collections, University of Vermont Libraries; below, courtesy of the Fletcher Free Library.)

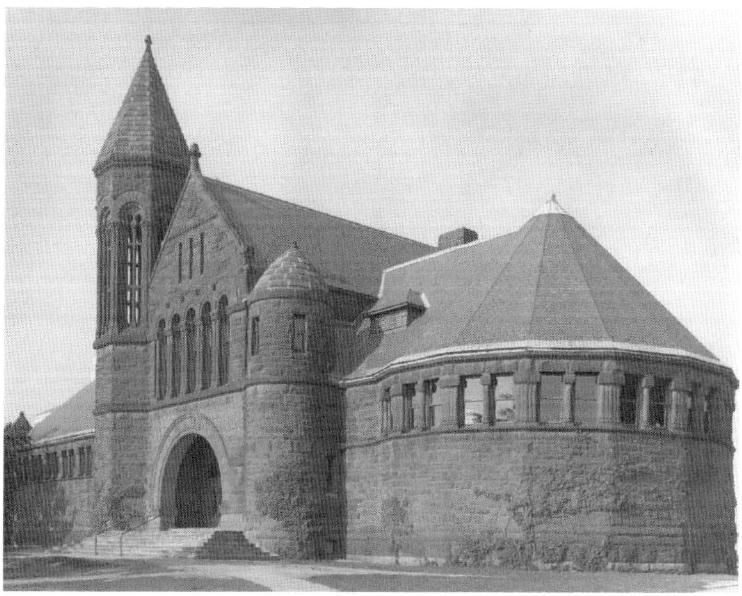

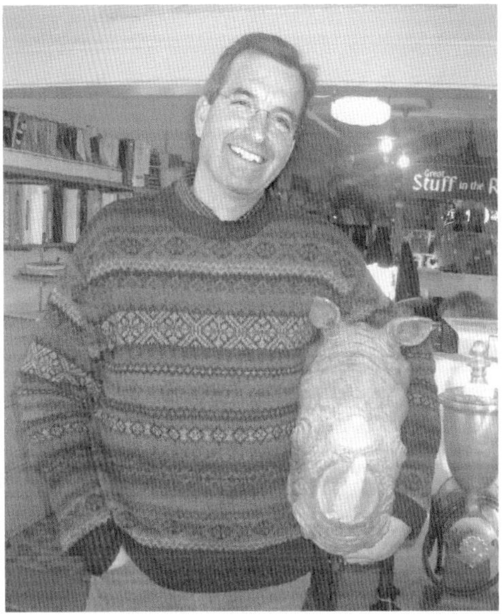

**Steve Conant and Rosie the Rhino**
When Steve Conant, the owner of a popular Burlington lighting and metal fabrication business, installed a fiberglass replica of a black rhinoceros head "bursting through" the second story of his Pine Street business, the resulting publicity was tremendous.

Thanks to his company's figurehead, Conant has learned about the desperate plight of rhinos around the world due to poaching and habitat destruction. Conant Metal & Light has donated to both the World Wildlife Fund and the International Rhino Foundation to help support the survival of the world's remaining rhinoceri. (Photographs by the author.)

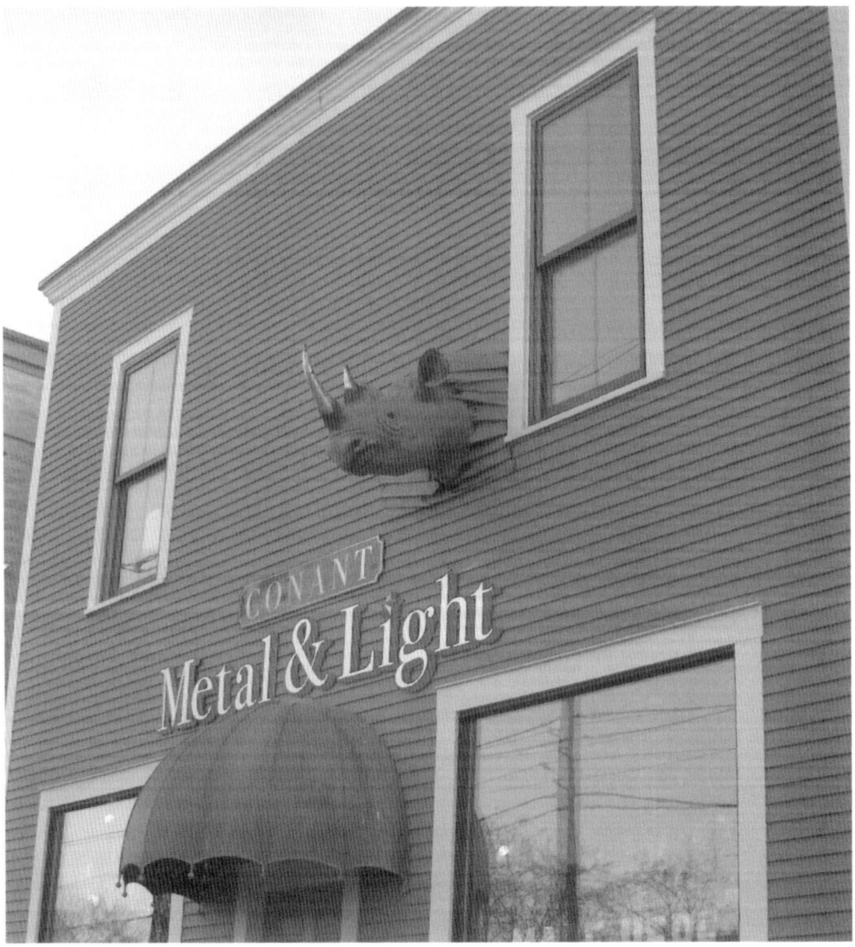

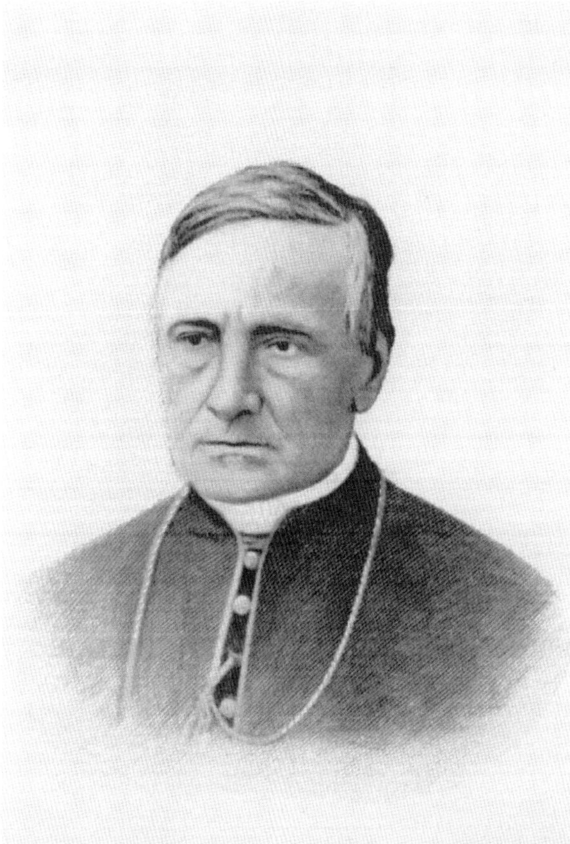

**Bishop Louis de Goesbriand**
Bishop Louis de Goesbriand (1816–1899), the first bishop of the newly created Diocese of Burlington, was also the driving force behind the design and construction of Burlington's Cathedral of the Immaculate Conception, the first church in New England designed and dedicated as a cathedral church. Construction of the structure lasted from 1862 to 1867, with the work often slowed or halted because many workers were called away to fight in the Civil War. Bishop de Goesbriand encouraged his parishioners by stating, "God will provide." These words were eventually carved over the main entryway. The cathedral, a Burlington landmark for more than 100 years, burned down in a suspicious fire on March 13, 1972. (Courtesy of the Fletcher Free Library.)

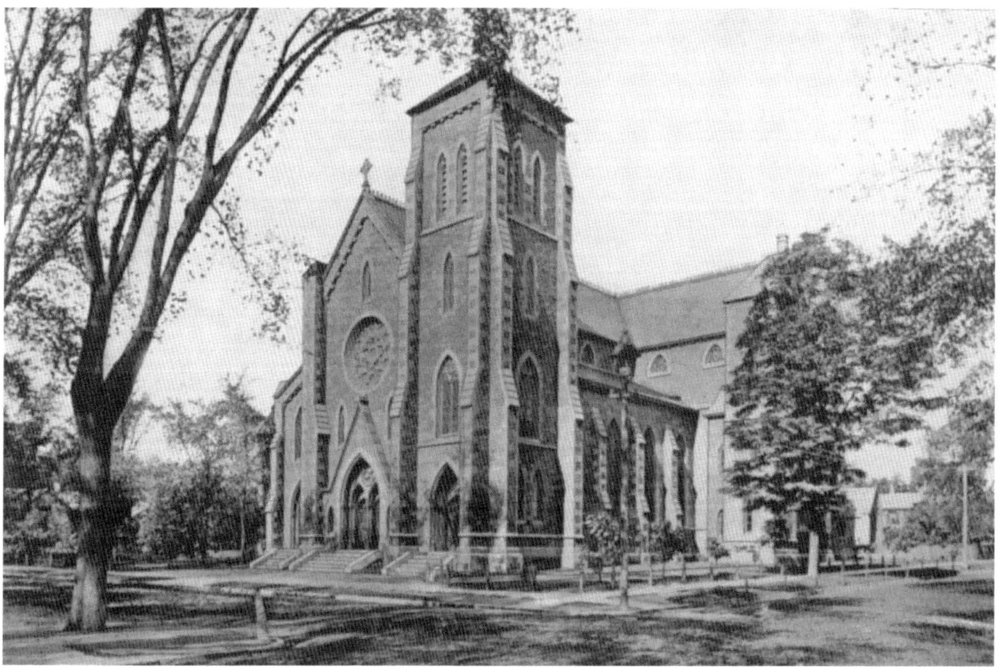

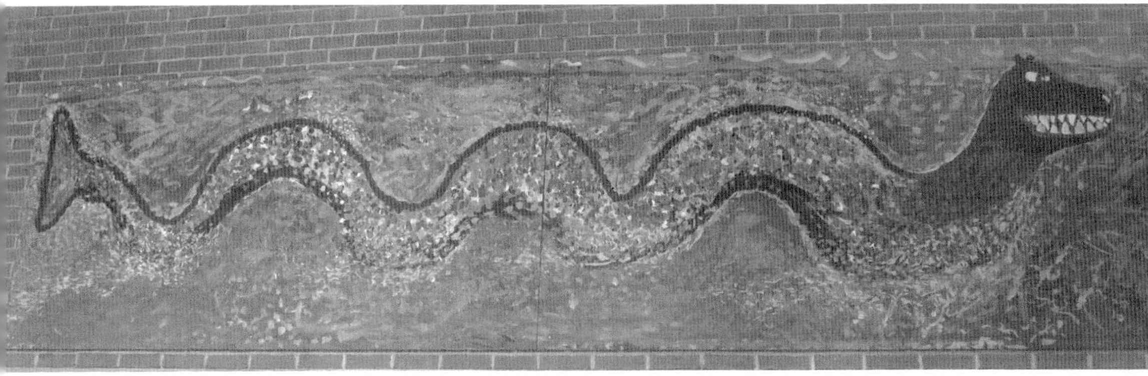

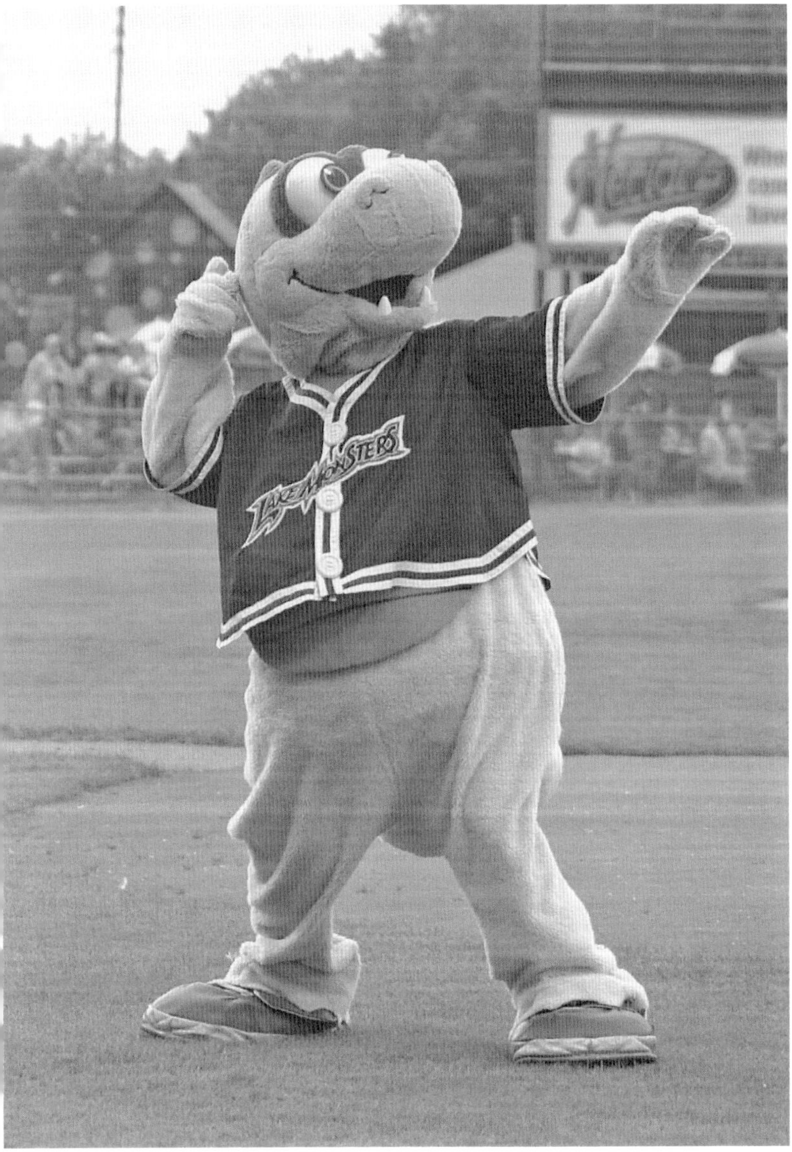


**The Lake Champlain Monster**

While most of the sightings of Champ, the fabled Lake Champlain monster, have not occurred in the "broad lake" near Burlington's waterfront, the legend is closely tied to every city and town that borders the lake. One of the earliest sightings at Burlington's end of the lake occurred in July 1873, when Clinton County, New York, sheriff Nathan H. Mooney reported spotting an "enormous snake or water serpent" 25 to 35 feet long. Champ is also the mascot of the Lake Monsters, Burlington's baseball team, and the namesake and inspiration for businesses and art projects all over Vermont. Just in case the monster turns out to be more than a folktale, the State of Vermont passed House Resolution 19 in 1982, protecting Champ "from any willful act resulting in death, injury or harassment." (Above, courtesy of the Fletcher Free Library; left, courtesy of the Vermont Lake Monsters.)

# CHAPTER TWO

# Stars of Media and Multimedia

Until the 1960s, Burlington was basically a "one paper and three station" town. It relied for news, weather, and entertainment on the *Burlington Free Press*, the city's longtime daily paper; radio stations WDOT, WJOY, and WVMT (originally WCAX, for "College of Agriculture Extension," launched by the University of Vermont in 1922); and television channels 3, 5, and 22.

Val Carter has the distinction of being one of Burlington's earliest radio personalities, hosting many shows on WJOY from the day the station went on the air in 1946, and on WDOT beginning in 1954. Carter also worked across the lake in Plattsburgh, New York, at WEAV-AM and FM in the late 1960s.

Jack Barry was another familiar radio host during the 1950s and 1960s. He became more famous later in his career as a television journalist and champion fundraiser for Vermont Educational Television and as a member of the Vermont State Legislature.

Marselis Parsons was the embodiment of local television news in Burlington as the anchor of the 6:00 p.m. newscast on WCAX-TV Channel 3 for almost 25 years and directing the station's award-winning news team.

The Burlington community still has access to all of the conventional media outlets, but it also has been lucky enough to benefit from the efforts of local media treasures who have made Burlington's "news and weather" anything but conventional.

Burlington journalists and newspaper visionaries Pamela Polston and Paula Routly met while working for the *Vermont Vanguard*, an alternative paper, in the early 1980s and had a hand in the publication of two other papers before launching *Seven Days*, Vermont's most successful news and arts weekly, in 1995. *Seven Days* columnist Peter Freyne brought local politics alive for many of his readers, and he was one of the many reasons that the paper appeals to a broad spectrum of readers.

Freeform videographer Eva Sollberger has produced hundreds of short and often humorous video journals about a wide variety of topics of local interest for her popular *Stuck in Vermont* series that airs on local television stations and online.

Maggie Maurice and Sally Pollak are beloved columnists at the *Burlington Free Press*. Both specialized in reporting on local personalities and events, but with very different approaches that reflect the changing times and tastes in local reporting.

For many Burlingtonians, Tom Messner *is* television weather. His sunny on-air personality has endeared him to generations of viewers, regardless of the forecast.

Lauren-Glenn Davitian, the founder and general manager of Burlington's Center for Media and Democracy and public access television channel 17, has been a champion for public access to the airwaves since 1984. She is responsible for hours of dynamic, locally produced television programming each week.

Far from being "just" media personalities, many of these journalists, news people, and programmers have contributed to making life in Burlington much more interesting, not only by informing the community but by helping to build it.

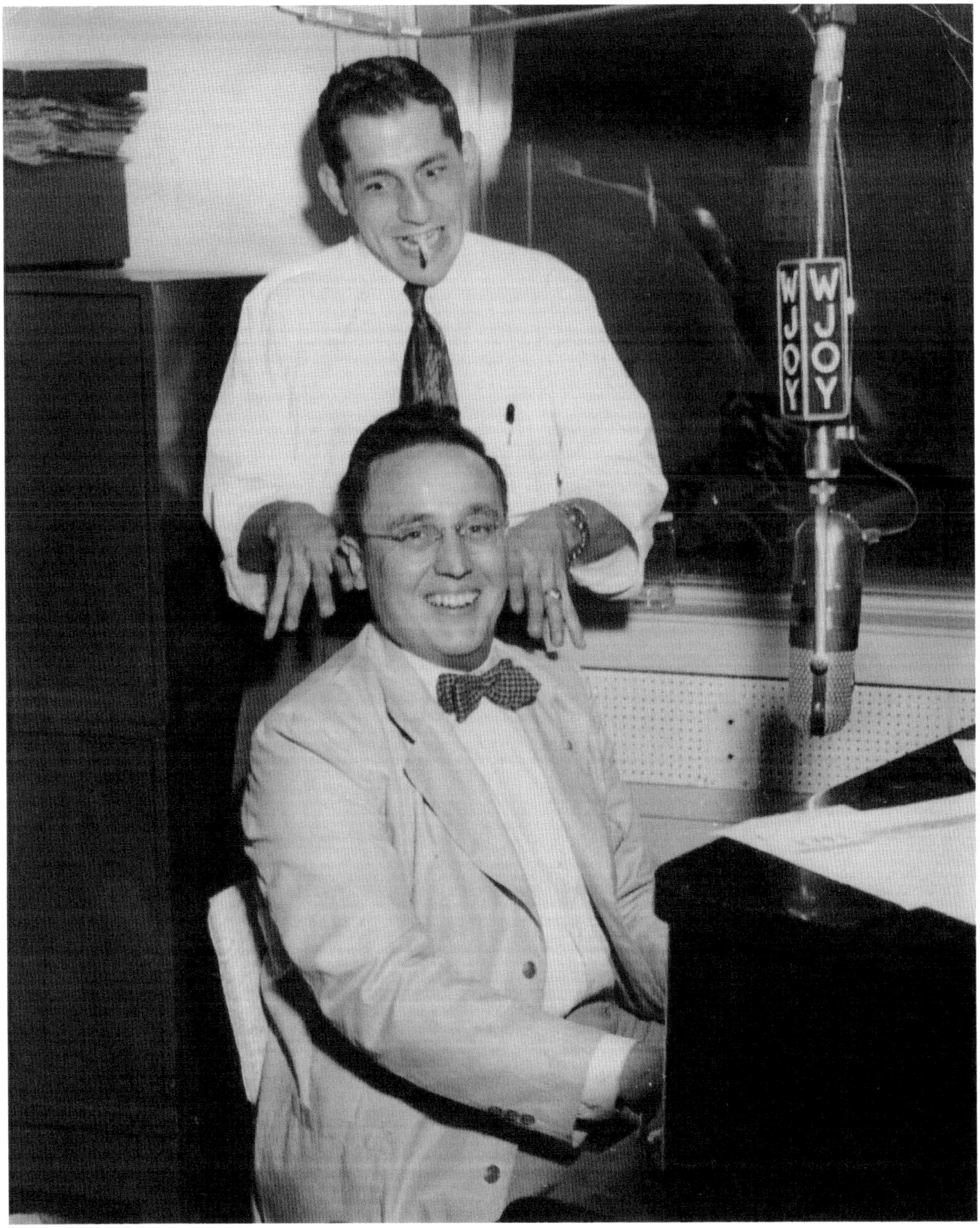


**Val Carter**

Val Carter (1920–1975) was one of Burlington's first radio personalities. When WJOY 1230 AM hit the airwaves in September 1946, Carter was there. He hosted the station's morning "drive time" show from 7:00 a.m. until 8:30 a.m., a program that featured, among other things, "Time signals, weather forecast, temperature, piano melodies and singing, and a complete variety of music." During his radio career in the Burlington area, Carter also worked for WDOT AM (where he served at station manager in the late 1950s) and WEAV AM and FM, just across the lake in Plattsburgh, New York. Carter is pictured here standing behind Orville "Goody" Goodrow, a favorite local musician, in the WJOY control room in 1951. (Courtesy of Hall Communications and Val Carter's family.)

**The Anchorman**
For many years, Marselis Parsons was the face of local television news in Burlington. He served as the anchor for the 6:00 p.m. news team on WCAX-TV Channel 3 beginning in the mid-1980s, and retired, after a 42-year career at WCAX, in 2009. Parsons's success can be attributed to much more than being a familiar face and knowing the local scene. During Parsons's tenure, his news team won many awards, including multiple Emmy awards for a monthly newsmagazine called *Dimension*, and an Edward R. Murrow Award for "The Best Television Newscast in the United States" in 2003. (Courtesy of WCAX-TV.)

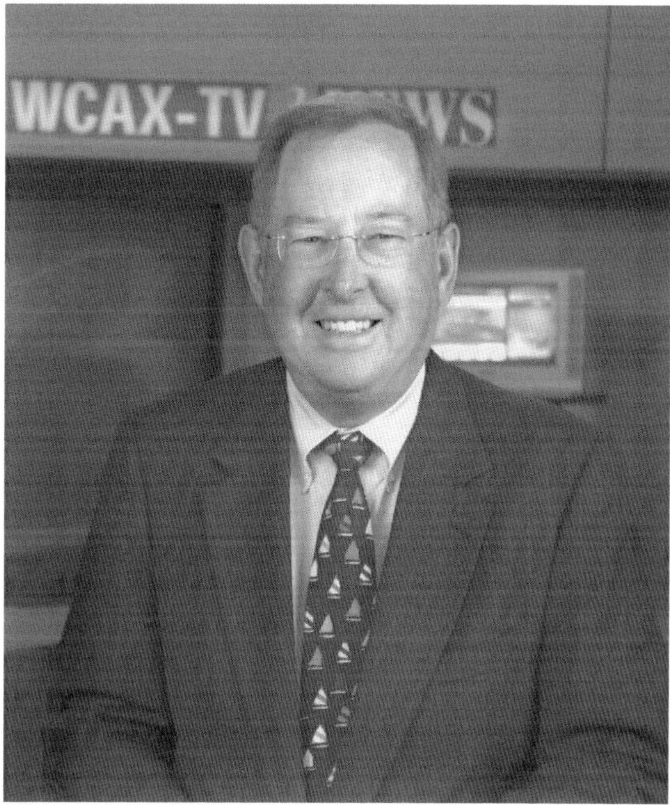


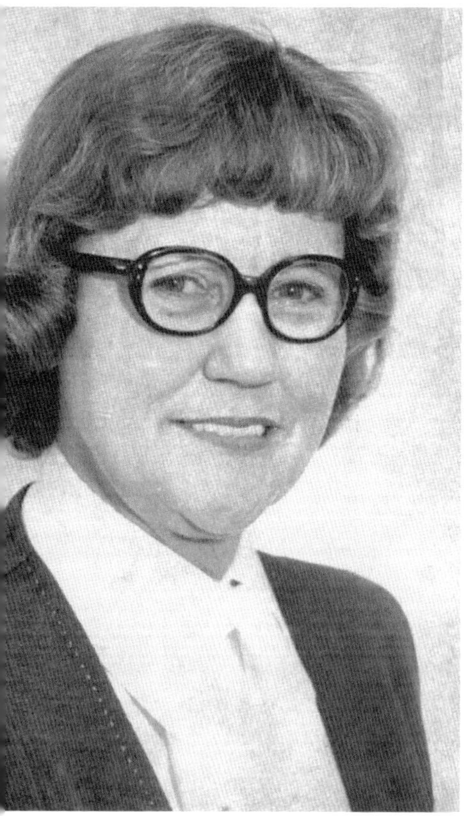

**Maggie Maurice**
Maggie Maurice (1925–2007) was a staff writer for the *Burlington Free Press* for 24 years, but it was her 14 years of observations and commentary about daily life under the headline "Maggie!" in the *Free Press*'s "Living" section that made her famous. Maurice paid attention to every detail and dutifully reported each tidbit of news about who's who and what's what in Burlington to her readers as if they were having a friendly chat. Maggie Maurice shaped Burlington's social scene every bit as much as she reported on it. (Courtesy of *Burlington Free Press*.)

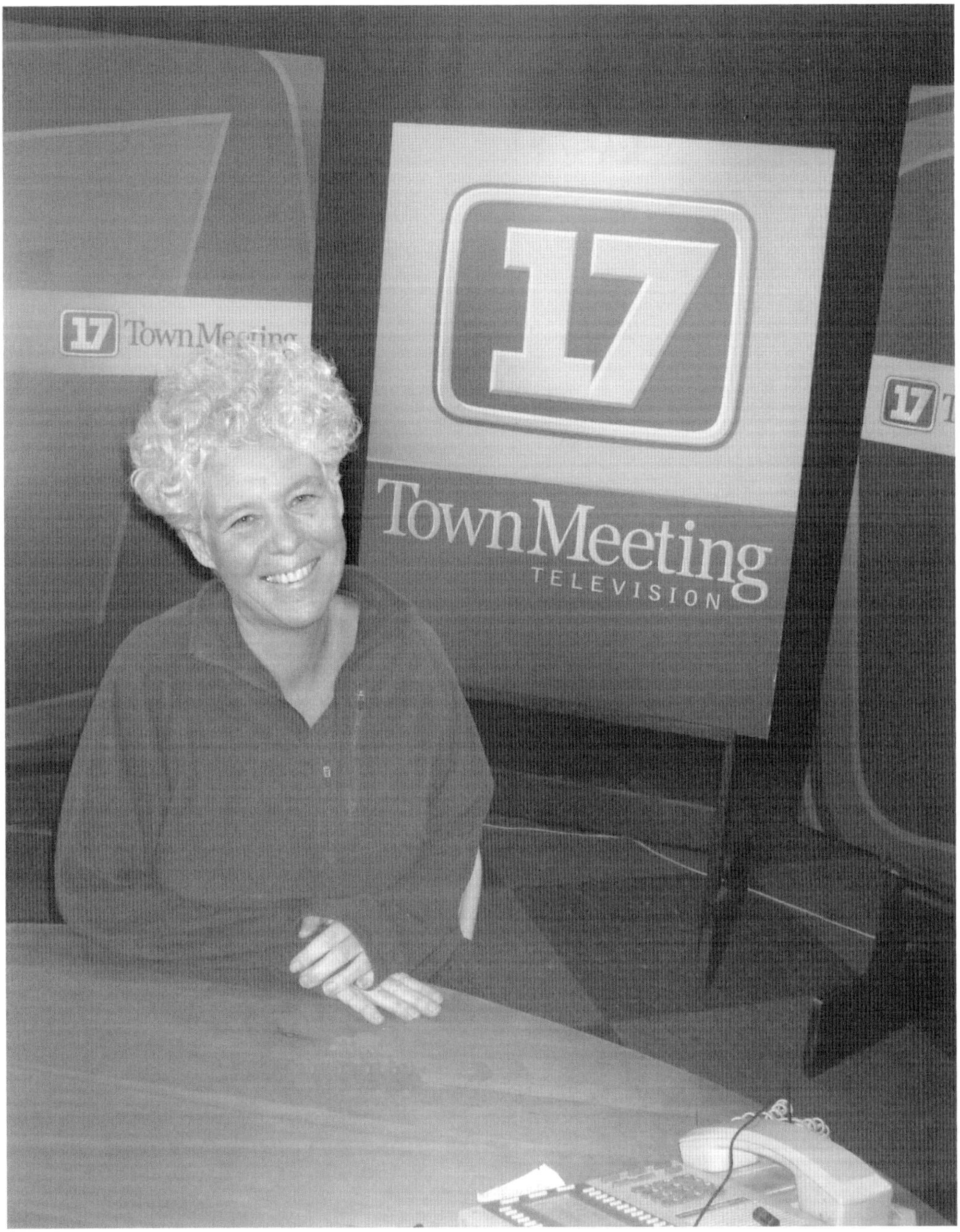


**Lauren-Glenn Davitian**

It is impossible to think of Burlington's CCTV Center for Media and Democracy, also known as Channel 17 and Burlington's Town Meeting Television, without thinking of Lauren-Glenn Davitian. LG, as she is affectionately known by friends, coworkers, and business associates, has been the driving wheel, the brain trust, and the executive director of CCTV since she launched the organization in 1984. Davitian is a champion of public media access in Vermont. She provides inspiration and support to 25 other community media centers operating more than 40 PEG (public, educational, and government access) television channels around the state. LG's Twitter motto is "Free Speech or Die!" (Photograph by the author.)

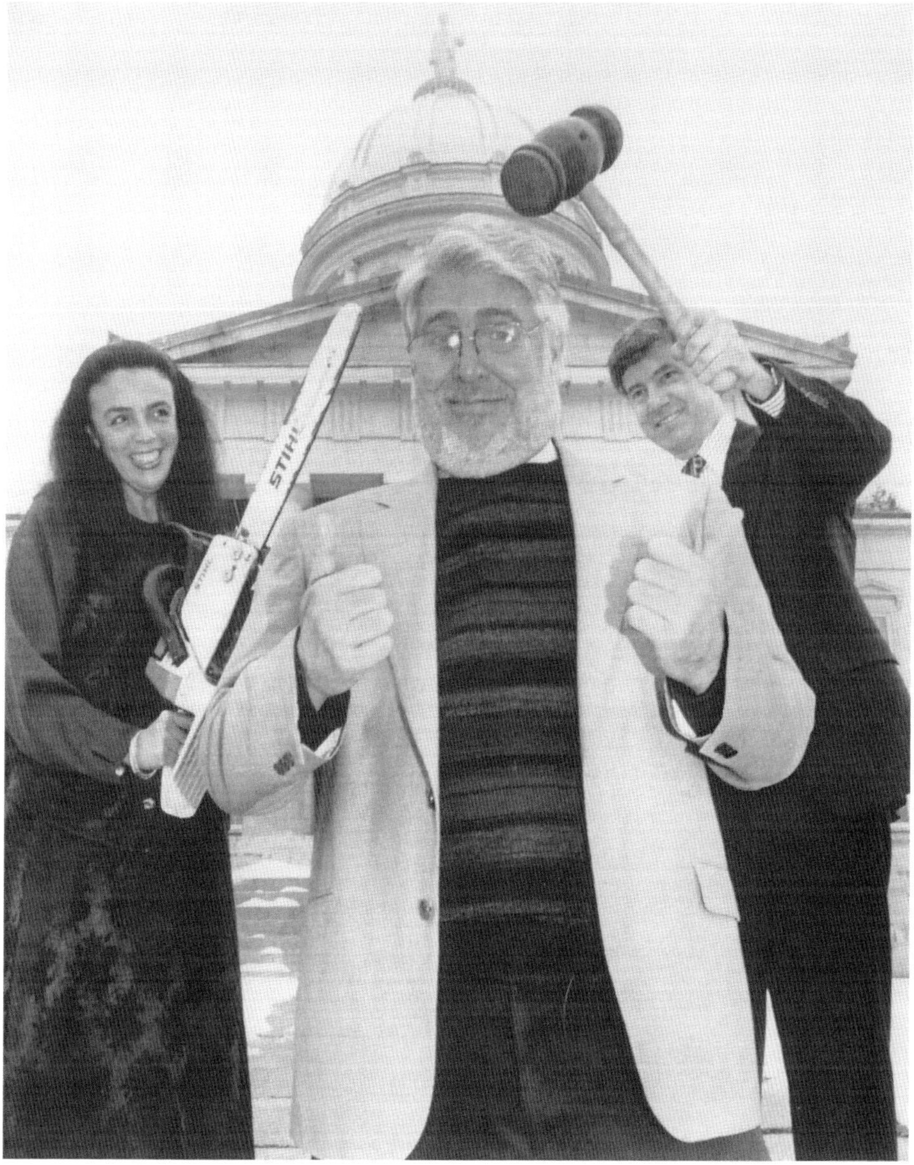


**Gonzo Politico**

Peter Freyne (pictured here cornered by state auditor Liz Ready and state senator Doug Racine) was one of Vermont's finest journalists and Burlington's favorite political commentators. Freyne began writing about local and state political figures in a column titled "Inside Track" for the *Vanguard Press*, Burlington's first alternative newspaper, and became a local celebrity when he continued the column for 13 more years in *Seven Days*, Burlington's popular weekly. Freyne often made up funny nicknames for local politicians: Vermont governor Jim Douglas got the title "Governor Scissorhands" for his expertise at cutting ribbons celebrating new projects around the state; and a pair of local state representatives became "The Self-Righteous Brothers" after denying accusations of ethical violations. No one remembers the accusations, but everyone remembers their nickname. After Peter Freyne's death at 59 following a long illness, Vermont politicians from both sides honored him for his humor and for his talents as a beloved gadfly. (Courtesy of *Seven Days*.)

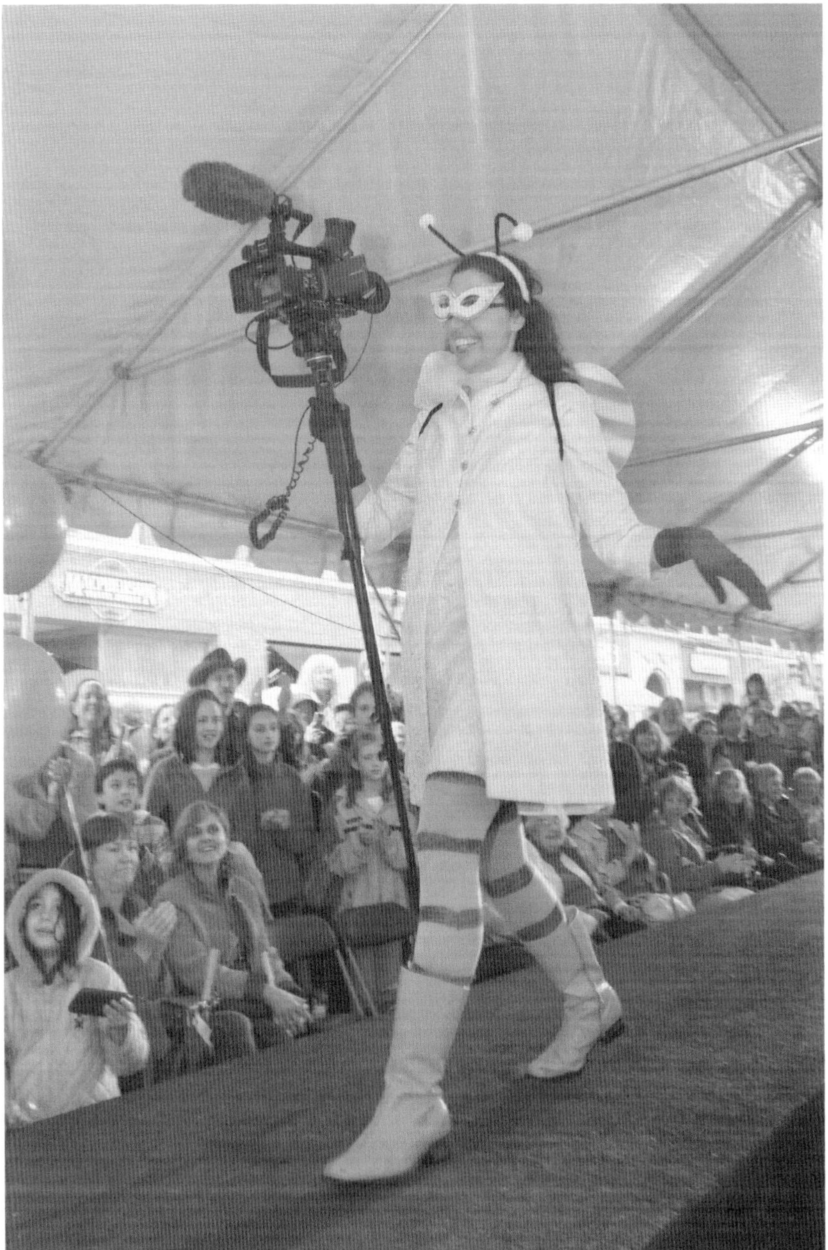

**Eva Sollberger**

Video whirlwind Eva Sollberger moved to Vermont less than 10 years ago. In that short time, she has become a well-known Burlington media maven. Sollberger has produced almost 300 editions of *Stuck in Vermont*, her regular online "vlog" (video blog) about life in the Burlington area. Recent vlog episodes include a celebration of the 75th anniversary of the publication of Tolkien's *The Hobbit* at a Burlington bookstore and a requiem for the Harbor Hideaway, a shuttered but fabled area restaurant on the verge of demolition. Sollberger's videos are always colorful and funny, and sometimes a bit quirky—just like their seemingly tireless producer. (Photograph by Josh Larkin, courtesy of Eva Sollberger.)

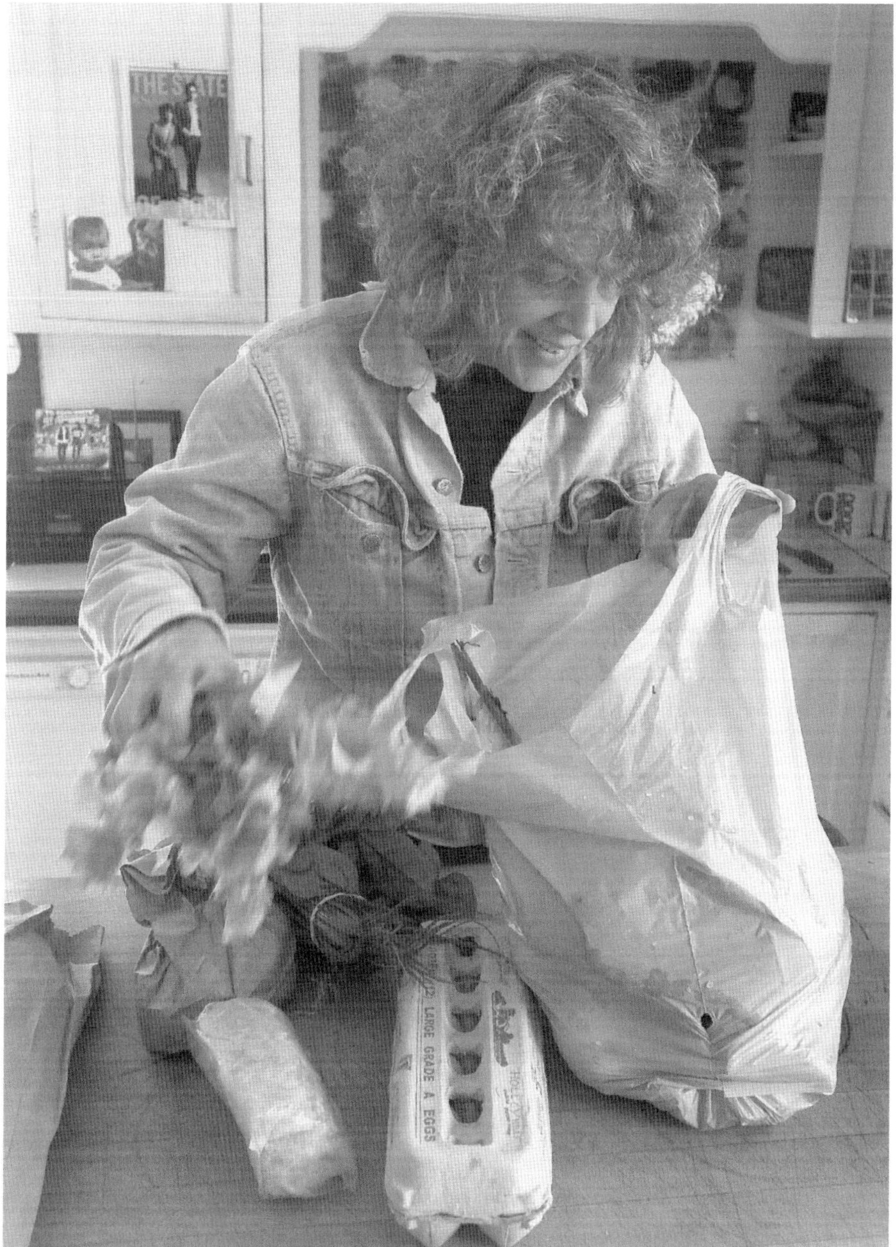


**Sally Pollak**

Many readers of Sally Pollak's columns in the *Burlington Free Press* would be surprised to learn that she was originally hired as a sportswriter. Pollak's local-interest stories have been appearing in the *Burlington Free Press*'s "Living" section since the 1990s, and it is hard to imagine Burlington's daily paper without her. Over the past decade, Pollak has written over 2,000 articles on subjects ranging from local 18th-century artist Charles Louis Heyde, to her attempts to survive on only locally produced food for an entire year. Pollak's warm style and often humorous approach has endeared her to a whole generation of local newshounds. (Photograph by Glenn Russell; courtesy of the *Burlington Free Press*.)

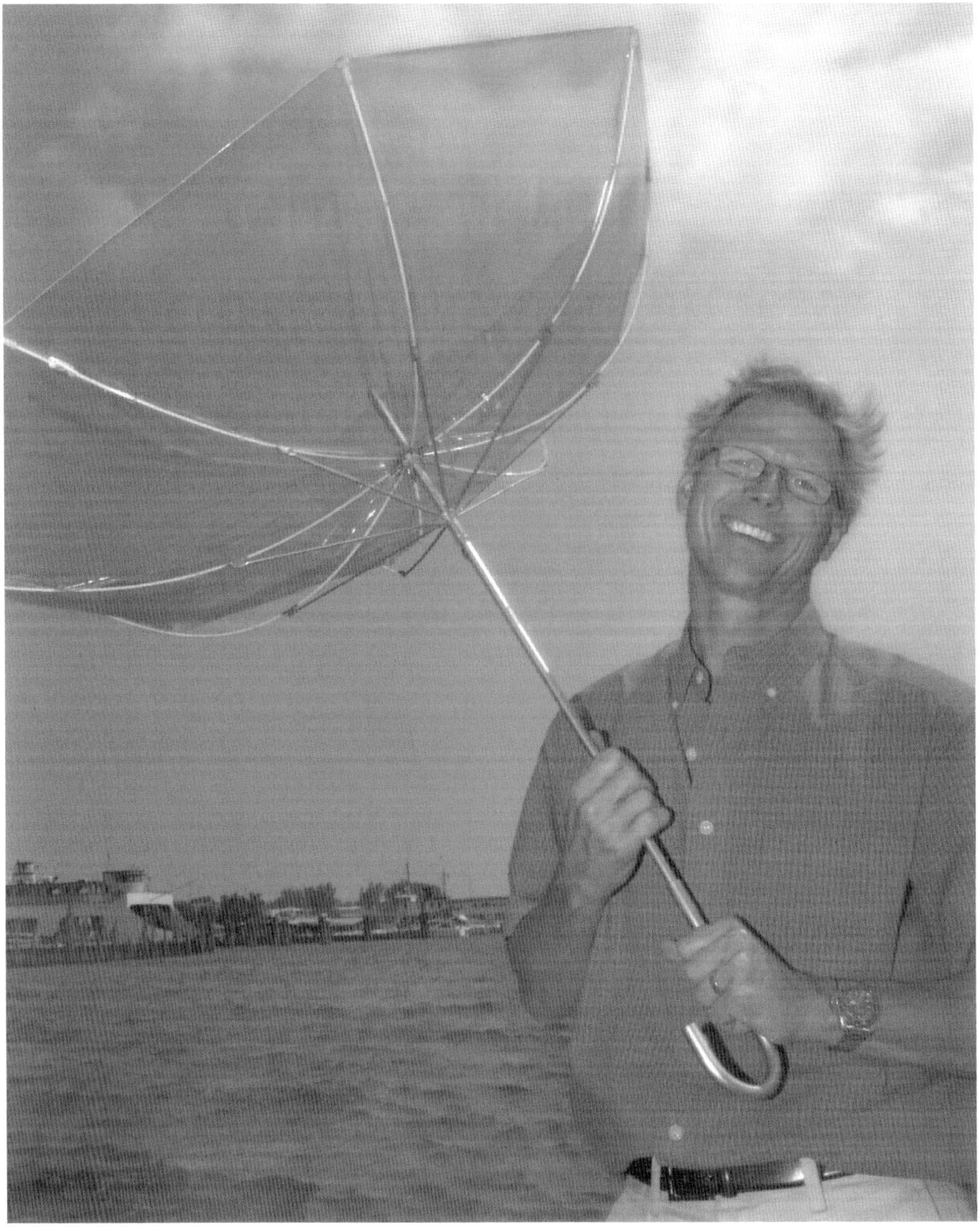

**Weather Superstar**
Meteorologist and local media personality Tom Messner has been forecasting the weather for the greater Burlington area since 1990 on WPTZ television, and in spite of the fact that the Champlain Valley receives some of the most varied and unpredictable weather anywhere, Tom has always delivered his forecasts with a smile. A whole generation of Burlingtonians has benefited from his sunny personality. There is more to Messner than what appears on the screen, however. Messner is well known for bringing the weather alive for schoolchildren thanks to many programs that he provides to local schools and for his support for many local charities, including the United Way, the American Heart Association, the Make-a-Wish Foundation, and the Alzheimer's Association. (Courtesy of Matt Thorsen.)

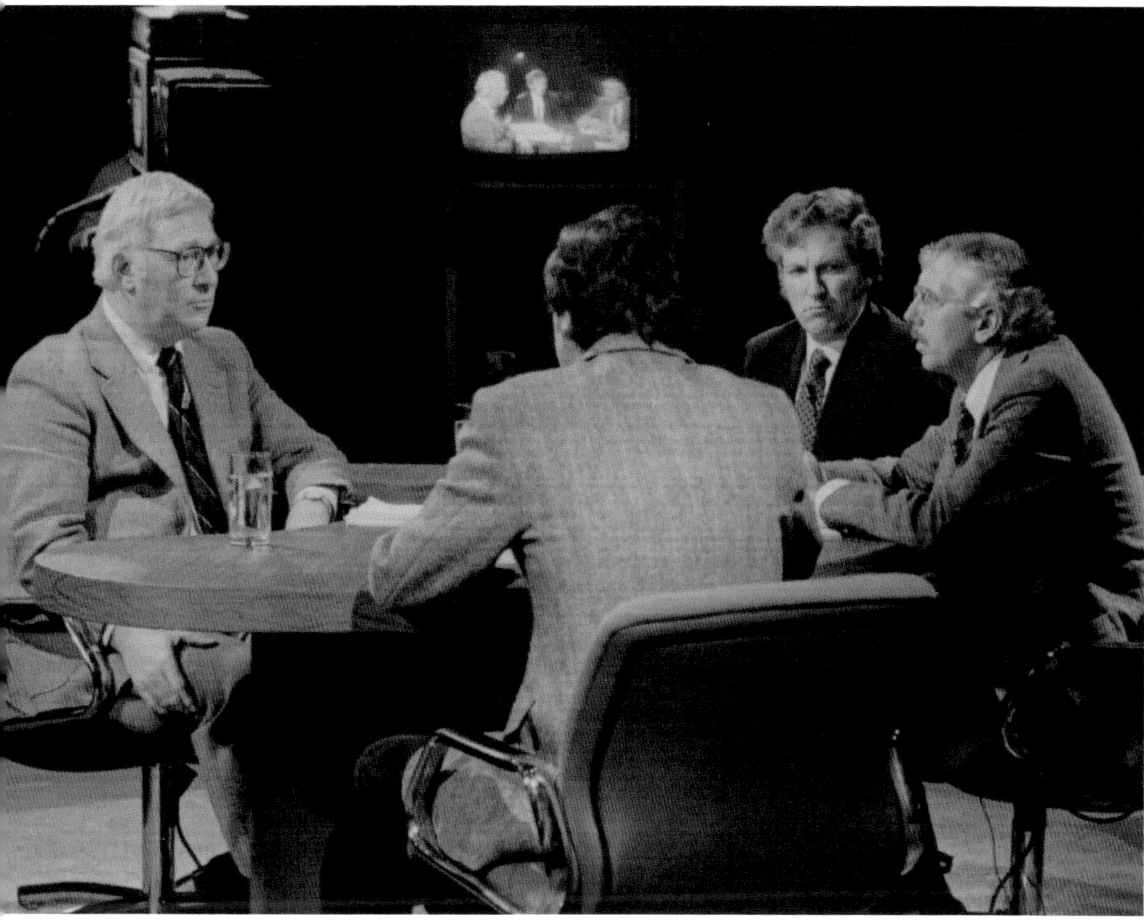

**Jack Barry**

Jack Barry (1926–1997) was one of Vermont's most beloved radio and television personalities. He was all over the airwaves in Burlington, hosting talk radio programs beginning in 1948 on WJOY, WDOT, WKDR, and WVMT, and producing and hosting television programs beginning in the early 1970s for Vermont ETV, the statewide public television station. Barry was cited as Vermont's Sportscaster of the Year in 1972, received a Distinguished Broadcasting Award in 1981 from the Vermont Association of Broadcasters, and was picked as *Rutland Herald*'s Vermonter of the Year in 1991. When he passed on after a long battle with cancer, Jack Barry was serving his third year in Montpelier as a state senator, surrounded by beloved state politics and politicians. He is seen here on October 15, 1982, hosting the first *Vermont This Week* program on Vermont Public Television. Shown with Jack (left) are Scott MacKay, *Burlington Free Press* (with back to camera); Hamilton Davis, *Rutland Herald* (second from right); and Tom Slayton, Vermont Press Bureau (far right). (Courtesy of Vermont Public Television.)

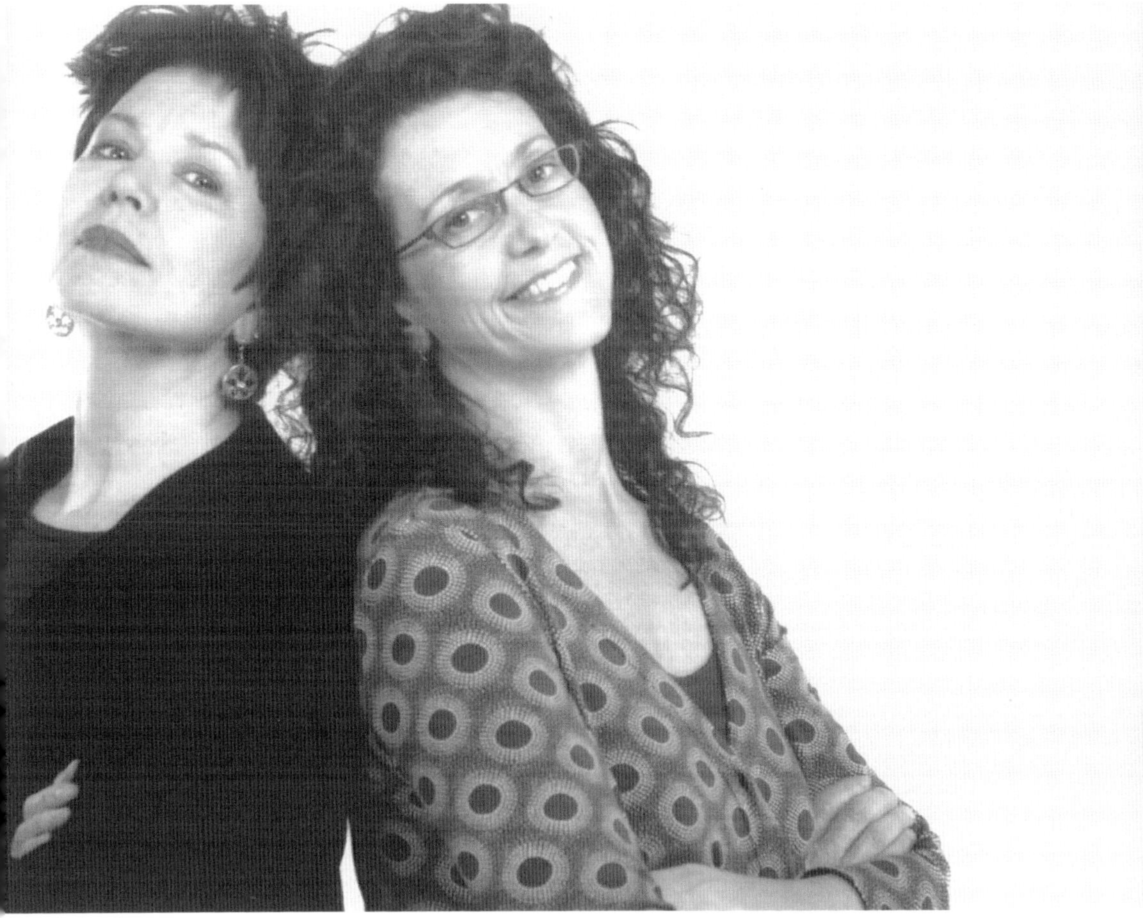

**The Mainstream Alternatives**

*Seven Days* is an apt name for the Burlington area's most popular weekly newspaper. Cofounders Pamela Polston (left) and Paula Routly have worked seven days a week for most of the past 17 years to create a "must-read" weekly newspaper that covers all the bases, from cutting-edge news stories to Burlington's arts and political scenes. Polston and Routly knew their potential audience well before they decided to start their own paper in 1995; the women had already worked together for nearly 10 years as writers and editors on three other local weeklies. In recent years, *Seven Days* has successfully expanded to cover much of northern and central Vermont while staying true to Polston and Routly's original vision: providing expertly written features that inform and entertain. (Photograph by Jordan Silverman; courtesy of *Seven Days*.)

# CHAPTER THREE

# Teachers, Historians, Archivists, and Other Keepers of the Flame

The City of Burlington has been a center of higher education in Vermont, and, at one time or other, the home of at least five colleges: The University of Vermont (UVM), Burlington College, Champlain College, Trinity College, and the Community College of Vermont. It is with the University of Vermont that some of the city's best-known teachers have been affiliated.

John Dewey, credited as the architect of modern educational theory, was a UVM graduate, as was Rev. T.A. Hopkins, the founder of Burlington's Rock Point School, and Effie Moore, one of the University of Vermont's first female graduates and one of Burlington High School's longest-serving teachers. Another beloved Burlington High School teacher is Leesa Guay-Timpson, affectionately known as "Frau," who has been teaching German and serving as the guiding light of the BHS theater club for 28 years.

Scholarly luminaries who have taught at UVM include: Ed Feidner, the founder of the Champlain Shakespearean Festival; Ken Rothwell, an expert in the field of Shakespeare on film; noted WPA artist Francis Colburn; Larry McCrorey, jazz saxophonist and charter member of the Vermont Human Rights Commission; Will Miller, a professor of politics who campaigned tirelessly for peace and justice; and Raul Hilberg, one of the world's foremost scholars on Holocaust studies. Bertha Terrill was the first female professor at the University of Vermont and the founder of the school's home economics department.

Burlington has had its share of notable historians, including Zadock Thompson, one of Vermont's first. His famous *History of Vermont* was published in 1833. Author and Vermontiana specialist Tom Bassett was the director of the University of Vermont's Special Collections. Bassett's masterwork is *Vermont: A Bibliography of Its History,* first published in 1981 and still a venerable reference book, even in these days of search engines and other electronic resources. Burlington preservationists Lilian Baker Carlisle and Ralph Nading Hill were both affiliated with the Shelburne Museum, a museum of folk art, paintings, and Americana located seven miles south of Burlington and collected by Electra Havemeyer Webb, a wealthy devotee of American folk arts. Lilian Carlisle's interest in all things historical was piqued during the time she spent as Webb's secretary and while she cataloged the museum's holdings. Ralph Nading Hill, who serves as trustee of the Shelburne Museum, is famous for saving the *Ticonderoga*, Lake Champlain's last passenger steamboat, from being scrapped. The "Ti" was eventually purchased by Webb, hauled overland using specially prepared train tracks and installed on the museum grounds.

Burlingtonian Chris Hadsel is another special Vermont preservationist. Her organization, called Curtains Without Borders, identifies and preserves hand-painted stage curtains that were originally used in opera houses, grange halls, and on stages throughout Vermont and nearby states.

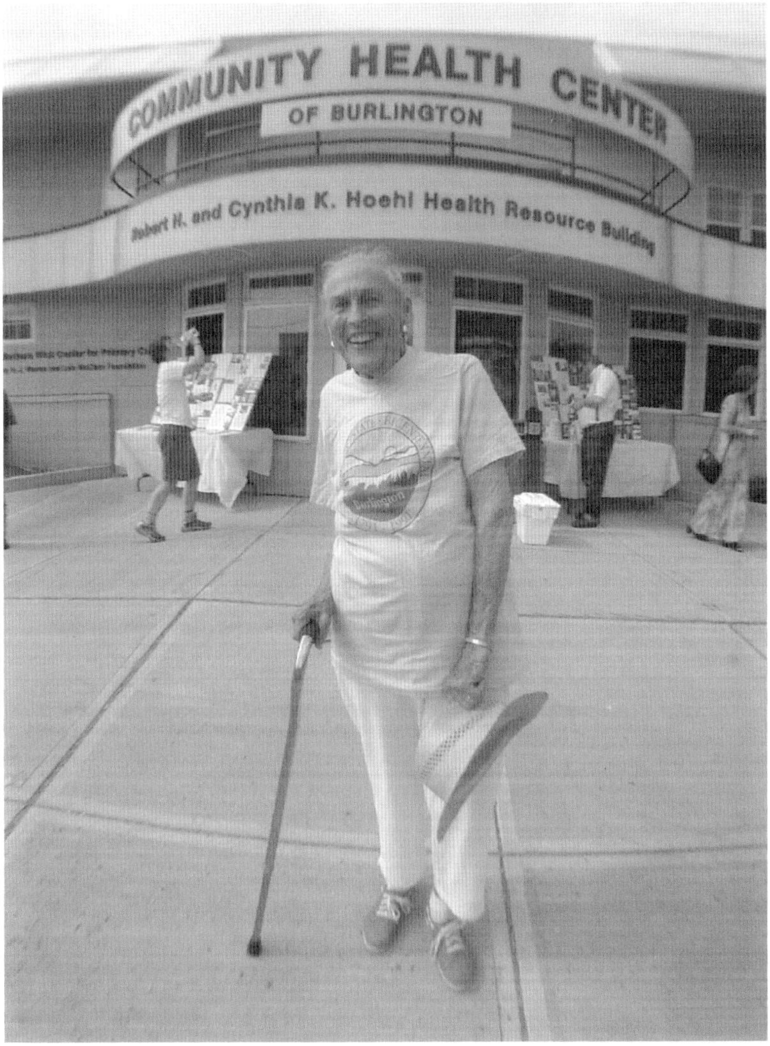


**Lilian Baker Carlisle**

Lilian Carlisle (1912–2006) always claimed that she "absolutely hated" history when she was growing up, but something apparently changed her mind! That "something" may have been Electra Havemeyer Webb, the founder of the Shelburne Museum, one of New England's great showcases of American folk craft, art, and historic buildings. Carlisle was hired part-time as Webb's social secretary in 1950, but soon was charged with the task of developing a cataloguing system for the thousands of items in the museum's collection. Over the next 11 years, Carlisle became an expert on quilts, historic hatboxes, and horse-drawn carriages, and wrote books on each of these subjects and on the examples of each that could be found in the Shelburne Museum's holdings. By the time she left the museum in 1961, Carlisle had discovered a love for all things historical, especially for local history. She founded the Chittenden County Historical Society after organizing a series of "historic walks" around downtown neighborhoods in 1965 to help celebrate the 100th anniversary of the establishment of the City of Burlington, and went on to edit a series of books about the history of cities and towns in Chittenden County. *Look Around Burlington, Vermont* was the first publication by the society, in 1972. Lilian Baker Carlisle delighted in sharing her knowledge and expertise, whether the subject was a long-gone Burlington building or coin silver jewelry. (Courtesy of Matt Thorsen.)

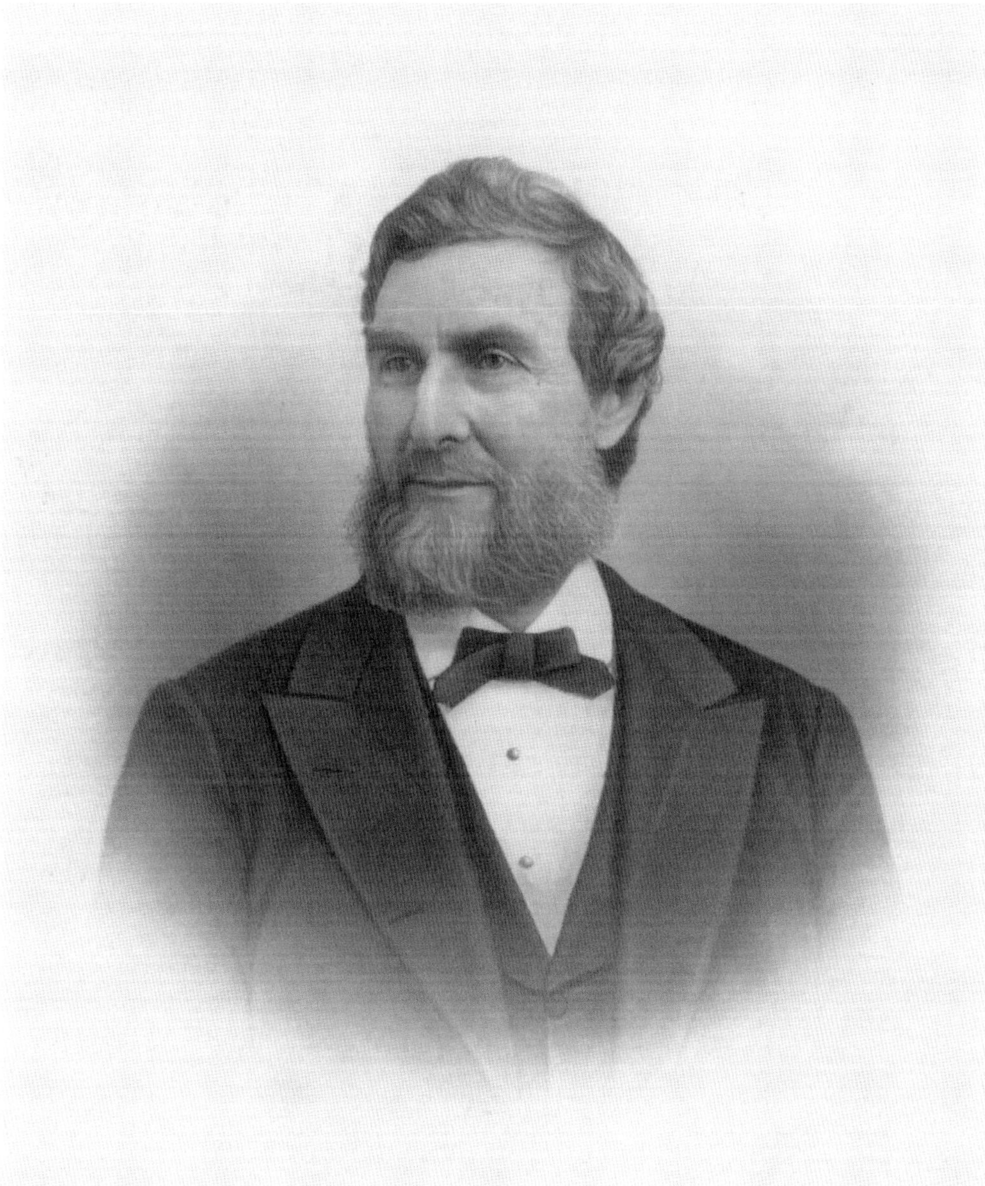

**Rev. T.A. Hopkins**

Theodore A. Hopkins arrived in Burlington at the age of four. His family moved from Pittsburgh, Pennsylvania, after his father, Episcopal Bishop John Henry Hopkins, lost a fortune in the national financial crisis of 1837 and established a farm on Rock Point, an undeveloped tract of land at the north end of Burlington's waterfront. In 1846, Hopkins entered UVM, eventually graduated from the General Theological Seminary in New York, and was ordained an Episcopal deacon. Hopkins returned to Rock Point in 1860 and dedicated himself to the establishment of the Vermont Episcopal Institute, a school for boys. Rock Point is still owned by the Episcopal Diocese of Burlington, and the Rock Point School continues as a private coed high school. Hopkins retired in 1881 to farm once again on five acres of his beloved Rock Point. (Courtesy of Fletcher Free Library.)

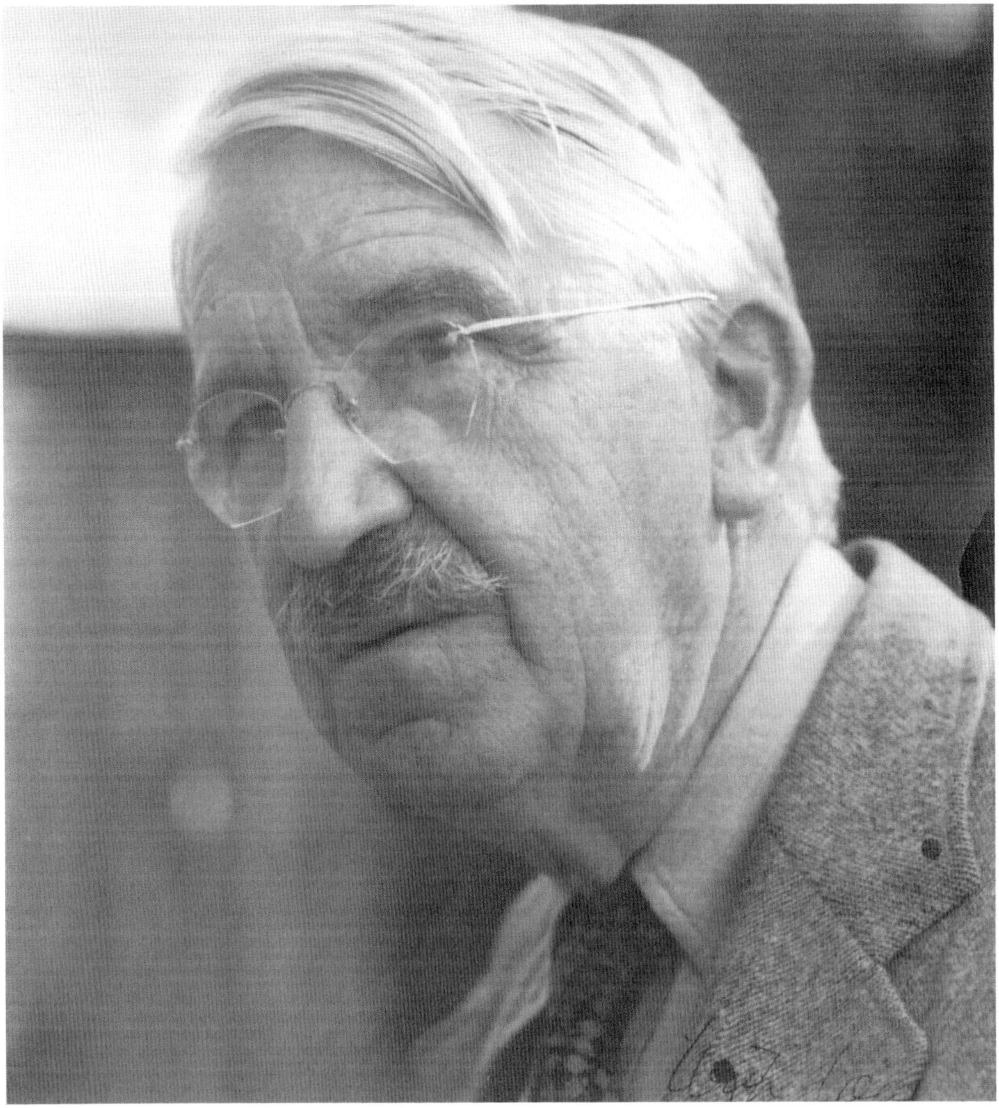

**Burlington's Great Educator**

Burlington-born John Dewey (1859–1952), philosopher, great thinker, and educational reformer, is virtually unknown today, even by many teachers. John Dewey is often confused with Melvil Dewey, the New York librarian who invented the Dewey Decimal System of book classification, and sometimes even with Adm. George Dewey, famous for his exploits in the Spanish-American War. John Dewey, a Phi Beta Kappa graduate of the University of Vermont, felt that the ability to solve problems, as opposed to memorizing dates, poetry, and times tables (standard classroom procedure at the time), was a necessary goal of education. Disregarding the divisions between subjects, Dewey's methods taught students to associate, identify connections, and form original insights. The memory of Dewey and his contributions to educational theory are commemorated in Burlington by John Dewey Hall, now serving as the home of UVM's psychology department. The building was erected in 1905 as the university's medical school (Dewey himself was present at the ceremony to lay the building's cornerstone) and was designed by Burlington architect Walter R.B. Wilcox, who also designed the city's Carnegie library building. (Courtesy of Special Collections, University of Vermont Libraries.)

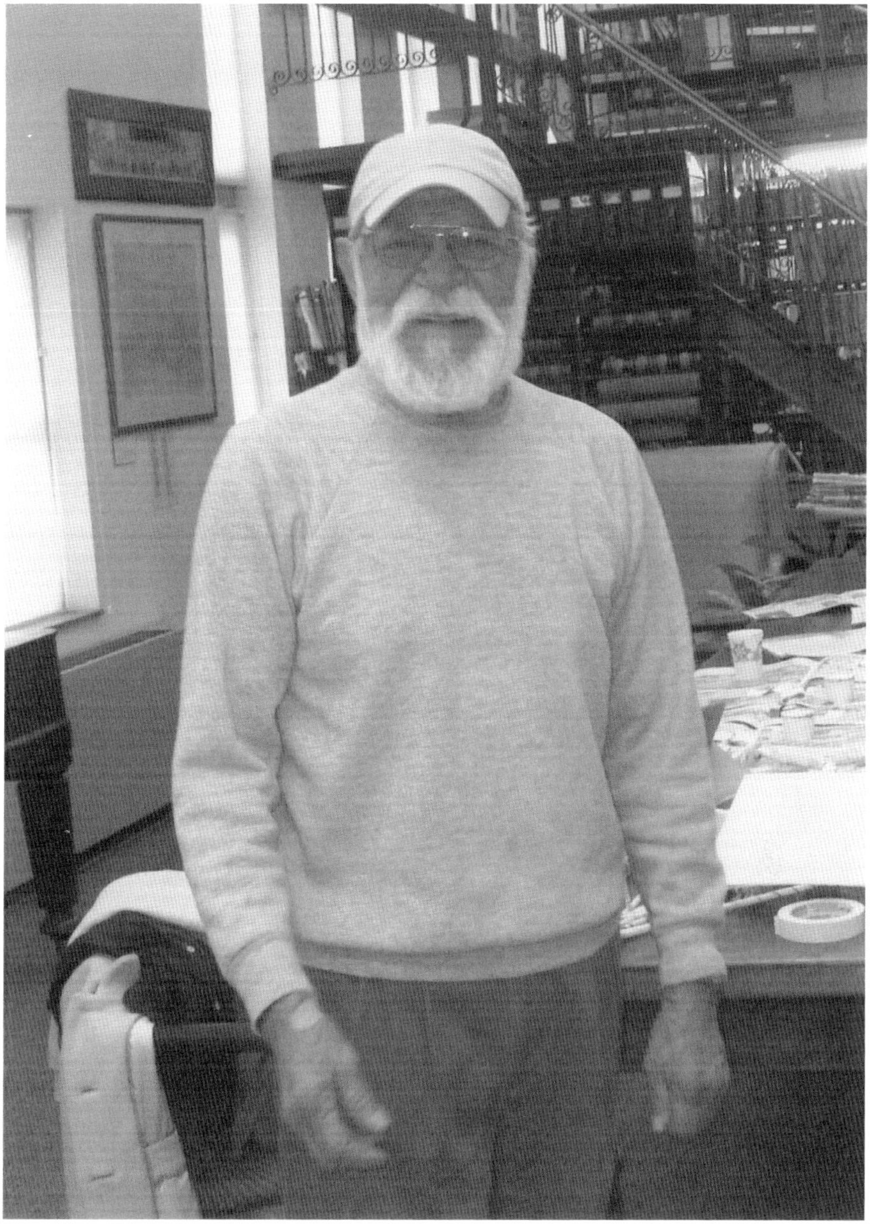

**The John Dewey Appreciation Society**
In the 1930s, Frank Gonzalez was one of three failing students placed in a John Dewey education program at his Pasadena, California, elementary school. In his new class, Gonzalez learned about the Greek myth of Icarus and got to see the drawings of Da Vinci. He also learned how to make paper gliders, launching them from a classroom window. Gonzales, now 86 years old, still makes amazing paper airplanes and can build practically anything out of newspaper. He uses tightly rolled pages to create a rigid skeleton on which to build. An art teacher who shares his joy of creating with Burlington children, Gonzalez attributes much of his success to John Dewey and his teaching methods. He organizes a John Dewey parade every year in Burlington, featuring a 20-foot-high puppet of Dewey that he has built of paper. (Courtesy of the Fletcher Free Library.)

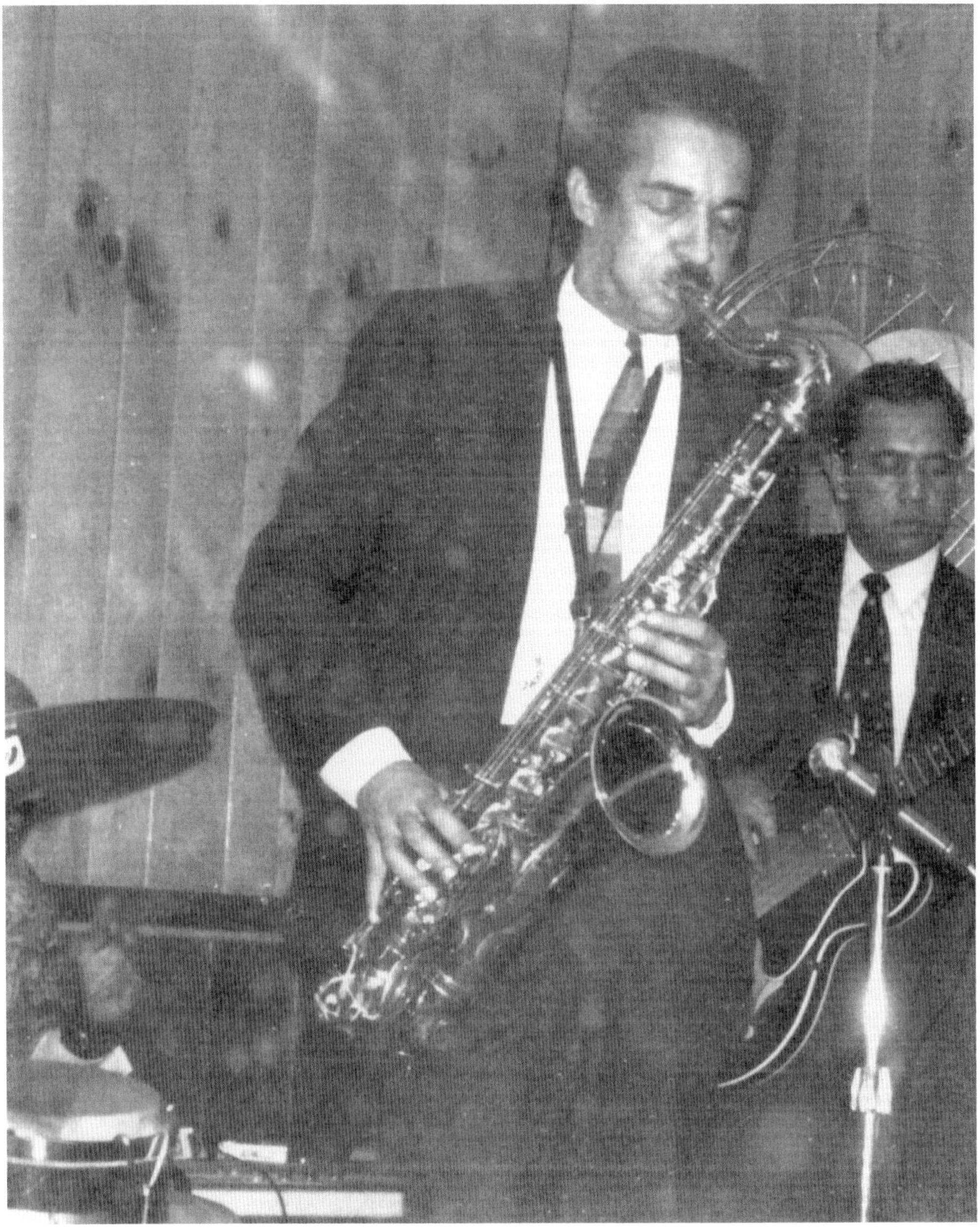

**Larry McCrorey**

In addition to being a celebrated professor in the University of Vermont's physiology department and the dean of UVM's School of Allied Health Sciences, Larry McCrorey (1927–2009) was an eloquent advocate for the social changes necessary to eradicate racism and was a charter member of the Vermont Human Rights Commission. Dr. McCrorey was also a shining light in Burlington's jazz community. He taught a series of popular courses on the history of jazz and was an accomplished saxophonist himself. When he retired from UVM in 1995, the college honored Dr. McCrorey by establishing the H. Lawrence McCrorey Multicultural Library Collection and Art Gallery. (Courtesy of Special Collections, University of Vermont Libraries.)

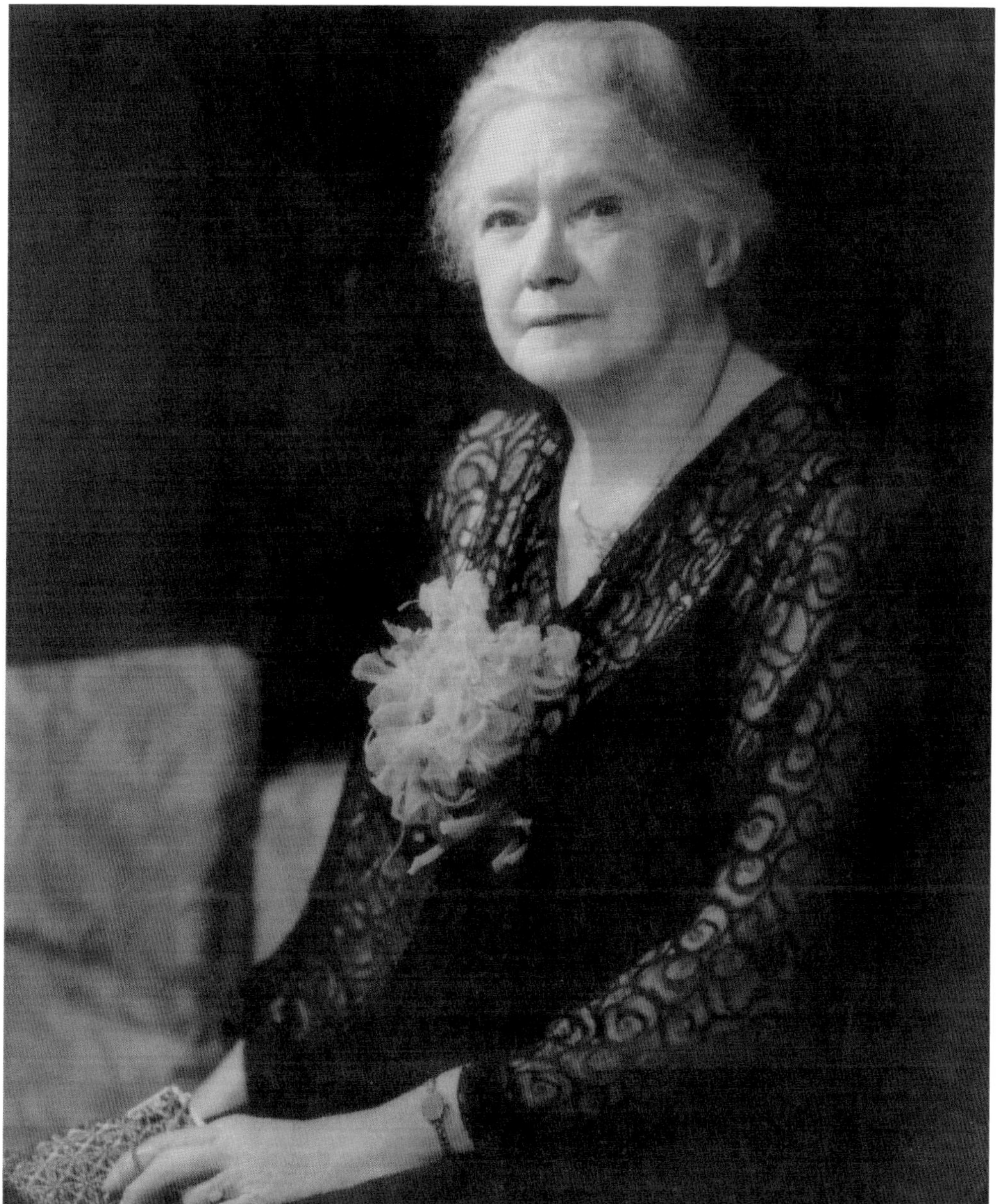

**Bertha Mary Terrill**
After studying at Yale and Harvard and undertaking a rigorous self-directed study program while teaching at the School of Religious Pedagogy in Hartford, Connecticut, Bertha Terrill (1870–1968) became the first female faculty member at the University of Vermont. She was hired in 1909 by UVM president Matthew Buckham to start a program based in the fledgling field of home economics. Professor Terrill built up the home economics department from one course taught in a former storage room to a comprehensive department known today as Family and Consumer Sciences Education. With her lifelong friend, UVM education professor Sara Holbrook (see page 93), Terrill also established the Burlington Community Center, now called the Sara Holbrook Center, an important educational and social resource for immigrants arriving in Burlington. (Courtesy of Special Collections, University of Vermont Libraries.)

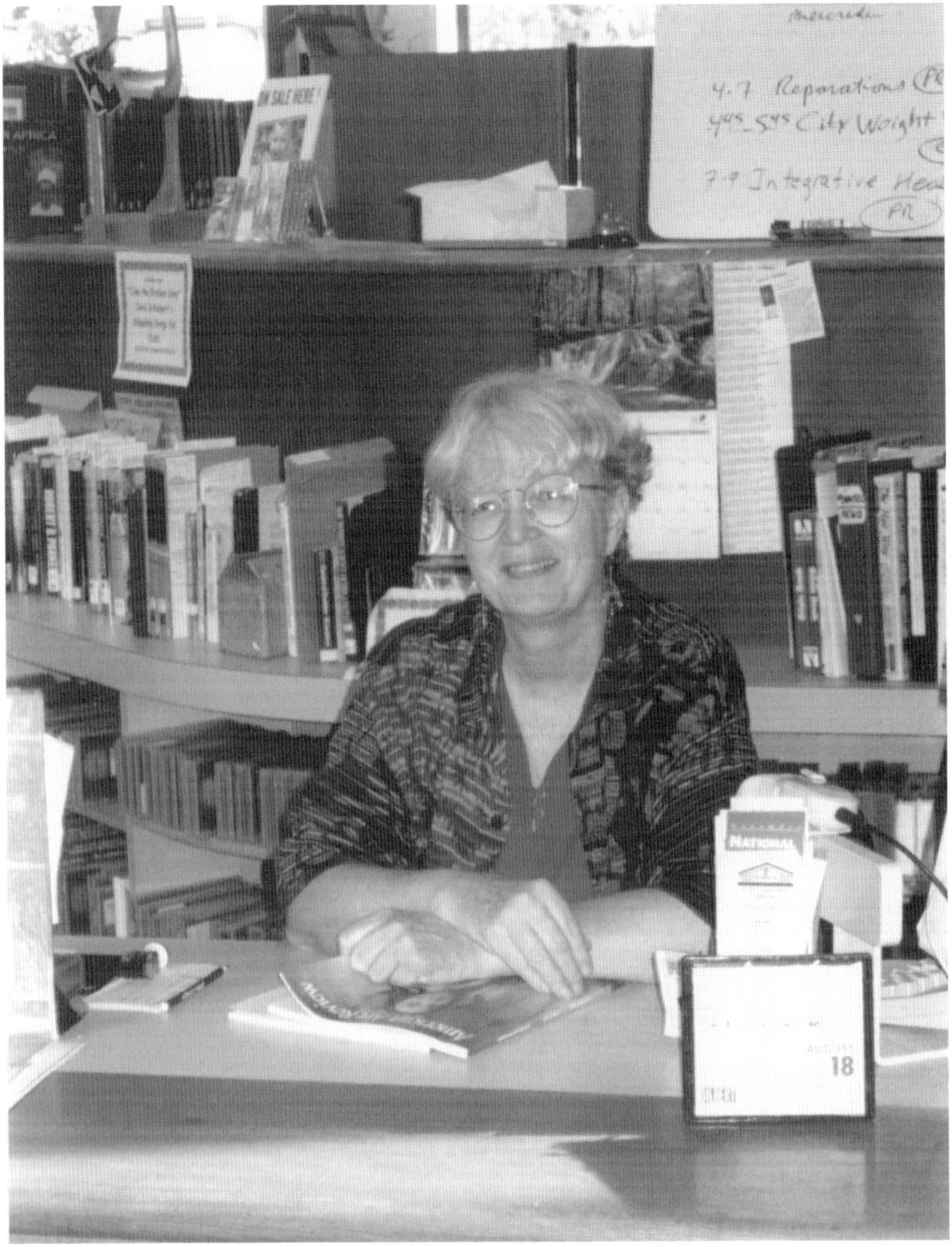

**The Library Lady**

Lorrie Colburn was a familiar and friendly face at the main desk of the Fletcher Free Library for nearly 25 years. In addition to serving as the library's circulation chief, Colburn freely dispensed book reviews, cheerful greetings, and friendly advice to library patrons and staff. Colburn's most memorable innovation, though, may have been her idea in 2002 of establishing a "lending library" of garden tools that could be checked out using a Fletcher Free Library card. Years after Colburn's retirement, the "library of tools" (which now also includes snow shovels) is still a big hit. (Photograph by the author.)

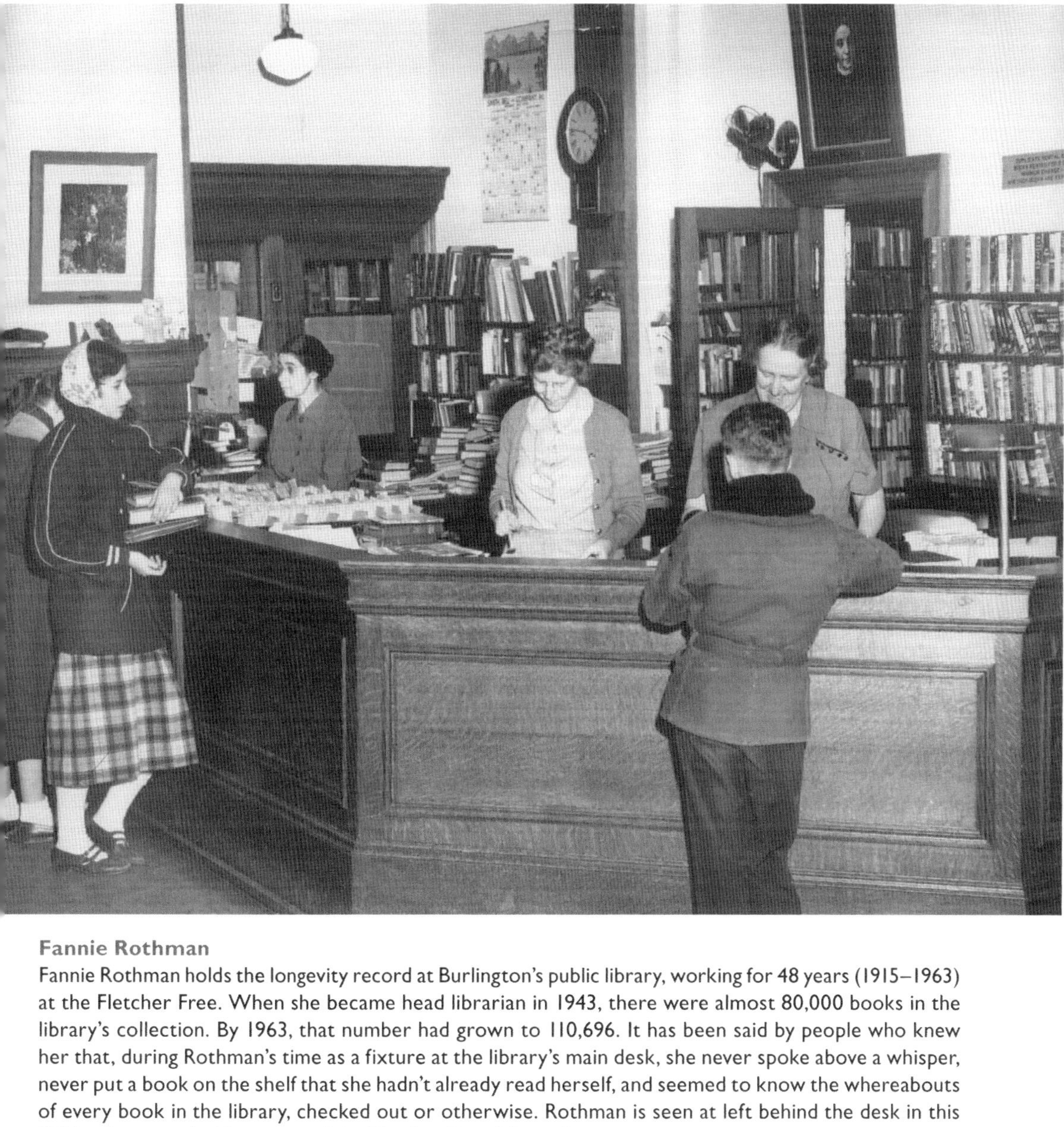

**Fannie Rothman**

Fannie Rothman holds the longevity record at Burlington's public library, working for 48 years (1915–1963) at the Fletcher Free. When she became head librarian in 1943, there were almost 80,000 books in the library's collection. By 1963, that number had grown to 110,696. It has been said by people who knew her that, during Rothman's time as a fixture at the library's main desk, she never spoke above a whisper, never put a book on the shelf that she hadn't already read herself, and seemed to know the whereabouts of every book in the library, checked out or otherwise. Rothman is seen at left behind the desk in this 1950s photograph. (Courtesy of the Fletcher Free Library.)

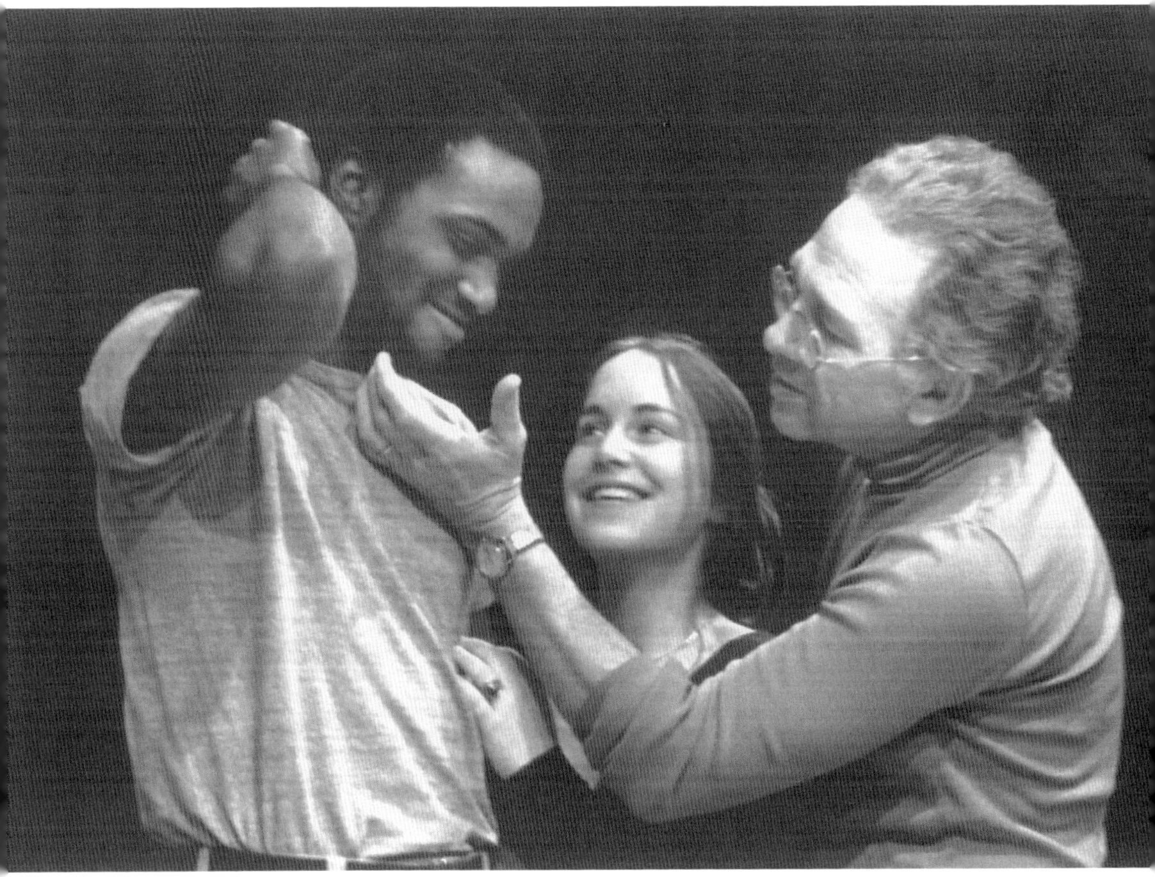

**Edward J. Feidner**

Ed Feidner (pictured here directing the play *When Bananas Grow on a Cherry Tree*) was the heart and soul of the University of Vermont's theatre department for 36 years. During that time, he directed, produced, or acted in more than 125 theatrical productions, including all but three of Shakespeare's plays. Feidner (1931–2008) simply loved Shakespeare and served as the producer and the artistic director for the Champlain Shakespeare Festival, Burlington's renowned summer theatre company, from 1962 until the festival disbanded in 1980. Ed Feidner was also instrumental in the conversion of the school's original gymnasium building into the Royall Tyler Theatre, a fine arts complex and permanent home for the school's theatre department. But his greatest achievement, at least according to the many students who remember him fondly, was the inspiration he provided. (Courtesy of Special Collections, University of Vermont Libraries.)

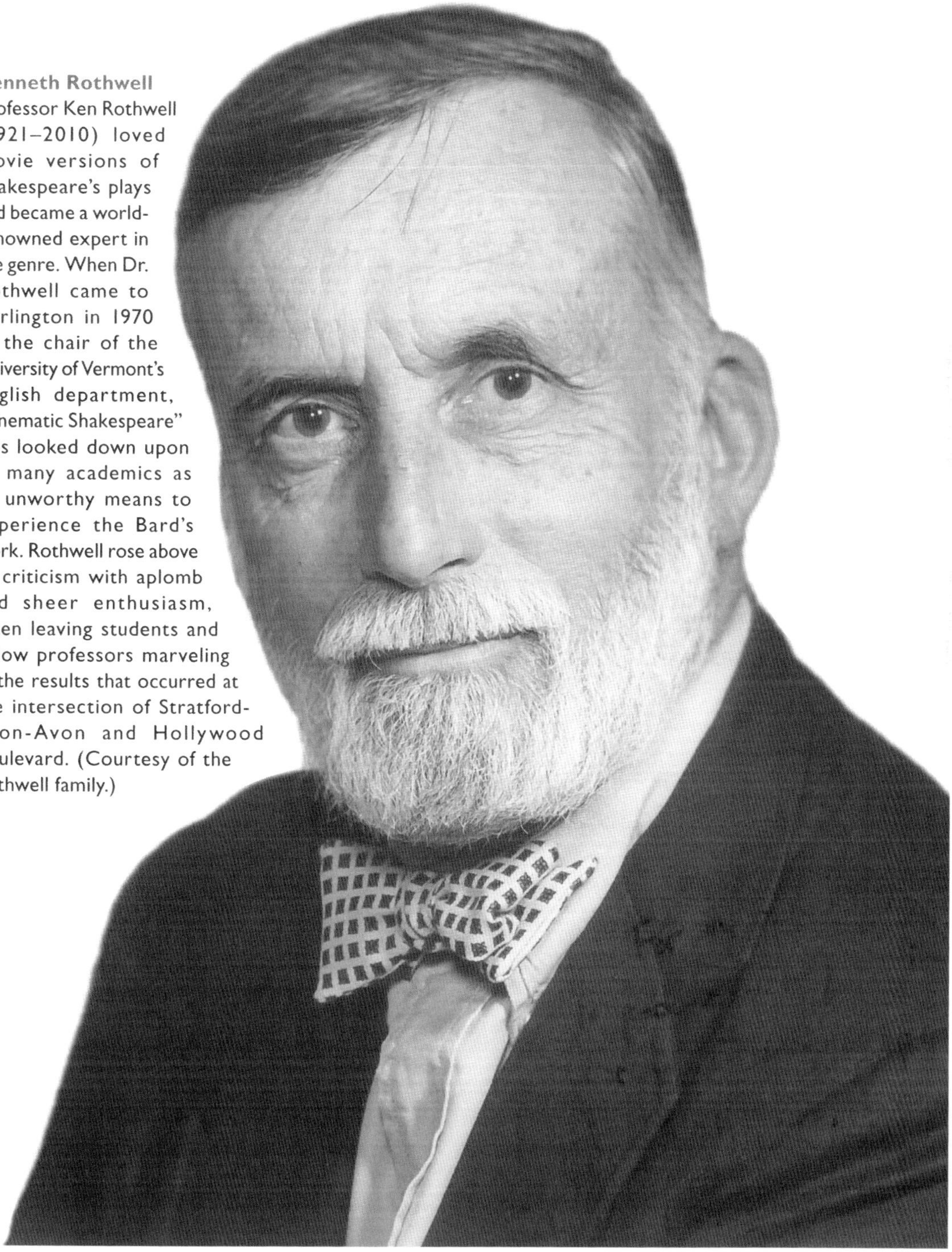

**Kenneth Rothwell**
Professor Ken Rothwell (1921–2010) loved movie versions of Shakespeare's plays and became a world-renowned expert in the genre. When Dr. Rothwell came to Burlington in 1970 as the chair of the University of Vermont's English department, "cinematic Shakespeare" was looked down upon by many academics as an unworthy means to experience the Bard's work. Rothwell rose above all criticism with aplomb and sheer enthusiasm, often leaving students and fellow professors marveling at the results that occurred at the intersection of Stratford-upon-Avon and Hollywood Boulevard. (Courtesy of the Rothwell family.)

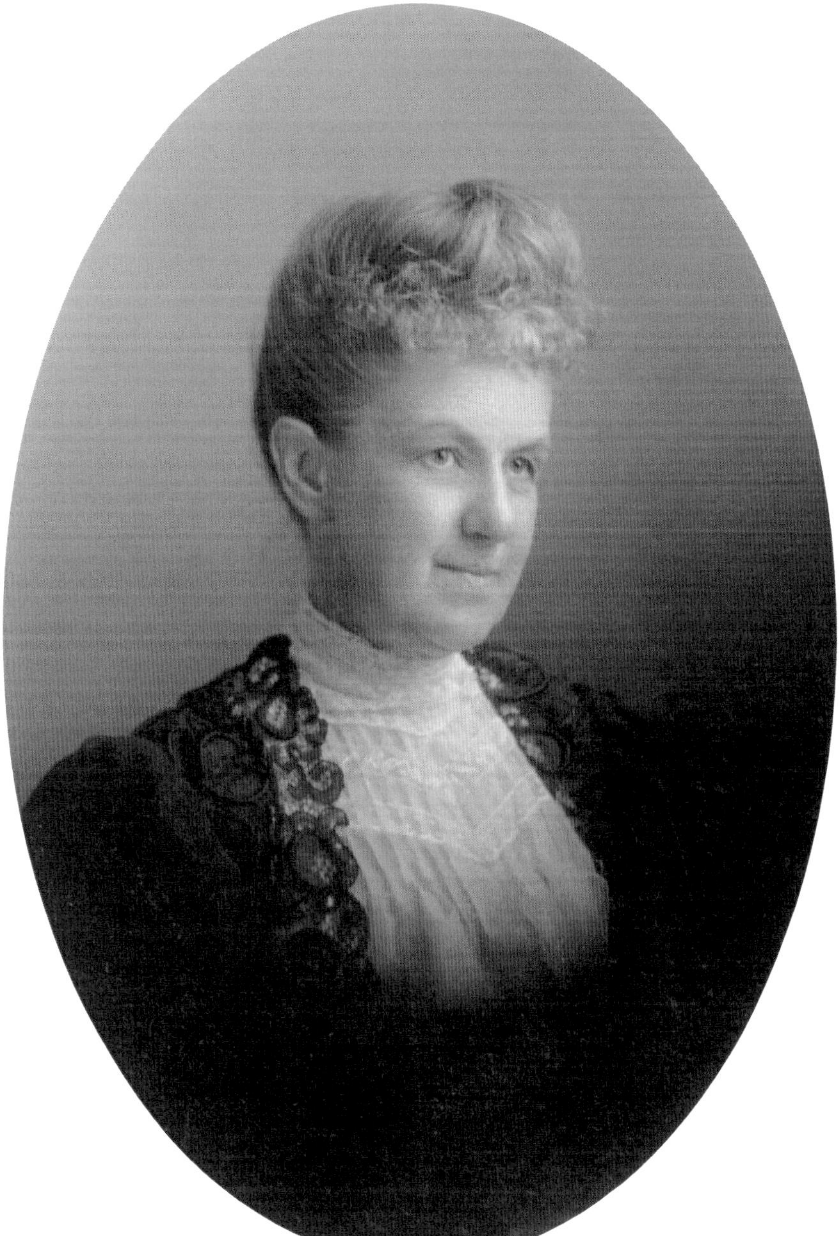

## Effie Moore

Effie Moore (1856–1921) spent nearly 40 years teaching Latin and serving as head of the English department at Burlington High School, the school she graduated from herself. Moore was also one of the first female graduates of the University of Vermont (in 1876) and a member of Phi Beta Kappa.

The 1921 *Oread*, Burlington High School's yearbook, was dedicated to Moore shortly after her death. The author of the *Oread*'s dedication noted that Effie Moore was the one to turn to "when any question arose depending for its answer on things that had been," and also pointed out the rarity of teachers who had been around long enough to have taught the parents of current students. (Courtesy of the Fletcher Free Library.)

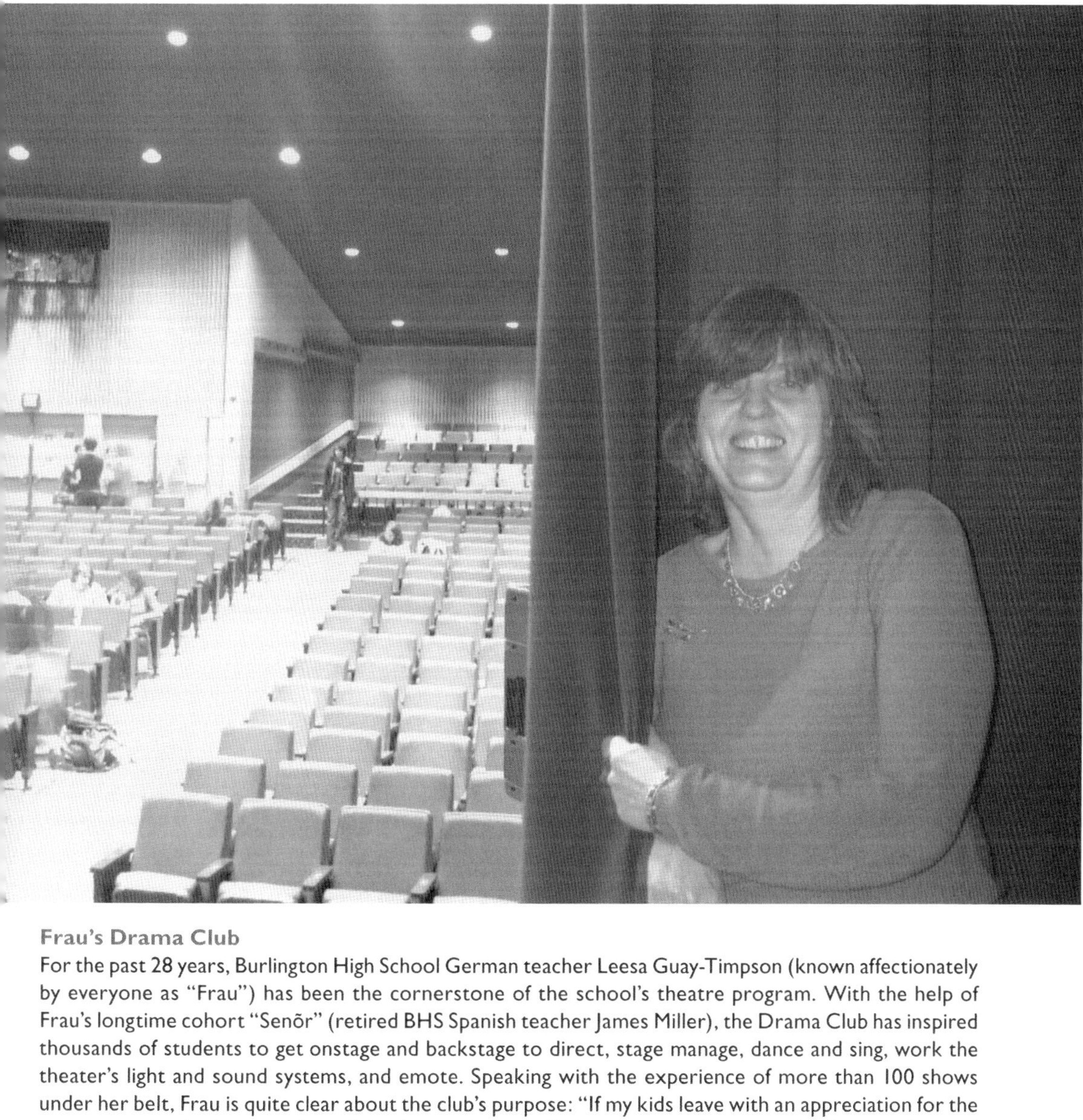

**Frau's Drama Club**
For the past 28 years, Burlington High School German teacher Leesa Guay-Timpson (known affectionately by everyone as "Frau") has been the cornerstone of the school's theatre program. With the help of Frau's longtime cohort "Senõr" (retired BHS Spanish teacher James Miller), the Drama Club has inspired thousands of students to get onstage and backstage to direct, stage manage, dance and sing, work the theater's light and sound systems, and emote. Speaking with the experience of more than 100 shows under her belt, Frau is quite clear about the club's purpose: "If my kids leave with an appreciation for the arts, remembering how much work it takes to do a good job onstage, and are not afraid to stand up and express themselves in public as adults, then we've done our job!" (Photograph by the author.)

## A Lover of Steamships and History

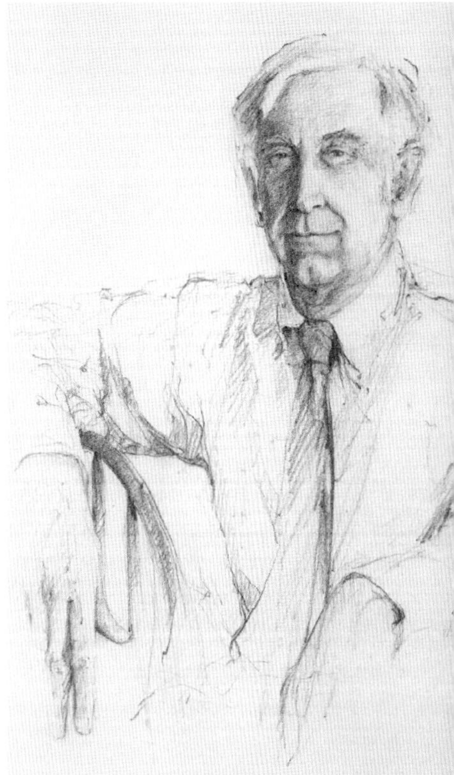

Ralph Nading Hill Jr. (1917–1987), a respected author and historian, was born and raised in Burlington. Hill had worked on the *Ticonderoga*, the last passenger steamship on the lake, and loved the boat so much that he had the study of his house built to the exact dimensions of the *Ticonderoga*'s wheelhouse. Since his home was situated on the lakeshore in Burlington's south end, the result was surprisingly like being aboard the "Ti" on Lake Champlain. Ralph Nading Hill served as longtime editor of *Vermont Life* magazine, and is famous for the many books that he wrote or edited, including *Contrary Country: A Chronicle of Vermont, Sidewheeler Saga* (based on his experiences aboard the *Ticonderoga*) and *Vermont, A Special World*, one of the state's all-time favorite books of scenic photography. Hill, at the time serving as a trustee of the Shelburne Museum, persuaded Electra Havemeyer Webb to buy the *Ticonderoga* and install it permanently on the grounds of the museum. The Ralph Nading Hill Literary Prize, one of Vermont's most coveted authorship prizes, is given annually by *Vermont Life* for a previously unpublished essay, short story, play, or poem focused on "Vermont—Its People, the Place, Its History or Its Values." (Above, portrait by Meri Bourgard, courtesy of Tony Hall; below, courtesy of the Fletcher Free Library.)

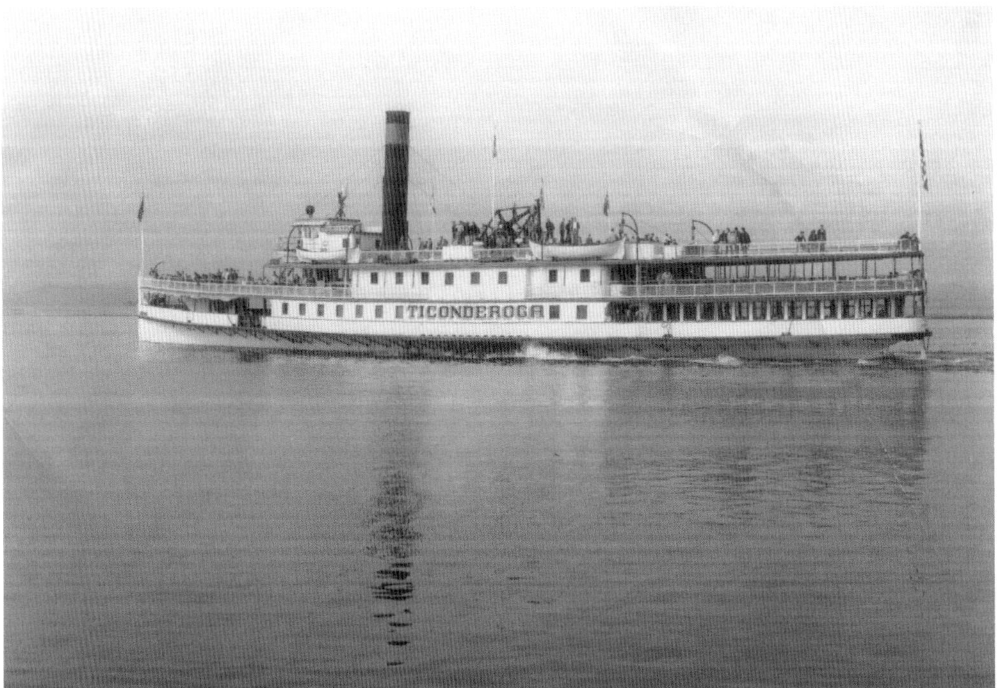

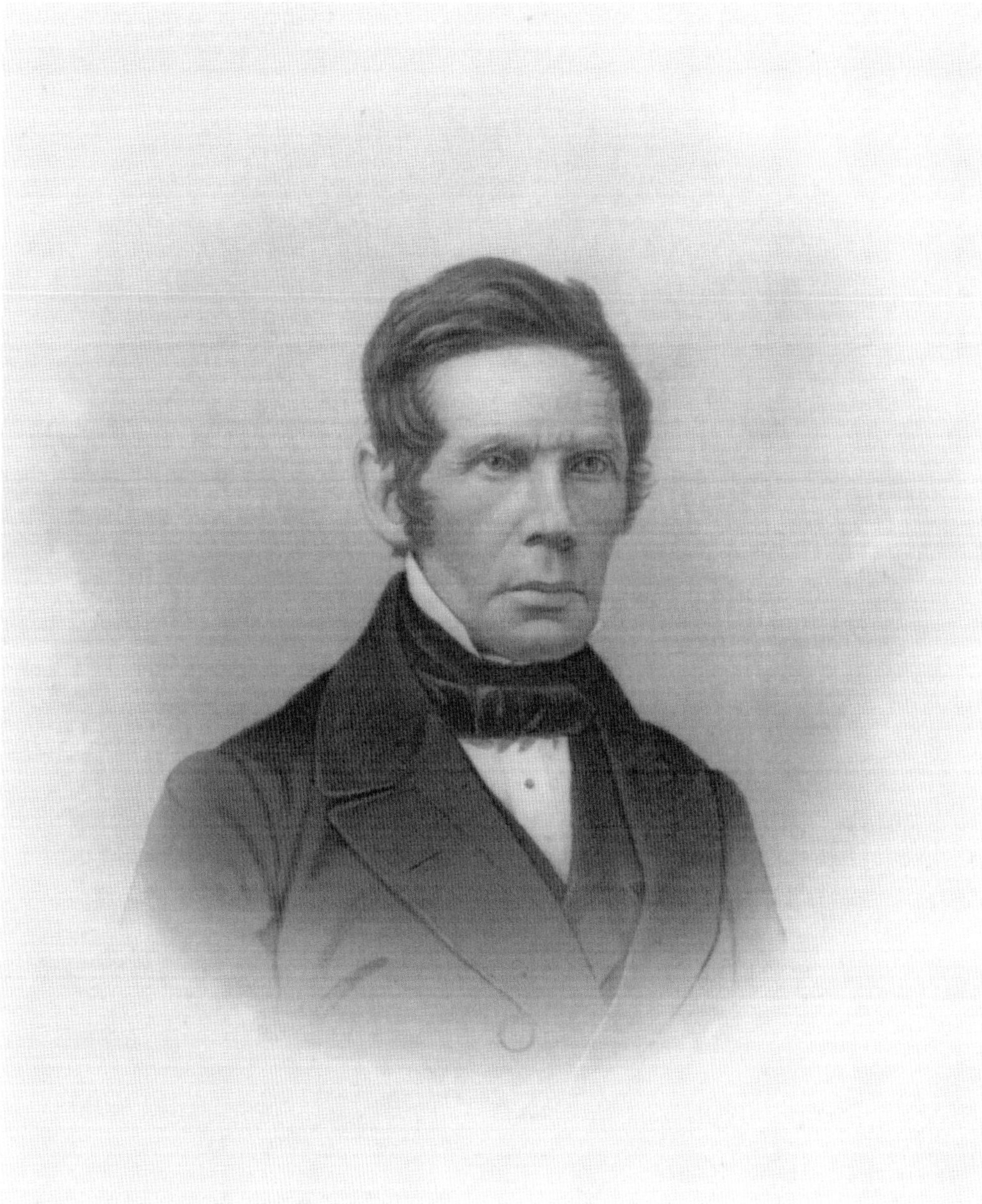

**Zadock Thompson**

Burlington naturalist and historian Zadock Thompson (1796–1856) was a University of Vermont graduate who taught at UVM during the 1830s and from 1851 to 1856. Thompson also served as the Vermont state naturalist in the 1850s. He was the first author to write about Vermont history and natural sciences. His books include *Gazetteer of the State of Vermont* (1824), *History of the State of Vermont* (1833), and *Natural History of Vermont* (1850). Thompson was a pioneer in the field of conservation, citing the damage caused by clear-cutting forests and warning against the effects that humans can have on Vermont's environment. He is memorialized, along with Vermont author Rowland Robinson and Vermont poet John Godfrey Saxe, in the Fletcher Free Library's 1904 stained-glass window as champions of "Science, Art, and Literature." (Courtesy of Special Collections, University of Vermont Libraries.)

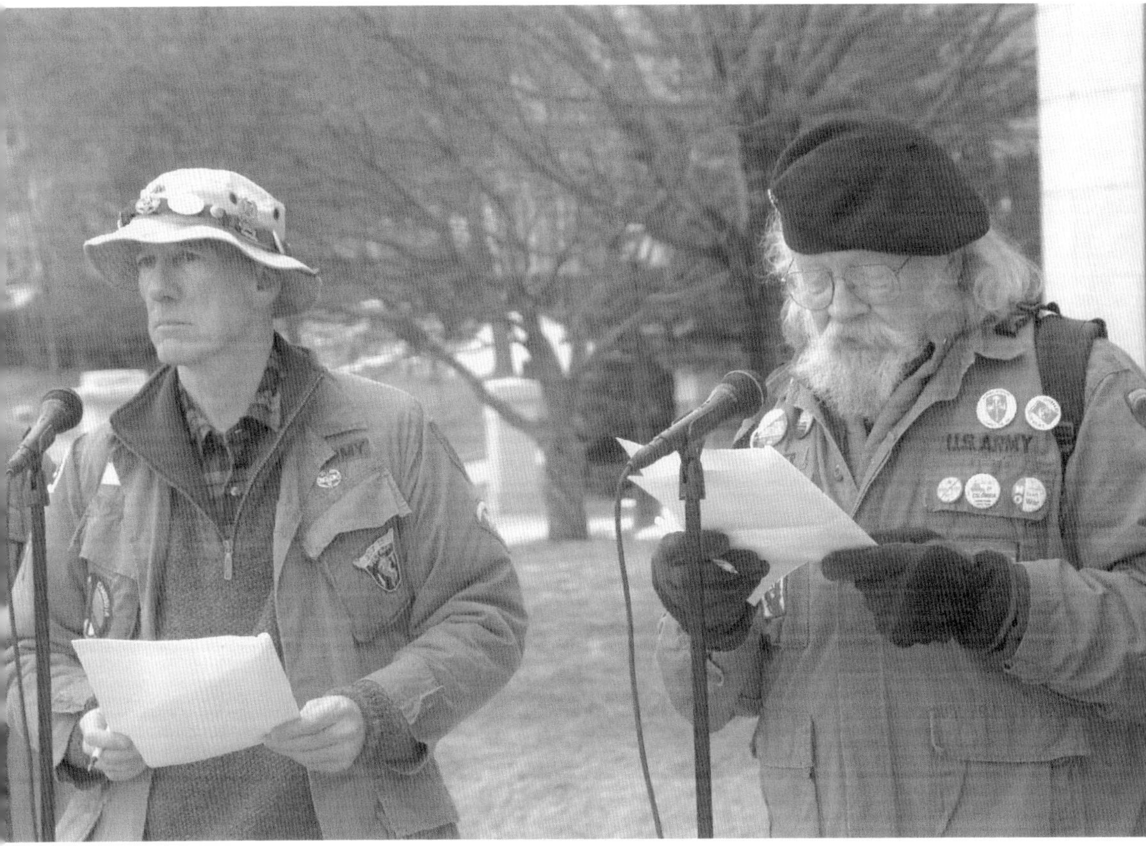


**Willard "Will" Miller**

Peace activist and beloved UVM professor and philosopher Will Miller (1940–2005) began teaching at the University of Vermont in 1969, after cutting his teeth as a signal analyst for the US Army in Eastern Europe during the height of the Cold War. He earned his PhD in philosophy at the University of Illinois. During his 35 years as a UVM professor, Miller was quick to offer help to any person or organization working for peace and social justice. His vast knowledge of political and economic theory made him a force to be reckoned with in all discussions about government and money. Will Miller died from lung cancer in 2005, but he left a legacy of informed resistance and many good examples about how and when to speak one's mind. In this photograph, Miller (right) speaks at an antiwar protest in Montpelier on March 20, 2004. (Photograph courtesy of Orin Langelle/GJEP.)

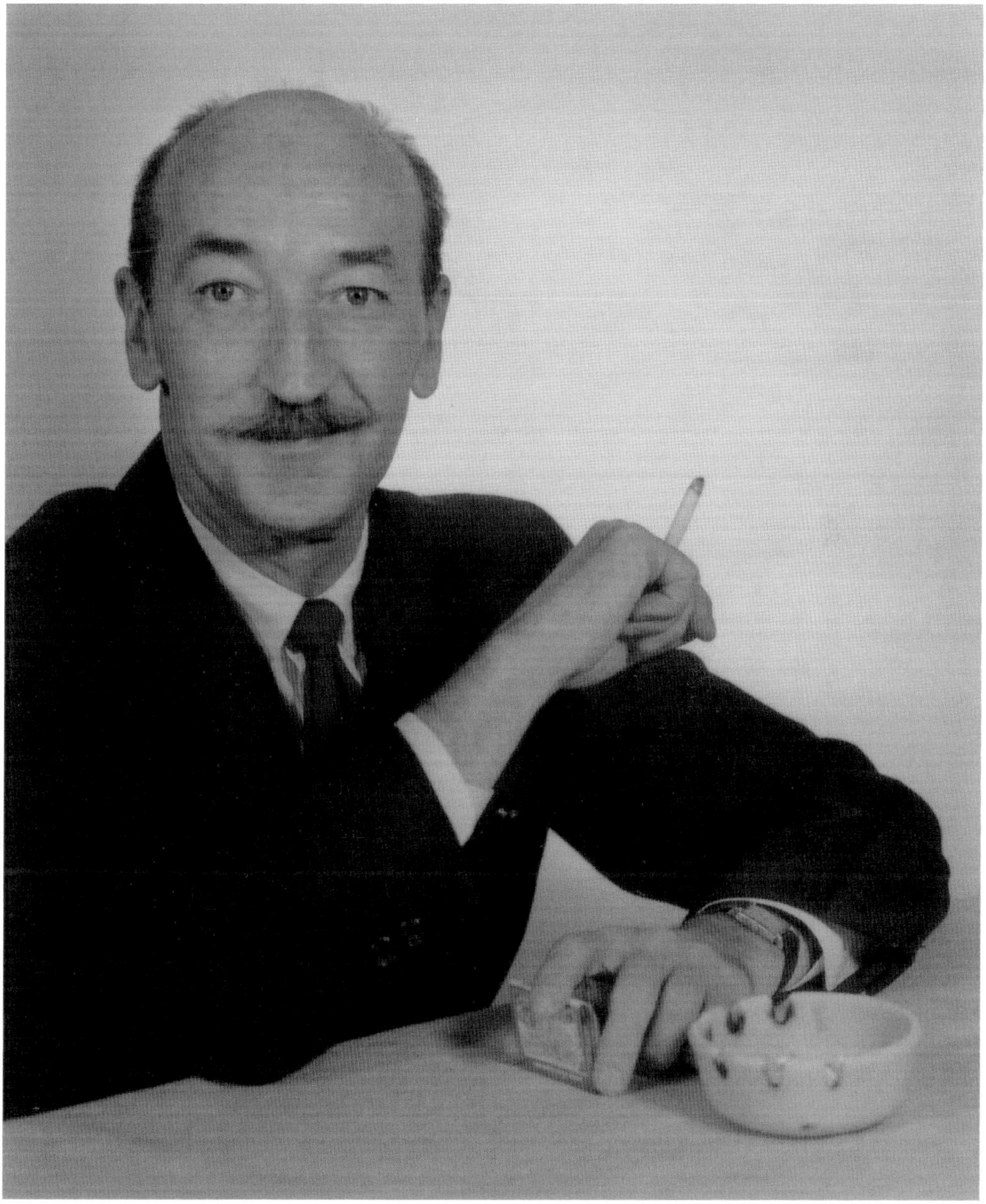

**A Droll Yankee Artist**

Francis Colburn (1909–1984) graduated from the University of Vermont in 1934. After studying at the Arts Students League in New York City, he returned to UVM as an artist-in-residence. Colburn founded the art department at the University of Vermont and worked with his friend, artist Ron Slayton, in FDR's Works Progress Administration Project (more commonly known as the WPA). Colburn was also one of the first native-born Vermont artists to experiment with Surrealism in his work. Colburn is well known for a series of humorous recordings that he made in the 1970s for Droll Yankee Records in Rhode Island, including his "Famous Graduation Address," which is available for listening online. The Colburn Gallery in Williams Hall, the home of UVM's art department, is named in his honor. (Courtesy of Special Collections, University of Vermont Libraries.)

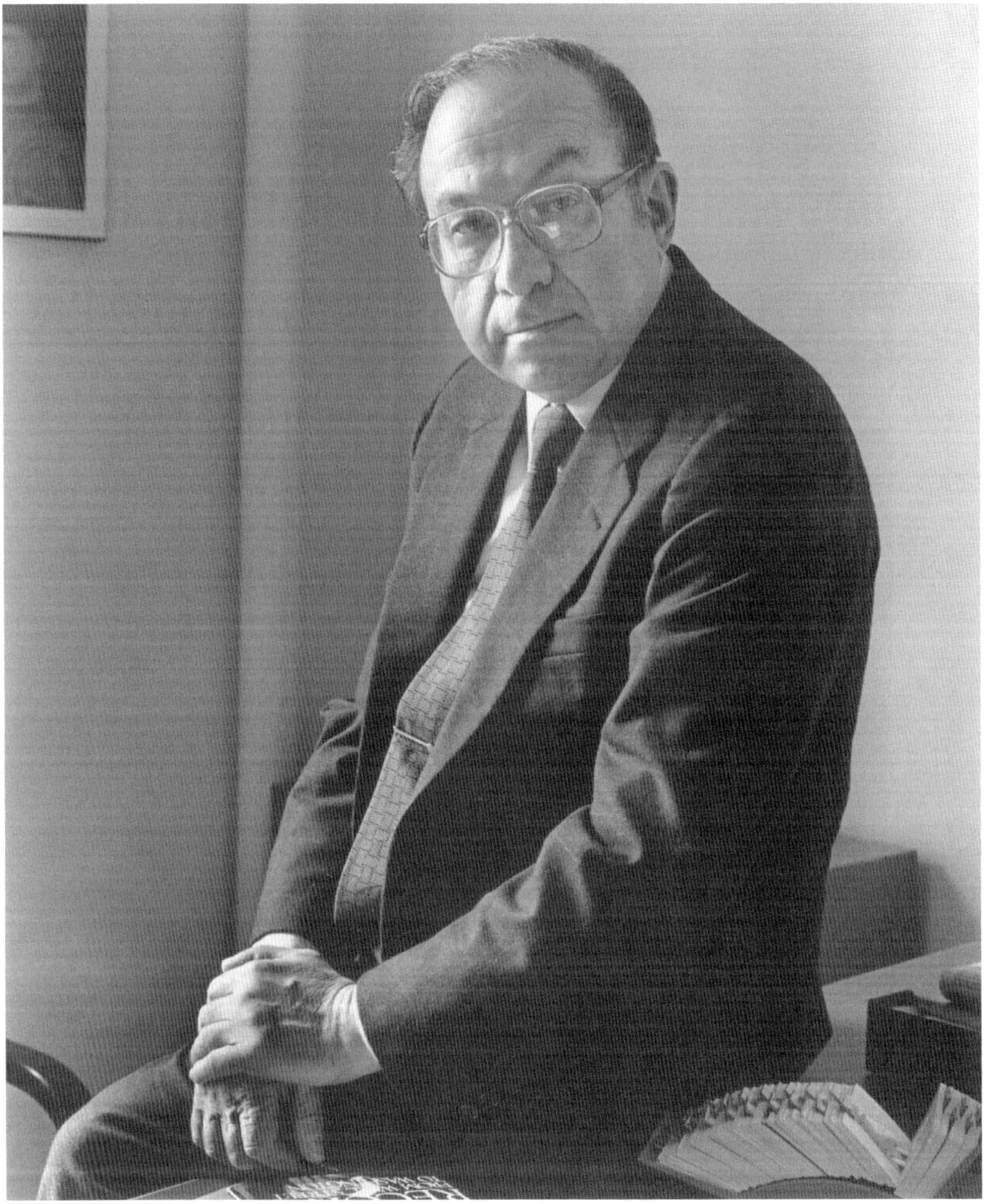

**Raul Hilberg**

Historian Raul Hilberg (1926–2007) was one of the world's foremost experts on the Holocaust and is the author of *The Destruction of the European Jews*, a definitive study on the subject. *Shoah*, the award-winning 1985 documentary by Claude Lanzmann about the nazi concentration camps, features interviews with Hilberg. When he was 13, Raul Hilberg and his family escaped from Vienna just before the beginning of World War II. After graduating from Columbia University in 1955, Dr. Hilberg moved to Burlington to begin his career in the University of Vermont's political science department, where he undertook further research and taught until retiring in 1991. To honor Professor Hilberg, the Raul Hilberg Distinguished Professorship of Holocaust Studies was established by the university in 2006. (Courtesy of Special Collections, University of Vermont Libraries.)

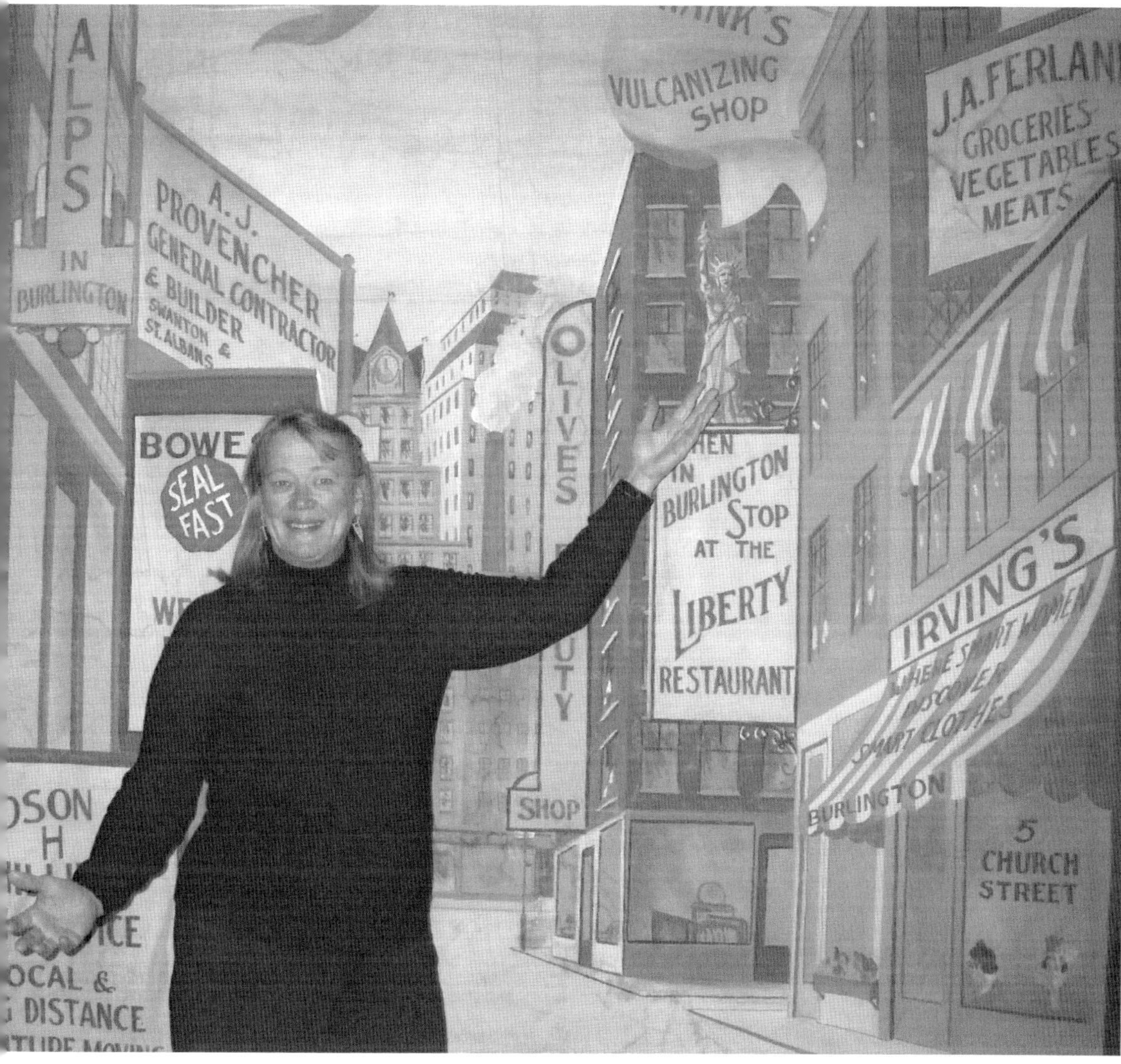


**Chris Hadsel**

Burlingtonian Chris Hadsel, then the director of the Vermont Museum & Gallery Alliance, was instrumental in launching the Vermont Painted Theater Curtain Project in 1996. The project began after the discovery of a few disused hand-painted theater curtains (mostly created between 1890 and 1940) around the state. Funding supplied by a matching grant from the National Trust for Historic Preservation allowed Hadsel and some of her fellow archivists and conservators to conduct a statewide survey to find more curtains and assess their condition. The project uncovered 185 historic painted curtains in Vermont, including the Burlington advertising curtain, shown here, painted by artist Lucretia Rogers of Plymouth in 1935. This curtain was found at an auction in Maine and has now been conserved and is on display on the stage in Burlington's City Hall Auditorium. Chris Hadsel and her team have since created Curtains Without Borders, an expanded project that already includes hundreds of antique curtains in New Hampshire, Maine, and northern New York. The discovery of so many beautiful and historic curtains has kindled renewed interest in the artists who painted them and in the buildings where they were on display. And as a result, some towns have been inspired to completely renovate venerable old auditoriums and stages. (Photograph by the author.)

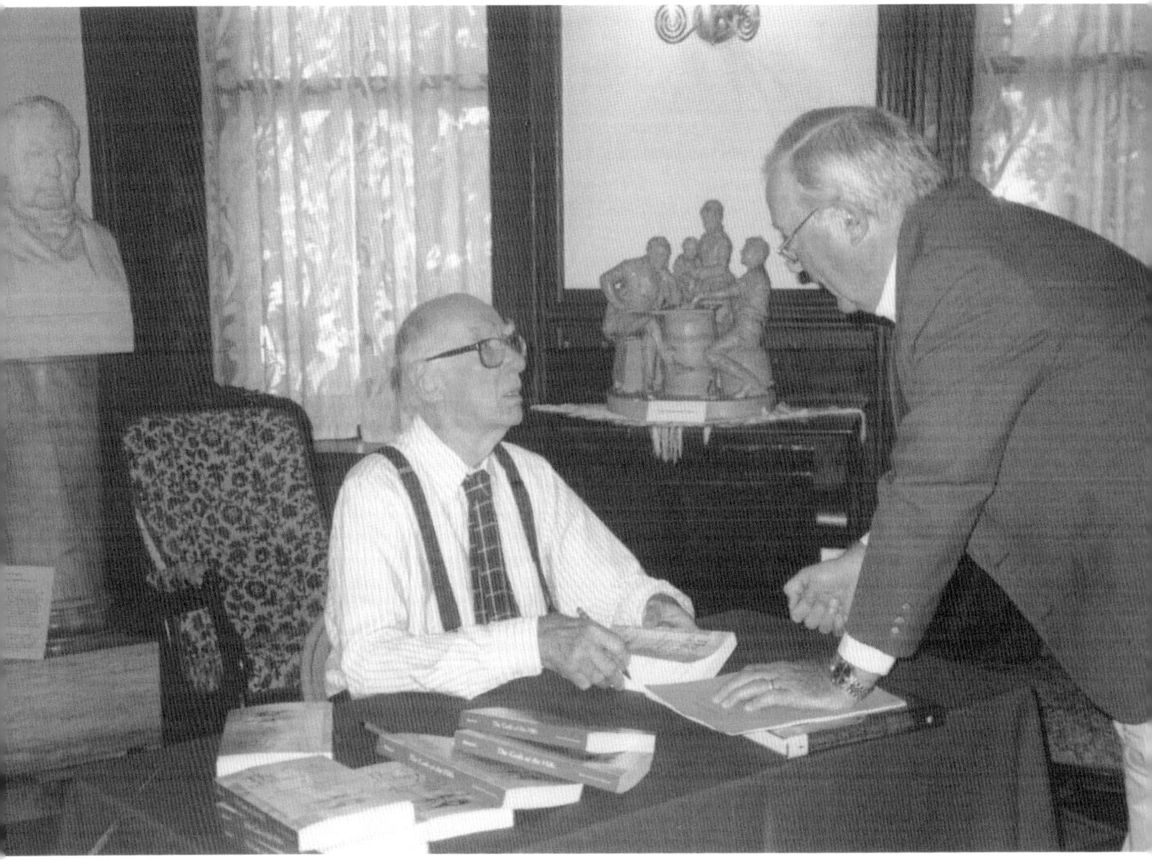

**T.D. Seymour Bassett**

World traveler, music lover, expert researcher, and Burlington character Tom Bassett (1913–2001) seemed to know everything there was to know about Vermont history. This is not surprising, as he was the author of *Vermont: A Bibliography of Its History*, a beloved reference book for Vermont librarians and anyone else trying to research days gone by in the Green Mountain State. Born and raised in Burlington, Bassett graduated from Yale, received his PhD in history from Harvard, and ended up moving back to his hometown in 1958 to teach history and ultimately to become the curator of Special Collections at the University of Vermont. Along the way, he founded the Burlington Friends Meeting, learned to play the clarinet, and canoed the entire length of Lake Champlain. It was said of Tom Bassett that he never stopped learning. He is shown here signing a copy of his book *The Gods of the Hills*. (Courtesy of Miriam French.)

# CHAPTER FOUR

# Entrepreneurs, Land Barons, and Businesses Large and Small

Burlington's growth from a small settlement in the 1760s to a bustling trading port in the 1860s was initially fueled by land speculation, and then by the lumber trade and manufacturing. Ira Allen moved to Burlington with three of his brothers, including Ethan, the eldest and most famous of the Allens, to establish the Onion River Land Company, a land investment business that eventually controlled 300,000 acres of prime farmland along the Winooski River. Garden Way cofounder and preservationist Will Raap created the Intervale Foundation to help foster the return of local agriculture on the same land that had belonged to the Allens.

Willard Crane lived and worked in Burlington during the late 19th century, a time when vast fortunes were made from lumber and shipping. Burlington grocer John McKenzie founded a specialty meat company in 1907 that, for nearly 100 years, provided the city with locally made hot dogs and maple hams.

Sid and Lou Mazel, members of a family that ran a downtown department store, opened Gaynes Shoppers World, one of Vermont's first discount department stores, in 1959. Gaynes was very popular with Canadian customers and was the beginning of an ongoing love affair between Montreal consumers and Burlington businesses. The town's reputation as a center for entrepreneurs was set in frosty sweetness with the success of Ben Cohen and Jerry Greenfield, who launched their ice-cream business in 1978.

Other notable local businesspeople include Jim Lampman, founder of the Lake Champlain Chocolate Company in 1983, and Nectar Rorris, a local restaurant owner who turned a rundown club on Burlington's Main Street into a legendary venue for live music. Dave and Jenny Rooke, two of Burlington's newest commercial brewers, launched their premium homemade root beer in 2005 and have already seen it become a favorite in restaurants throughout northern Vermont.

Burlington has been home to many locally owned bookstores. The Everyday Book Shop closed in 2008, but it will be a long time before Burlington book lovers forget Elizabeth Orr, who ran the shop all by herself for umpteen years. Crow Bookshop on Church Street features a broad selection of interesting new and used books, and Phoenix Books, Burlington's newest bookshop, has launched an energetic campaign, urging Burlington readers to buy local.

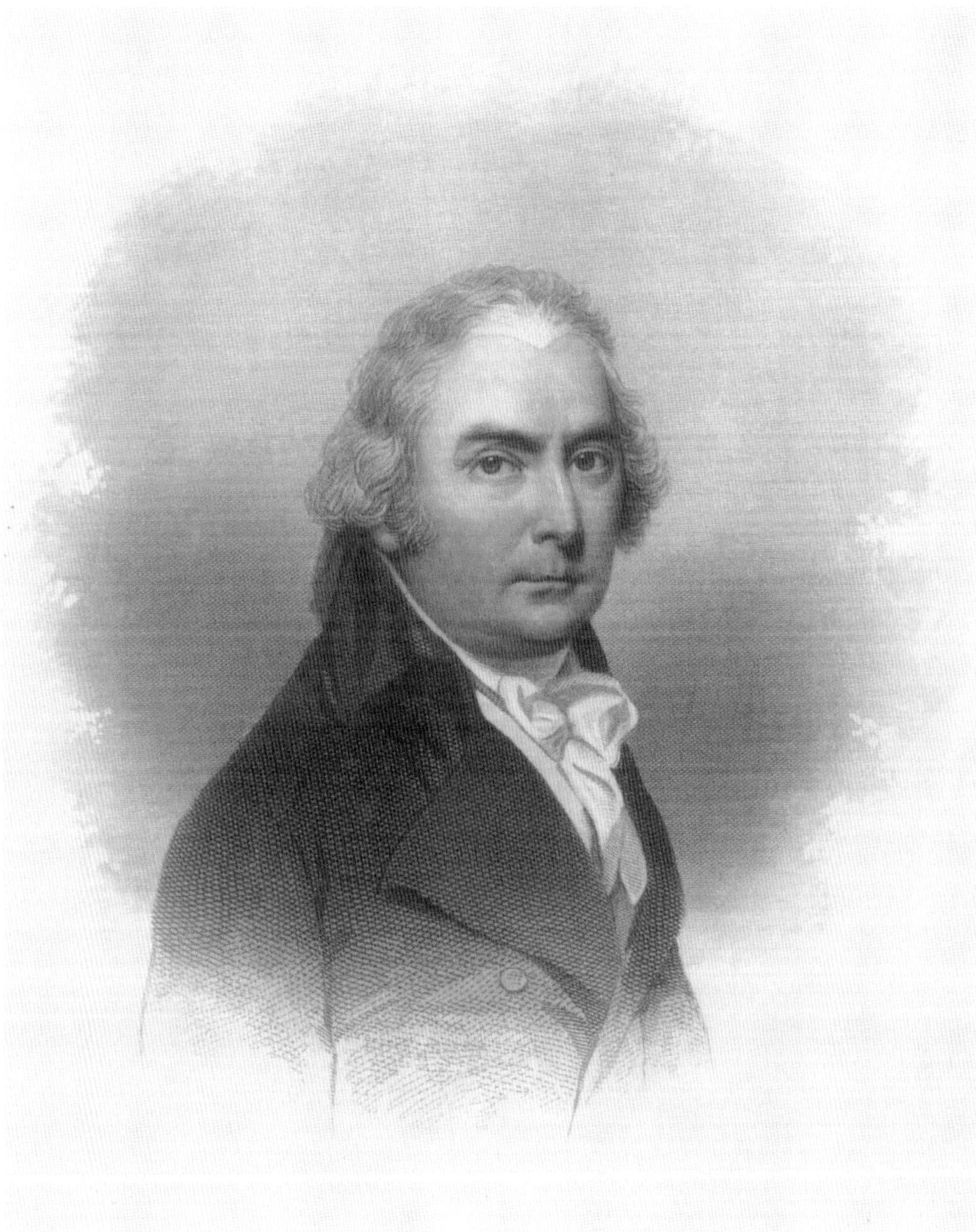

### Ira Allen

Ira Allen (1751–1814) was the youngest of the five brothers of Ethan Allen. Ira moved to the Burlington area in 1771 to serve as the surveyor for the Onion River Land Company, a family business venture for purchasing land from the New Hampshire Grants. By the 1790s, Ira and his wife, Jerusha Allen, owned 20,000 to 30,000 acres of land, seven mills, two forges, and a ferry across the Winooski River. Ira Allen is the designer of the Great Seal of the State of Vermont and the seal of the University of Vermont, which he helped found with a gift of 50 acres of land in 1780. In spite of his apparent business acumen and his wealth, Ira Allen was bankrupted by a disastrous purchase of French guns in 1795. He was buried in a pauper's grave in Pennsylvania. (Courtesy of Special Collections, University of Vermont Libraries.)

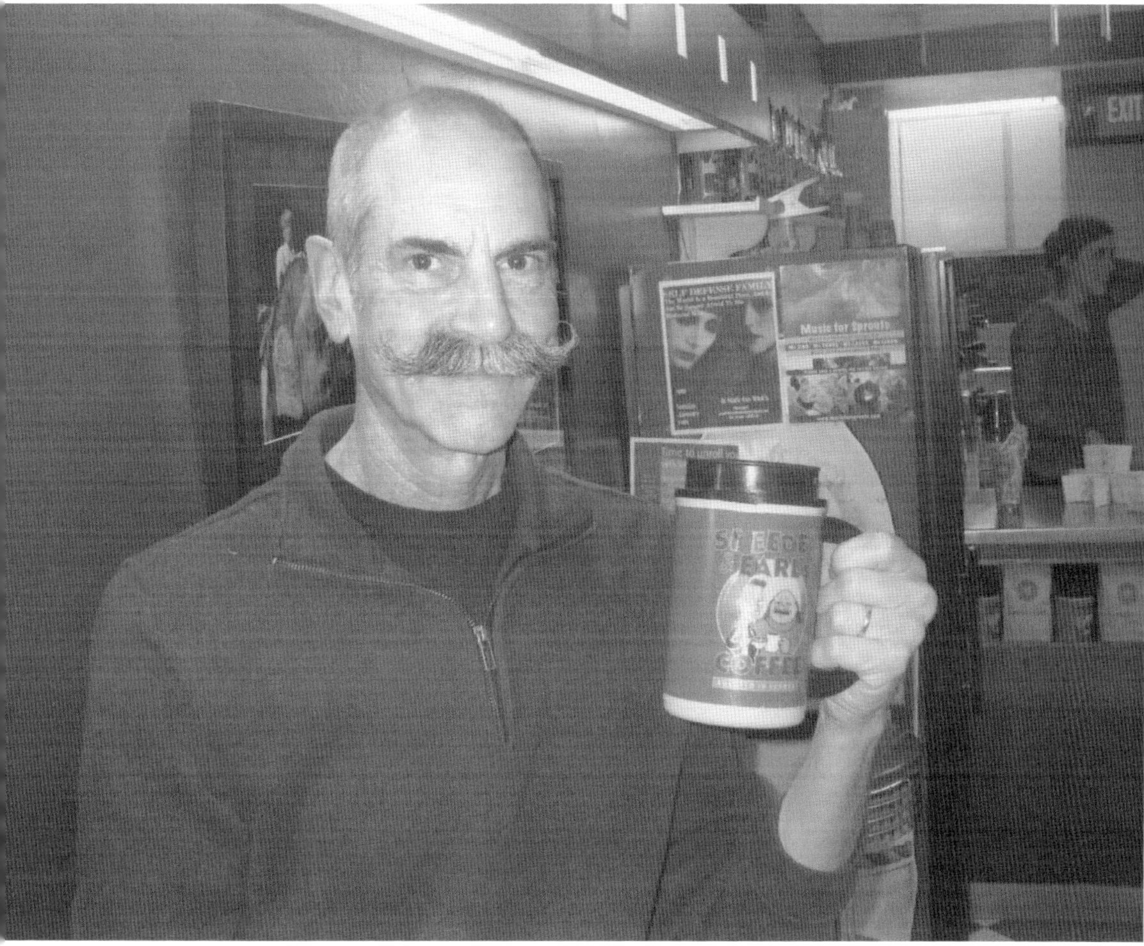


**Mr. Earl**

Doug Montgomery has owned the tiny storefront that is the Church Street home of Speeder & Earl's, one of Burlington's first and favorite coffee shops, for the past 15 years. Even though he is not the original owner, many people think that Montgomery is "Earl," one of the two fictional namesakes of the business (as in "They often call me Speedo, but my real name is Mr. Earl"), because they both share substantial and unique moustaches. Doug Montgomery loves good coffee, loves the variety of regular customers who frequent his little "coffee-to-go" location, and prides himself on having provided many young people with their first and, he's often been told, their favorite job. (Photograph by the author.)

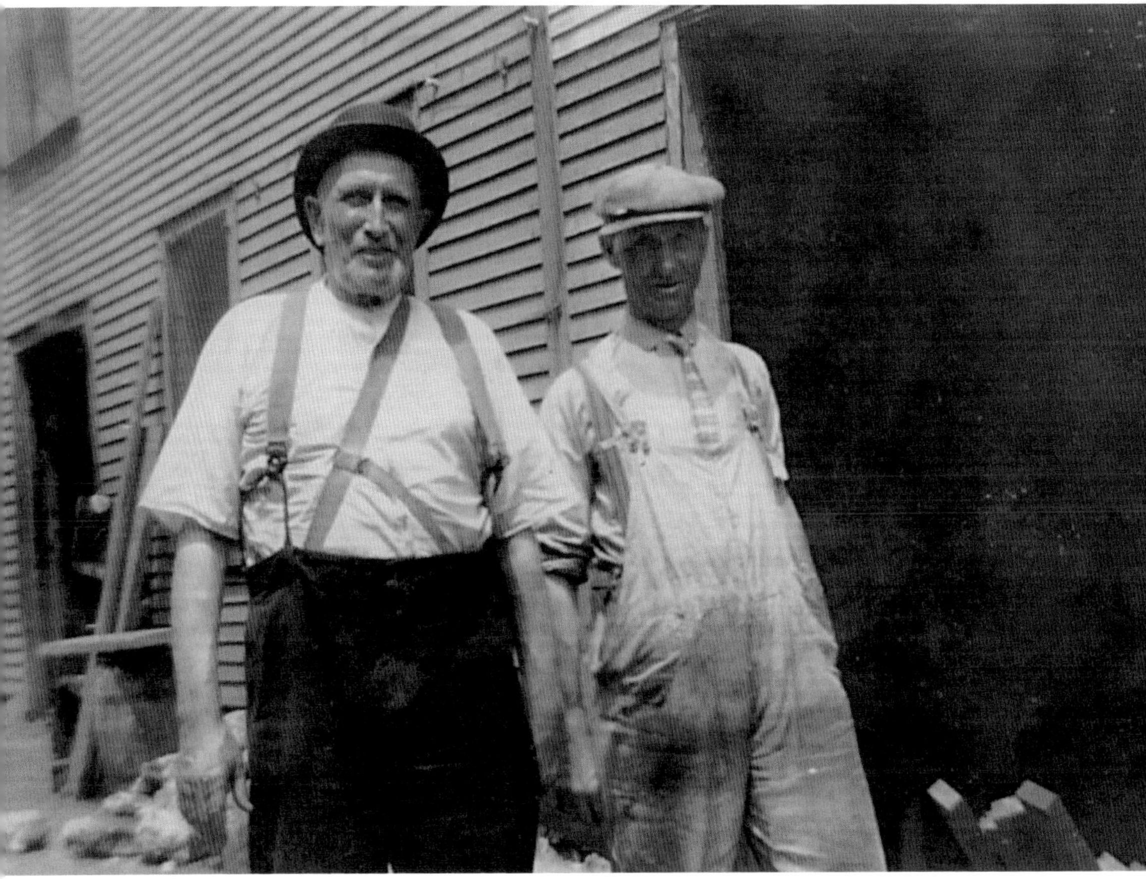

**Burlington's Own Hot Dogs**
Burlington grocer John McKenzie (pictured on the left in front of his "Shop," as everyone referred to the John McKenzie Packing Co. at 40 George Street) founded his specialty meat company in 1907. McKenzie's natural-casing hot dogs are still the standard for local picnics. The company's radio jingle, sung by Johnny Cash himself, was to the tune of *Casey Jones:* "Old John McKenzie was a dedicated man, made the best pork sausage in all the land!" By the 1980s, the McKenzie Packing Company had built a 30,000-square-foot building in Burlington's south end. McKenzie was sold to Kayem Foods in Chelsea, Massachusetts, in 1999, but the "McKenzie Country Classics" line of products is still available, featuring John McKenzie's maple cured ham and bacon (using only Vermont maple syrup), and of course those famous hot dogs. (Courtesy of Peter J. Beck.)

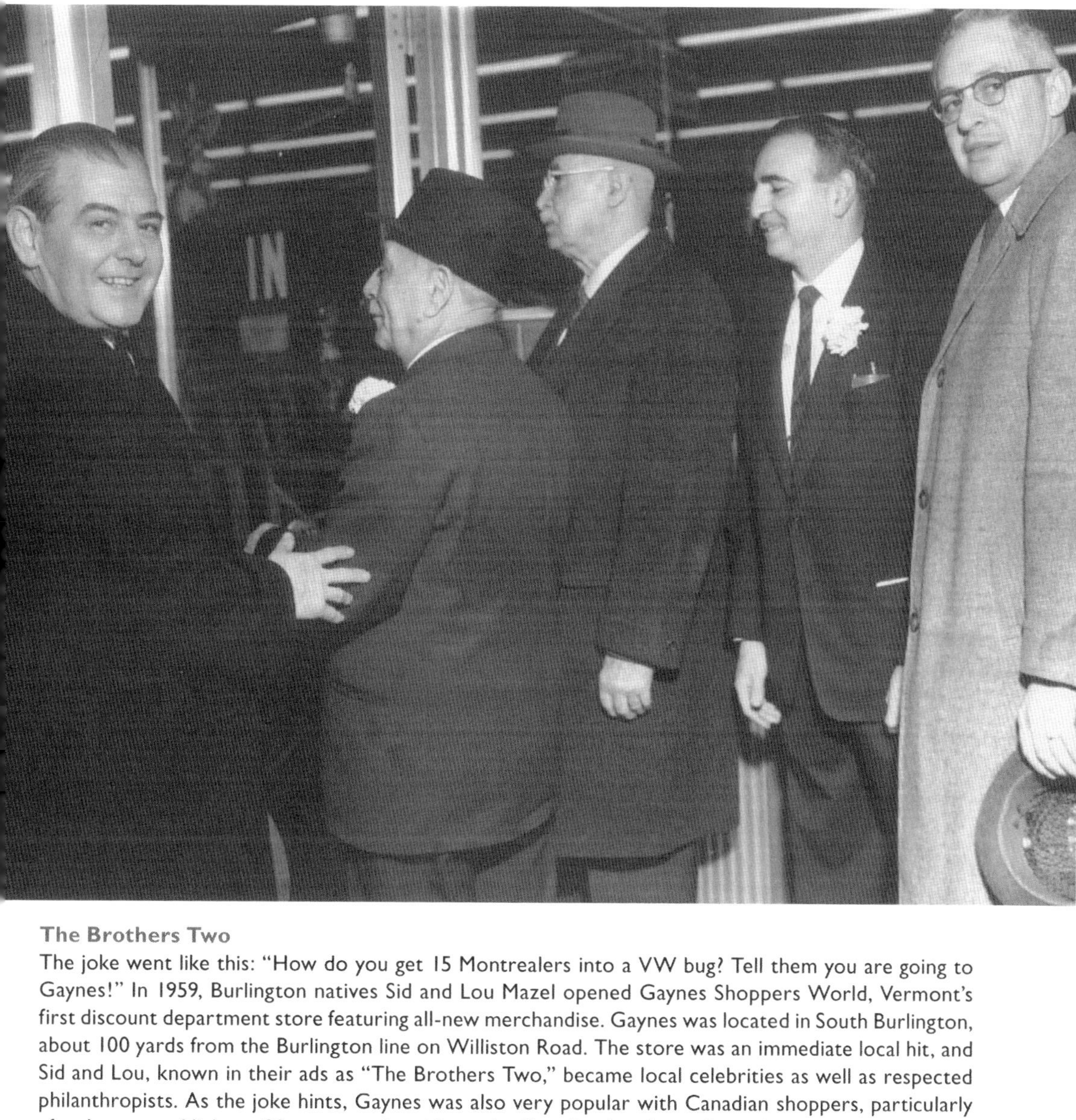


**The Brothers Two**

The joke went like this: "How do you get 15 Montrealers into a VW bug? Tell them you are going to Gaynes!" In 1959, Burlington natives Sid and Lou Mazel opened Gaynes Shoppers World, Vermont's first discount department store featuring all-new merchandise. Gaynes was located in South Burlington, about 100 yards from the Burlington line on Williston Road. The store was an immediate local hit, and Sid and Lou, known in their ads as "The Brothers Two," became local celebrities as well as respected philanthropists. As the joke hints, Gaynes was also very popular with Canadian shoppers, particularly after Interstate Highway 89 was completed from the Canadian border to Exit 14W (next to the Gaynes parking lot) in the mid-1960s. Pictured at the 1959 Gaynes ribbon-cutting ceremony are, from left to right, Sid Mazel, Morris Mazel, unidentified, Lou Mazel, and real estate developer Tony Pomerleau. (Courtesy of Nancy Mazel-Tiffany.)

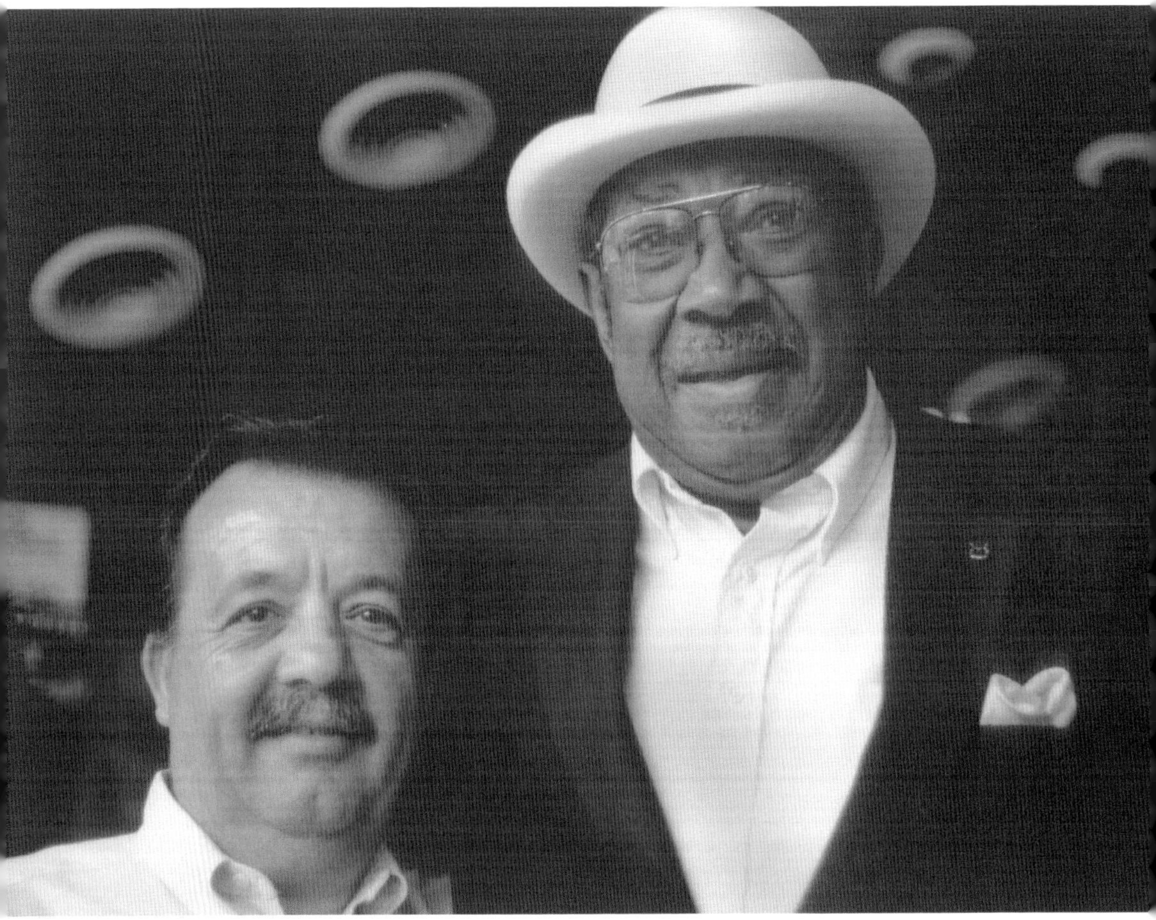

**Nectar Rorris**

Before opening the now-famous Burlington restaurant that bears his name, restaurateur Nectar Rorris used to own a classic burger joint called The Lure on Williston Road in South Burlington. Nectar purchased a building located at 188 Main Street in 1975 and opened Nectar's at the site of the Hi-Hat, a dimly lit lounge slightly past its prime. Nectar's soon became famous for hand-carved turkey sandwiches and spectacular gravy fries in the dining room, and live music seven nights a week on a crowded stage in the adjacent barroom. The restaurant entered jam-band immortality when Phish named its second album *A Picture of Nectar* in honor of the place where they played many of their early gigs. Nectar's still features live music every night, and its gravy fries are still the best. Nectar Rorris (left) is pictured with "Big" Joe Burrell (see page 90). (Courtesy of Matt Thorsen.)

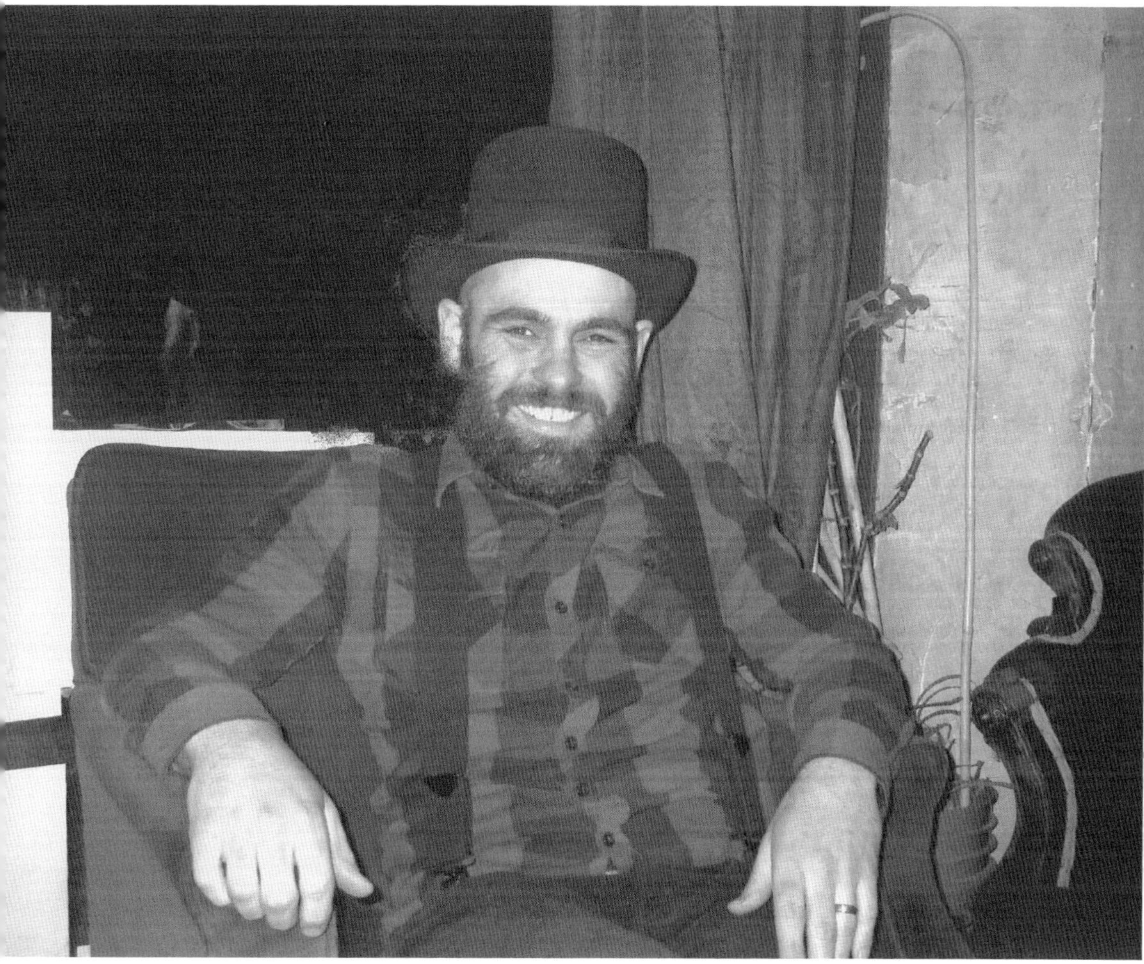

**Radio Bean**
Artist and performer Lee Anderson opened Radio Bean, a north end coffee shop and bar, in 2000 with the belief that "there's no 'higher culture' without a vast subculture, and that incredible performances rise from small and experimental acts." Things have taken their own path since then. Almost on its own, Radio Bean has become one of Burlington's most popular venues for live music: Irish jam sessions on Wednesday evenings, honky-tonk or gypsy jazz on Sunday afternoons, and a series of bands playing everything from rock to space music almost every night of the week. Anderson is "too busy to be amazed at all the success, but I have moments of clarity amid the cacophony!" For experimental artists, anarchists, and all sorts of aspiring musicians, Anderson's Radio Bean is the center of Burlington. (Photograph by the author.)

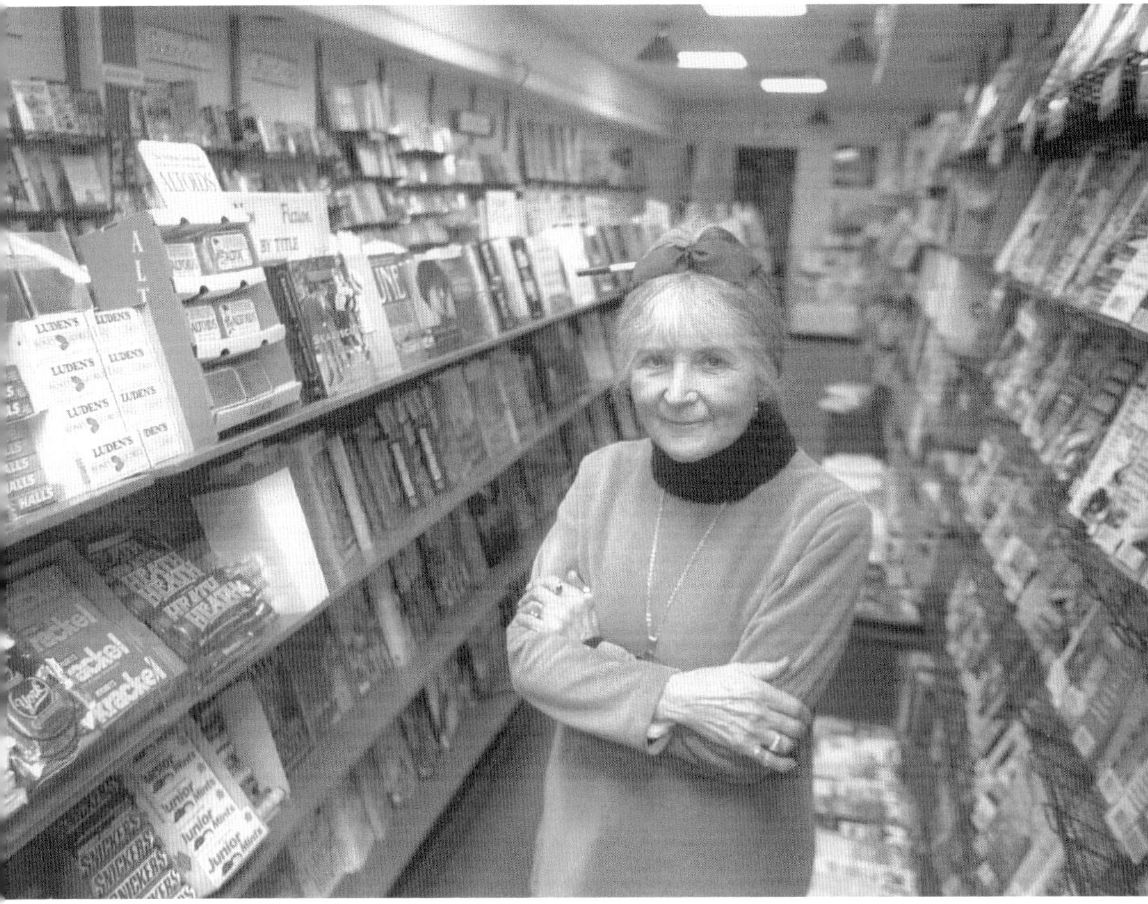


**Every Day for 40 Years**

Elizabeth Orr was a very classy lady, often looking as if she had been getting ready to have a cup of tea in a Victorian garden. Beyond her genteel exterior and the soft English accent, however, was a backbone of iron. For as long as anyone could remember, Orr had run the Everyday Book Shop as a one-woman, seven-day-a-week operation on College Street. Her downtown space was a bookstore, newspaper stand, and convenient local stop for fans of hard-to-find European chocolate bars. Orr ran an old-fashioned bookshop: no computers, just handwritten receipts and plenty of time to relax and chat. When Elizabeth Orr closed up shop in 2008 at the age of 81, everyone, including Orr, was a little sad. Burlington will not see her like again. (Courtesy of Jordan Silverman.)

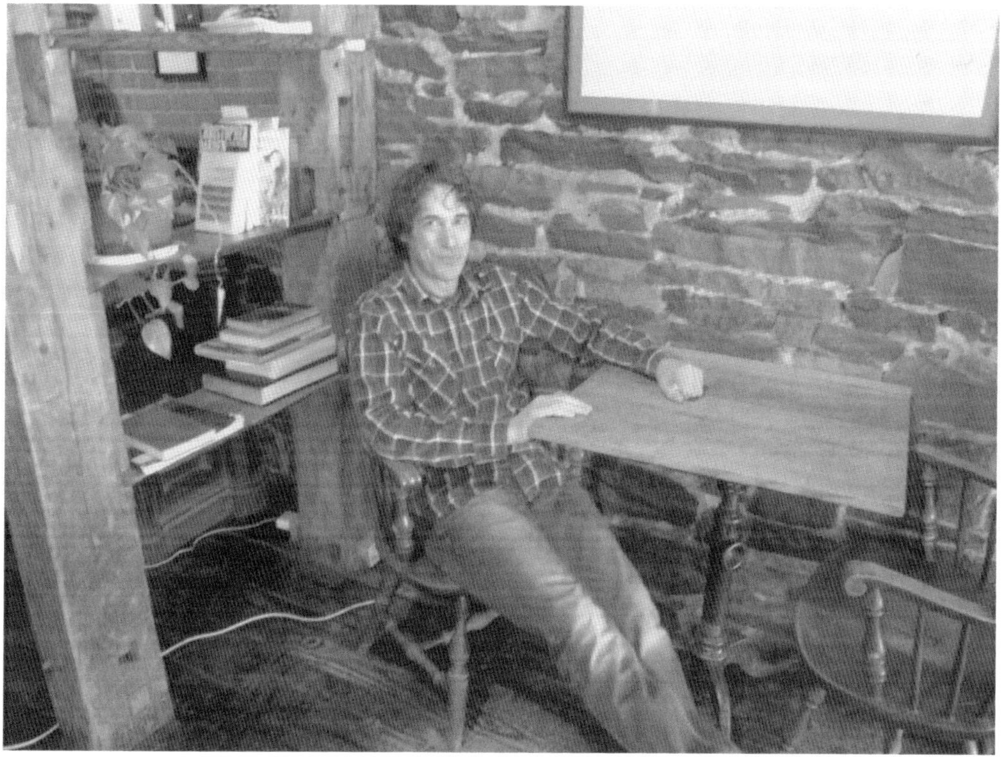

**Muddy Waters**
Mark MacKillop is the owner and one of the founders of Muddy Waters, one of the coziest downtown coffee shops in Burlington. "Muddys" opened in 1994 and was modeled after coffeehouses that MacKillop had seen in Santa Cruz, California. No matter the season, Muddys seems to fill up quickly with youthful regulars who seem to be in no hurry to be anywhere else. MacKillop describes his shop as "not a business for people looking to succeed in the conventional way; it is an exercise in esthetics, and as much a social mission as a business." Social mission or not, Mark MacKillop's shop seems to be just the way his customers like it. (Photograph by the author.)

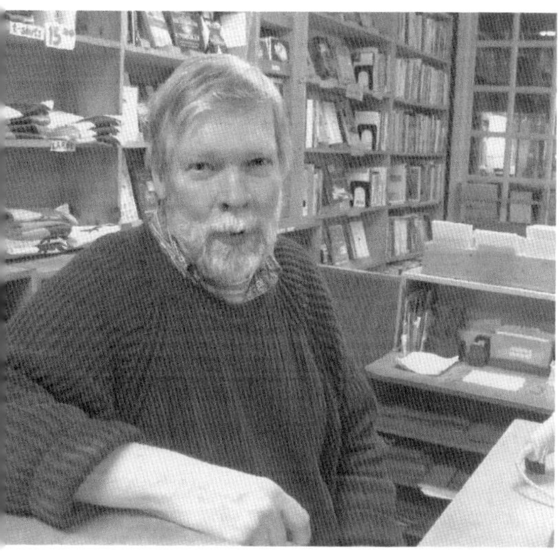

**The Bookman**
Ed Beckwith was a real man of letters. He loved to read, was famous for creating funny birthday cards and Facebook posts, and was the "front man" for almost 10 years at Crow Books, one of Burlington's two locally owned bookstores. Unfortunately, Beckwith cannot be found at Crow's counter anymore. He died unexpectedly at the age of 59 en route to the 17th hole at a local golf course on Father's Day. Friends took solace in the fact that he left on a sunny day while doing something he enjoyed, but they were devastated to have lost such a sweet and quietly humorous character. (Courtesy of Crow Books.)

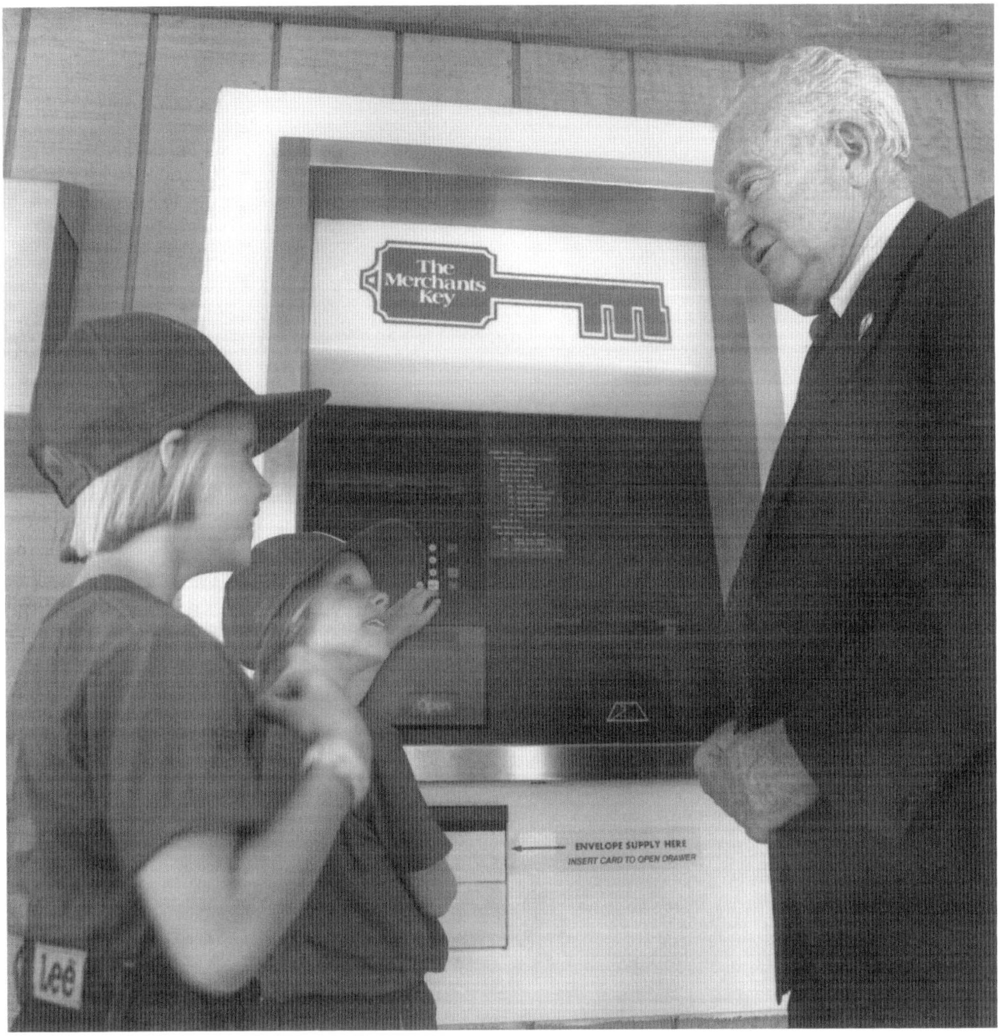


**Dudley Davis**
Dudley Davis called Burlington home for his entire life and did much to help his hometown. After graduating from UVM, Davis began his working career as a cashier at the locally owned Merchants Bank. He retired from Merchants in 2004 after serving as the bank's president for 36 years. During that time, he provided financial backing for some of the area's most successful businesses, including Ben & Jerry's, IDX Systems, and Rhino Foods. Dudley Davis championed the cause of affordable housing in the Burlington area and served as president of the Lake Champlain Regional Chamber of Commerce and the Greater Burlington Industrial Corporation. Just before his death in 2004, Davis's lifetime of service to the Burlington community was honored by a commitment to name the university's new $61 million student center the Dudley H. Davis Center. He posed with his grandchildren, Courtney and Hillary, for a Merchants Bank advertisement around 1980. The caption read, "Now all you have to do, Granddad, is put in your card and push this button!" (Courtesy of Jeff Davis.)

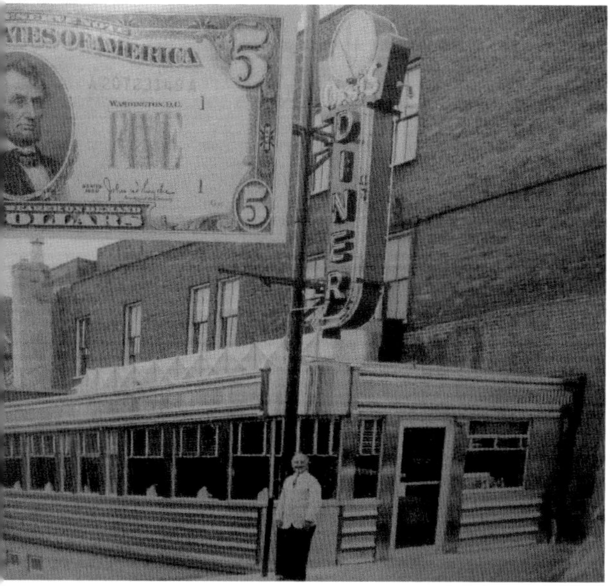


### The Oasis Diner

Harry Lines opened a brand-new restaurant on Bank Street in January 1954. The classic diner was constructed by the Mountain View Diner Company of Singac, New Jersey. Lines named it the Oasis. He is shown in the photograph to the left, which used to sit by the cash register. The first $5 bill paid on opening day is also seen in the photograph. For the next 53 years, the Oasis was a local favorite for breakfast and lunch and for discussing politics. In the photograph below, President Clinton stops by for a visit in 1995. When Harry's son Stratty retired in 1997, his own sons Jon and David did not change a thing, which was just fine with the customers. The brothers finally sold the business in 2007. The classy building is now a Mexican restaurant that stays open late and is still very popular, but it is certainly not at all the same. (Courtesy of the Lines family.)

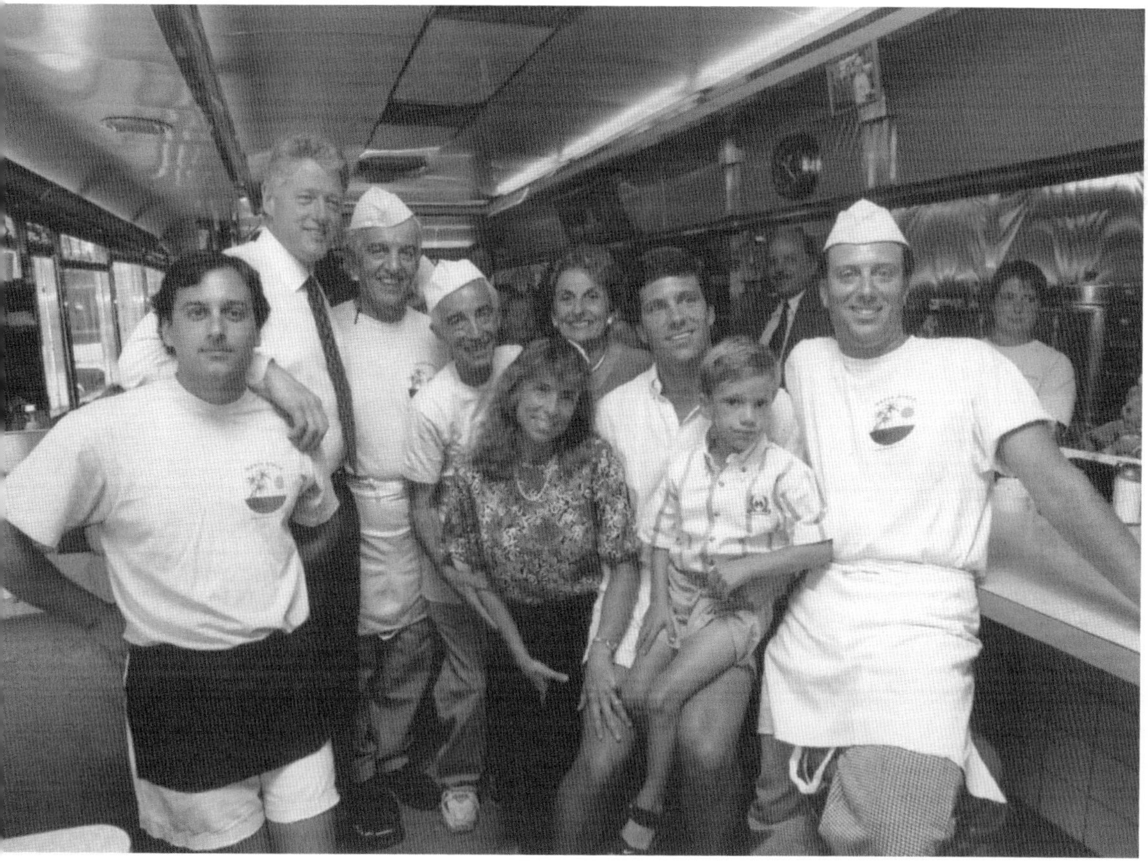

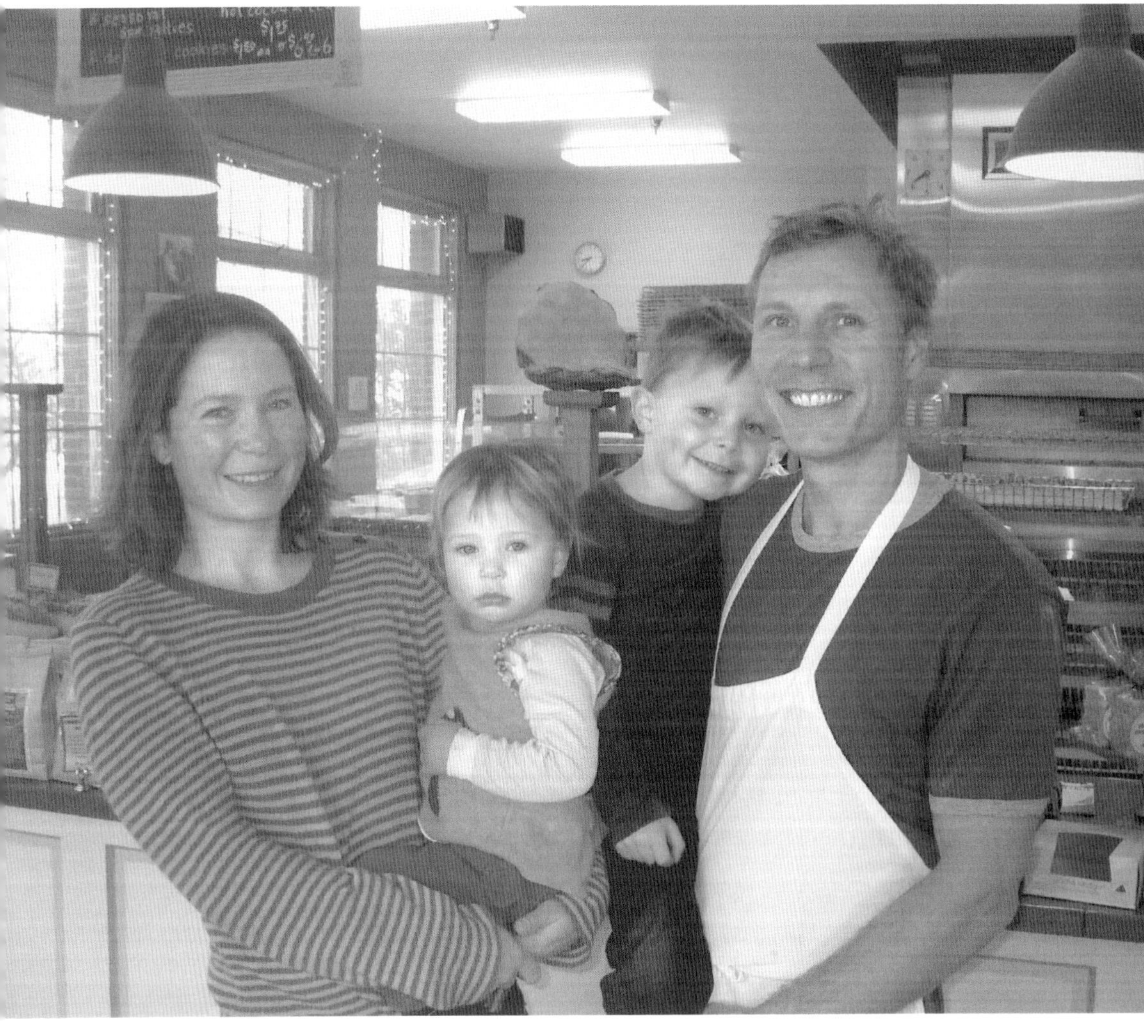

**Bread and Community**

Sara Goodwin Brown and her husband, Ethan, moved to Burlington from Missoula, Montana, in 2002 and opened their Great Harvest Bread Company a year later. The bakery boasts the high ceilings and beautiful wide-plank floors that can be found in many of Burlington's converted factories. Sara and Ethan have become committed members of the Burlington community, holding fundraising events like their "Baker for a Day" contest to help raise money for local charitable organizations. They found their home, located right around the corner from Great Harvest, by posting a sign on the store's bulletin board. Sara and Ethan's glazed cinnamon buns and generous free samples of warm buttered whole-grain bread and muffins have also become the stuff of local legend. (Photograph by the author.)

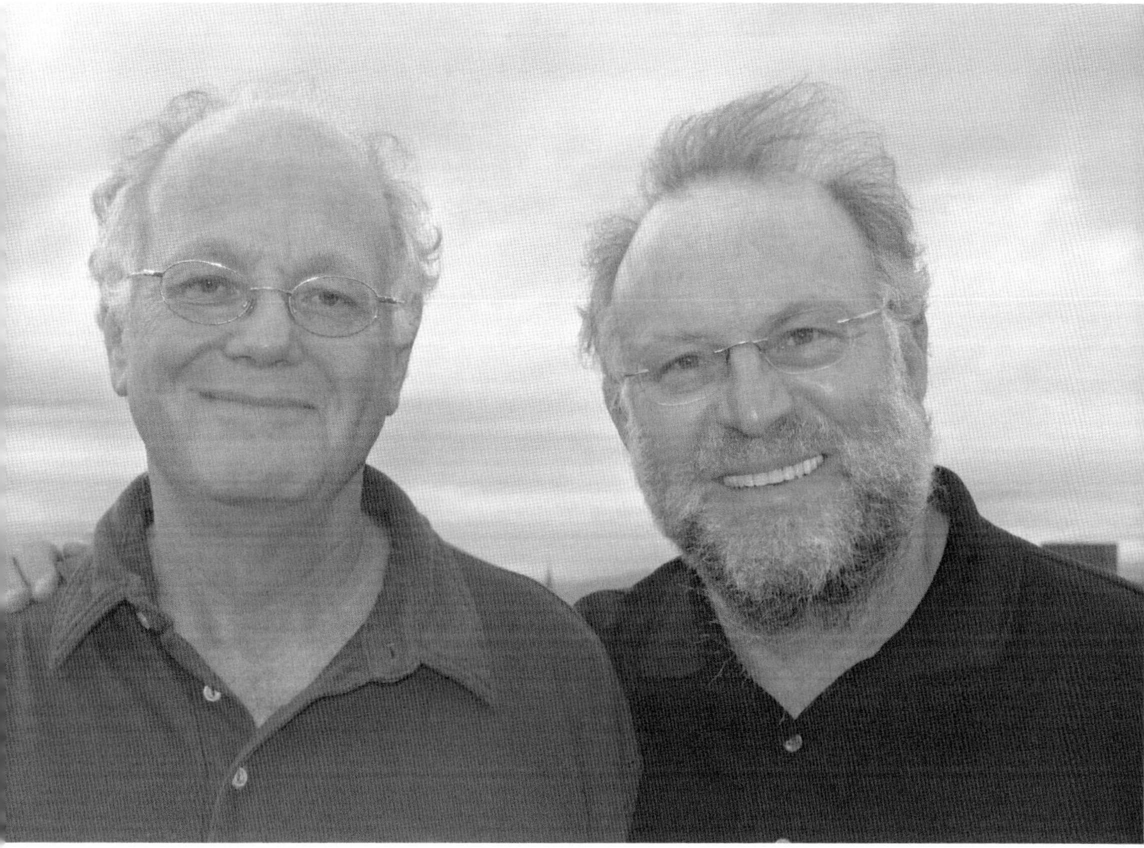

**Ben and Jerry**

The legacy of Ben Cohen (on the left, naturally) and Jerry Greenfield goes far beyond Chunky Monkey and Cherry Garcia. What started in a barely renovated gas station at the corner of St. Paul and College Streets in Burlington in 1978 is an inspiration for countless young entrepreneurs to try something new, and to try it with something that they and others like to eat. A trademark of this beloved local company is a socially conscious approach to business, with an accent on buying locally and giving back to the community. To this day, Ben & Jerry's has a "Free Cone Day," when they treat Burlington to free ice cream to mark each anniversary of their business. As Jerry Greenfield always used to say, "If it's not fun, why do it?" (Courtesy of Ben & Jerry.)

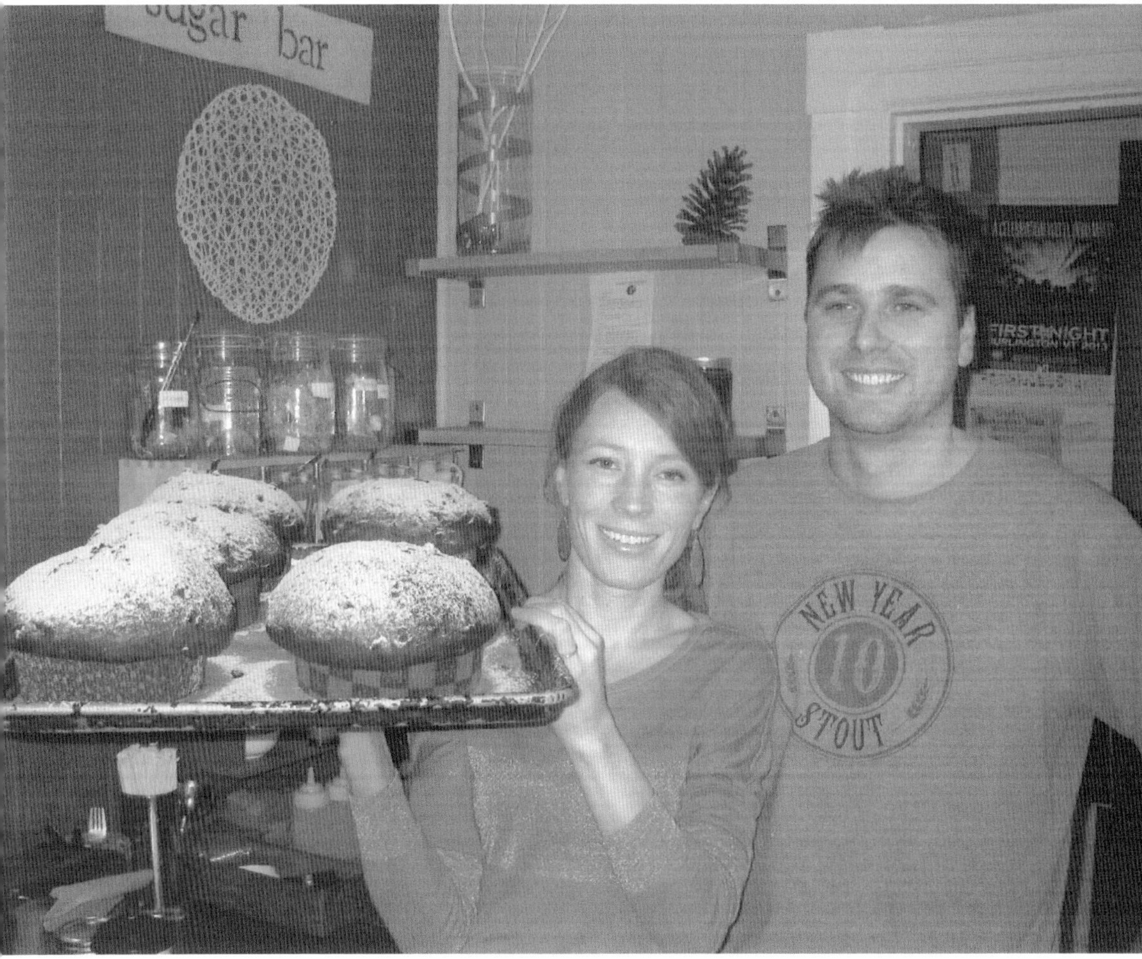


**Bakery of Their Dreams**

Shortly after Jessica and Ryan Bunce moved back to the Burlington area (Jessica grew up nearby in Jericho, Vermont), they agreed that both had always wanted to own a bakery. Their dreams were answered when Panadero, a tiny bakery located in a brightly colored apartment building in Burlington's Old North End, came up for sale. Ryan and Jessica took over the business in 2010 and have recently expanded into a space next door, previously occupied by a much-loved coffee shop. The Bunces' new addition—now called Barrio Bakery—was an instant hit in the neighborhood. Its new storefront has large picture windows, a variety of interesting lunch items, freshly baked breads, and what may be the best sour cherry tarts in North America. The Bunces have proved once again that saying your dreams out loud can sometimes make them happen. (Photograph by the author.)

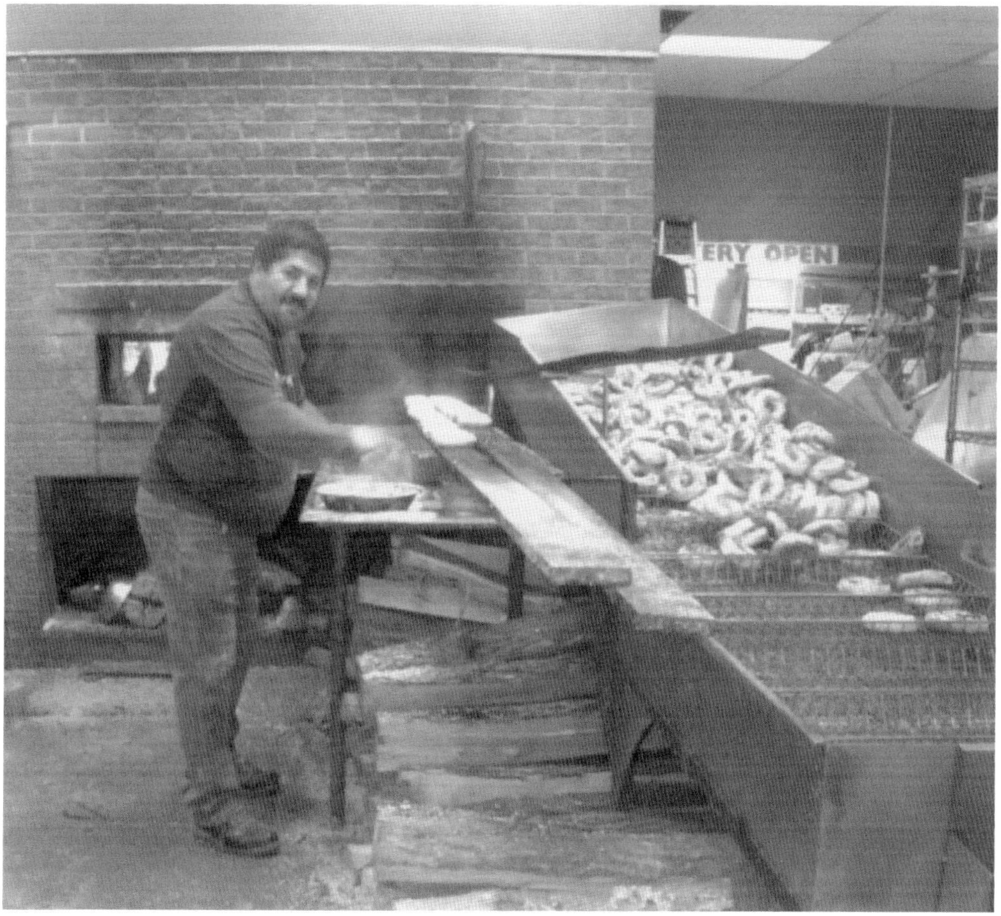


**Lloyd's Bagels**
Lloyd Squires has hand-rolled over 40 million bagels in his life, many of them at Myer's, his bakery located in an old industrial building on Pine Street. Squires learned his craft at Mijer Lewkowicz's bagel business in Montreal, and opened his own bakery in Burlington in the late 1990s, at first commuting daily from Montreal because of difficulties getting a permit to live in the United States. His bagel shop opens every morning at 4:00 a.m. Lloyd dreams of moving to Nova Scotia and opening up a smaller version of Myers. In the meantime, Burlington gets to enjoy old-world bagels hot out of a wood-fired oven. (Photograph by the author.)

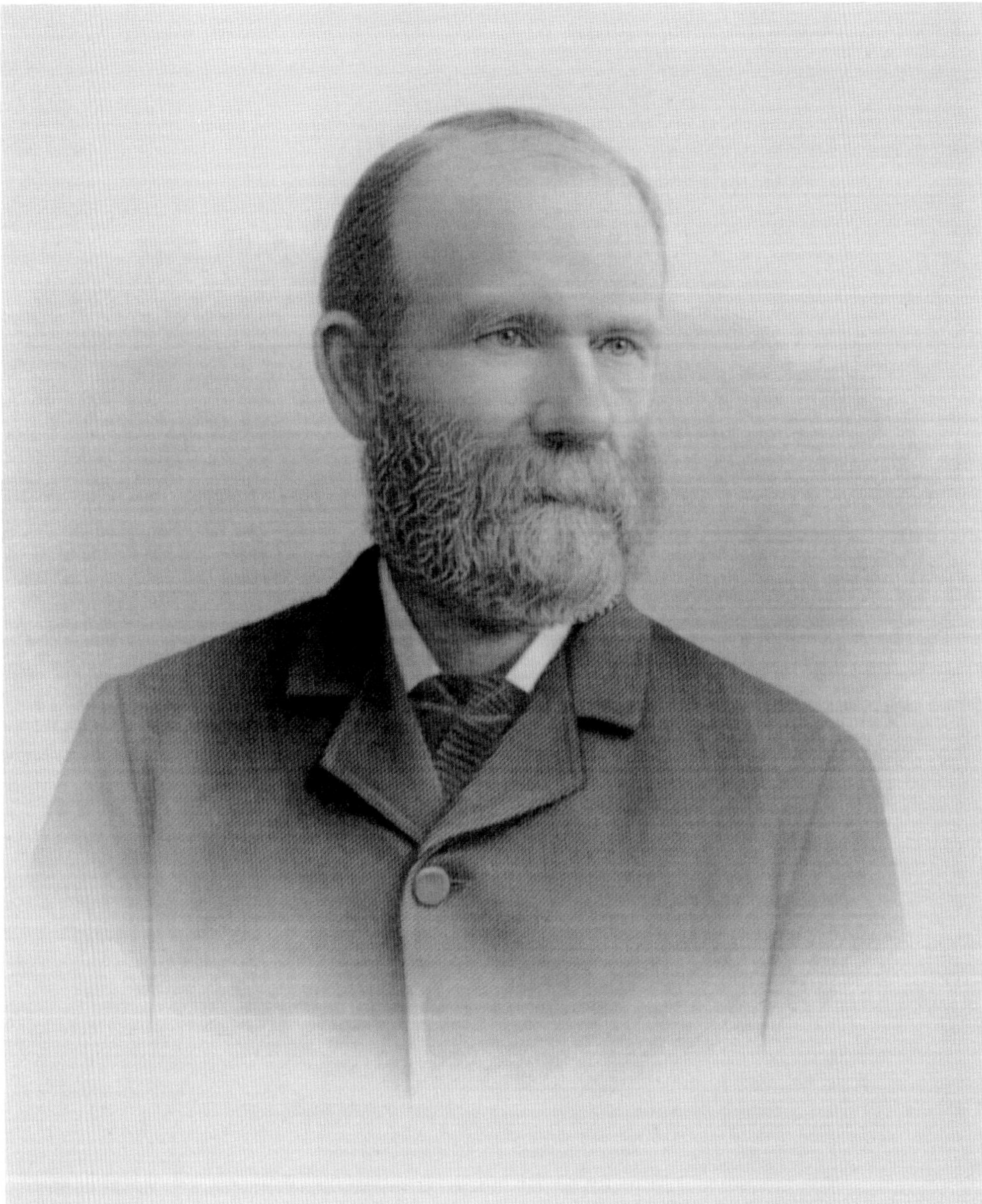

**Willard Crane**

Willard Crane, a 19th-century lumber executive, was a perfect example of how local businessmen of the era had wide-reaching influences in the recently established city of Burlington. After learning the ropes of the lumber industry in Nashua, New Hampshire, New York City, and Trois Rivieres, Quebec, Crane opened his own business in Burlington with his brother David in 1858. By 1902, a time when Burlington was the third-largest exporter of lumber in the United States, W. & D.G. Crane was one of Burlington's most successful lumber firms. At the same time, Willard Crane was either the director or a board member of the Queen Anne Screen Company, the Burlington Venetian Blind Company, the Vermont Shade Roller Company, The Lang & Goodhue Manufacturing Company, the Burlington Savings Bank, and the Vermont Electric Company. (Courtesy of the Fletcher Free Library.)

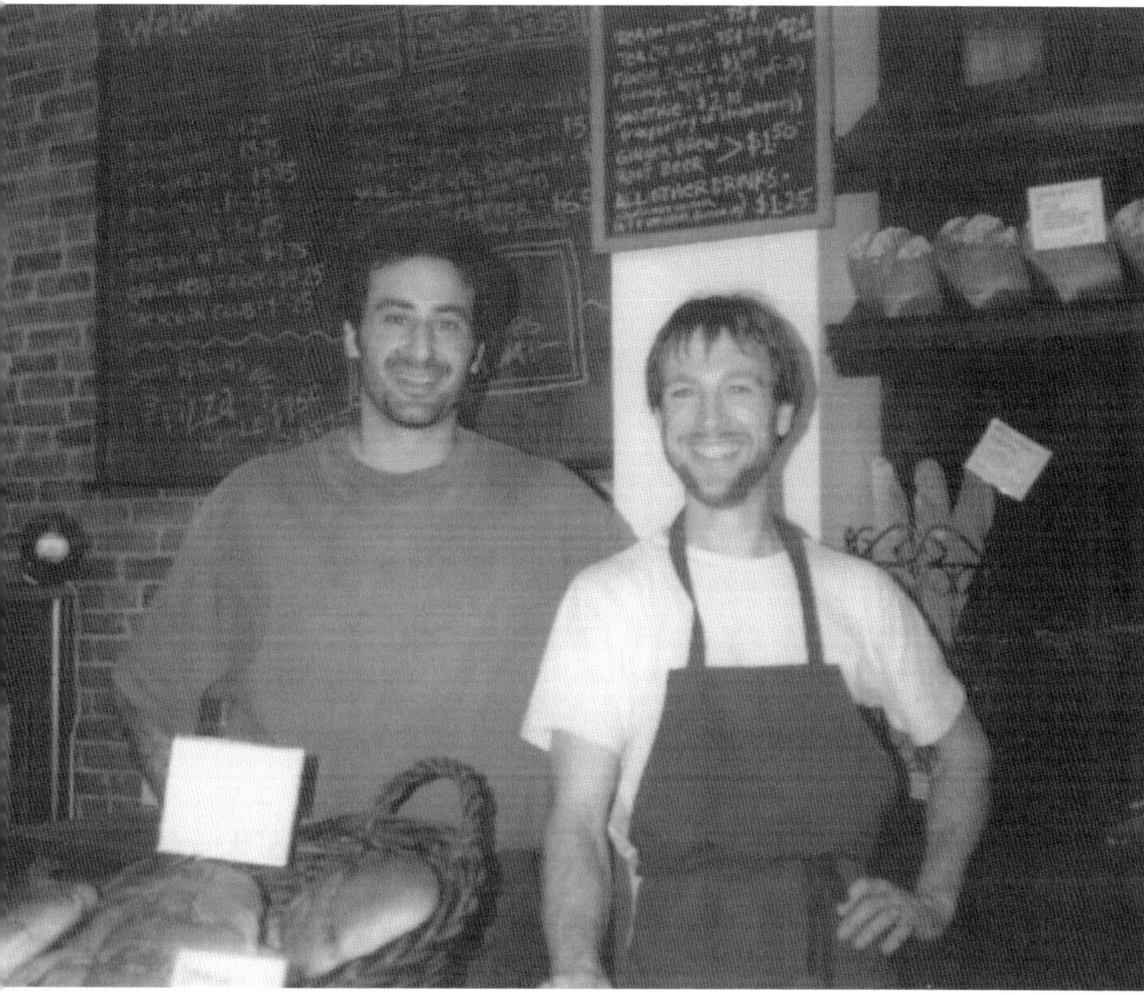

**From Asparagus to Ziti**

After two months of meetings over many helpings of Nectar's famous french fries, Avery Rifkin (left) and Tim Elliott, pictured here on a typical Friday morning with freshly baked challah, opened Zabby & Elf's Stone Soup, an eclectic eatery on the block of College Street east of Church in 1997. Their restaurant's name comes from a famous children's story in which everyone contributes a little bit of food to make a heavenly soup. Elliott and Rifkin are enthusiastic food lovers as well as top-notch chefs. Their ongoing success is a testament to their restaurant's delicious food and cozy atmosphere, and also to the way they have catered to Burlingtonians' adventurous palates. Stone Soup features downtown's most colorful salad bar, its own bread, and everything from curly kale to its fabled chopped-liver sandwiches. (Courtesy of Stone Soup.)

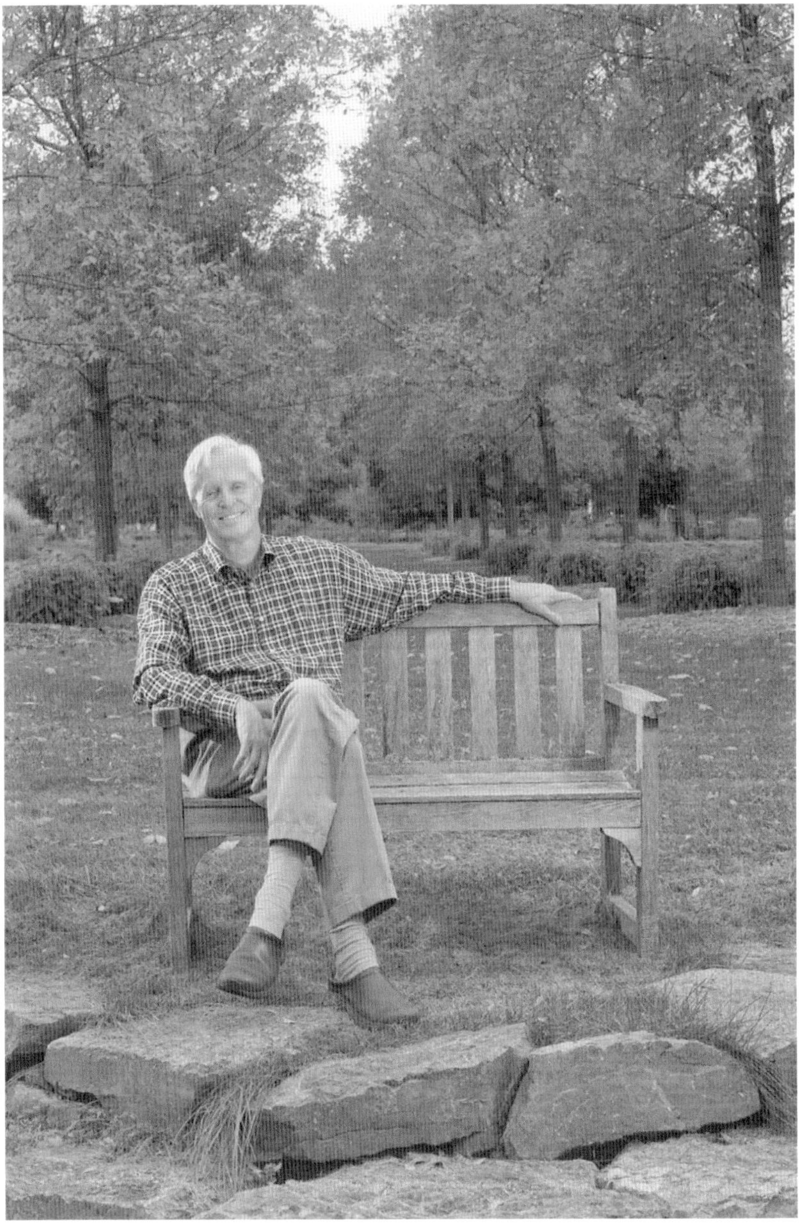

**The Champion of the Intervale**
Will Raap founded Gardener's Supply Company, now one of the world's largest online and catalog gardening retailers, in 1983. Since then, he has become a leader in efforts to reinvigorate local agriculture in Burlington's Intervale, the Winooski River floodplain that has been the home to many farms over the past 250 years, including Ethan Allen's. In 1987, Raap launched the Intervale Center, a Burlington nonprofit that is responsible for the development of 12 small privately owned farms as well as other environmentally responsible projects in the Intervale. Hundreds of acres of floodplain, used primarily for growing feed corn and as a garbage dump just 20 years ago, have become dynamic farmland again. Raap is still hard at work improving the planet, designing similar projects in Costa Rica based on his successes in Burlington's Intervale. (Courtesy of Jon Shenton/Champlain Housing Trust.)

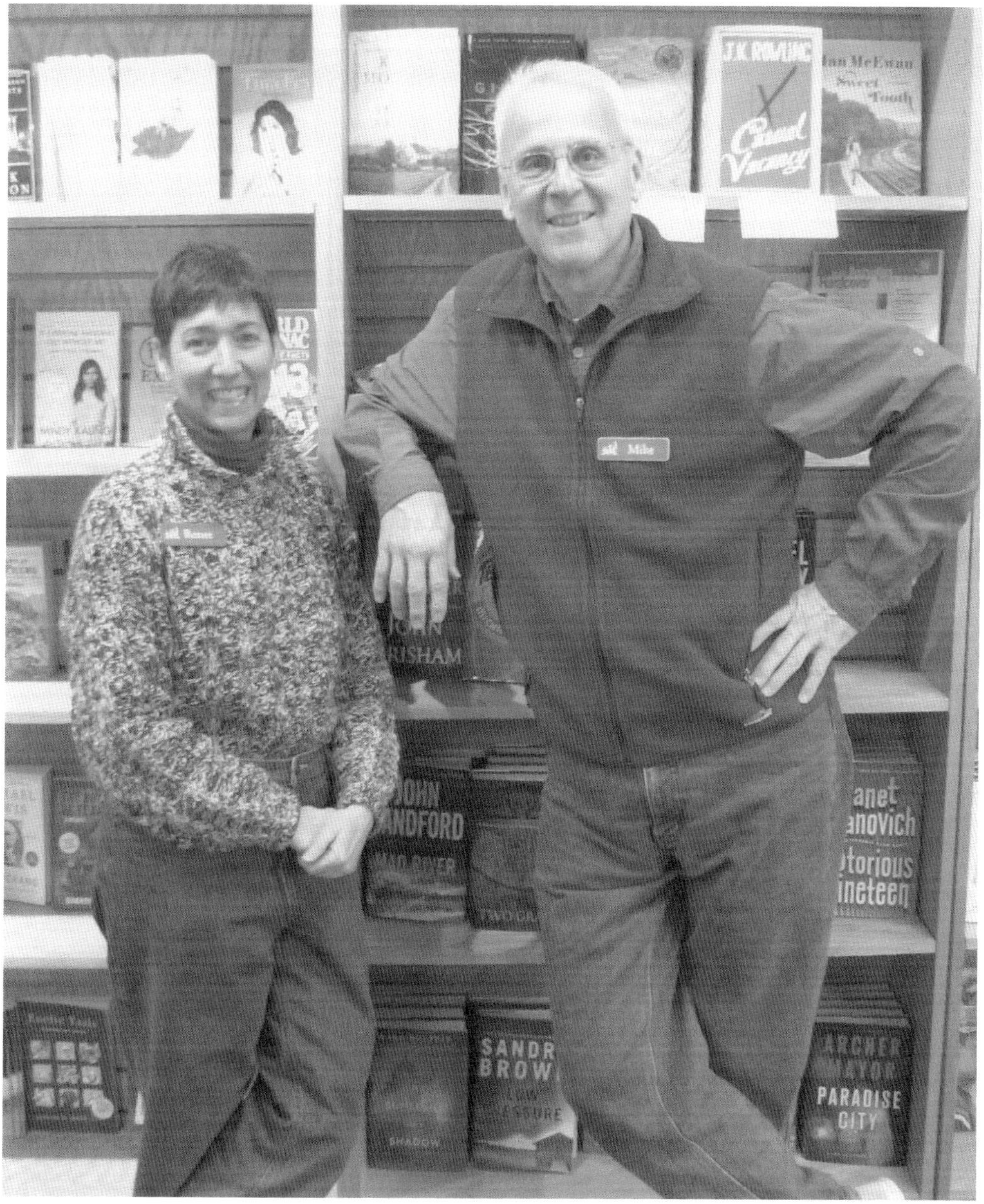


**Find It Here, Buy It Here, Keep Us Here!**
Renee Reiner and Michael DeSanto opened Phoenix Books, Burlington's newest bookstore, in the spring of 2012, less than a year after Borders Books and Music closed its Church Street location. Reiner and DeSanto don't seem to be too worried. They have more than 20 years of experience selling books in the Burlington area. Their previous stores, The Book Rack and Children's Pages in Winooski and Essex and an earlier version of Phoenix Books in Essex, have all been local favorites. Phoenix Books in Burlington features regular author readings and occasional live music performances, as well as a beautiful and provocative selection of books. Reiner and DeSanto, knowing that bookstores now face stiff competition from online booksellers, have created their own store website and have adopted a motto for the new retailer: Find it here, buy it here, keep us here! (Courtesy of Phoenix Books.)

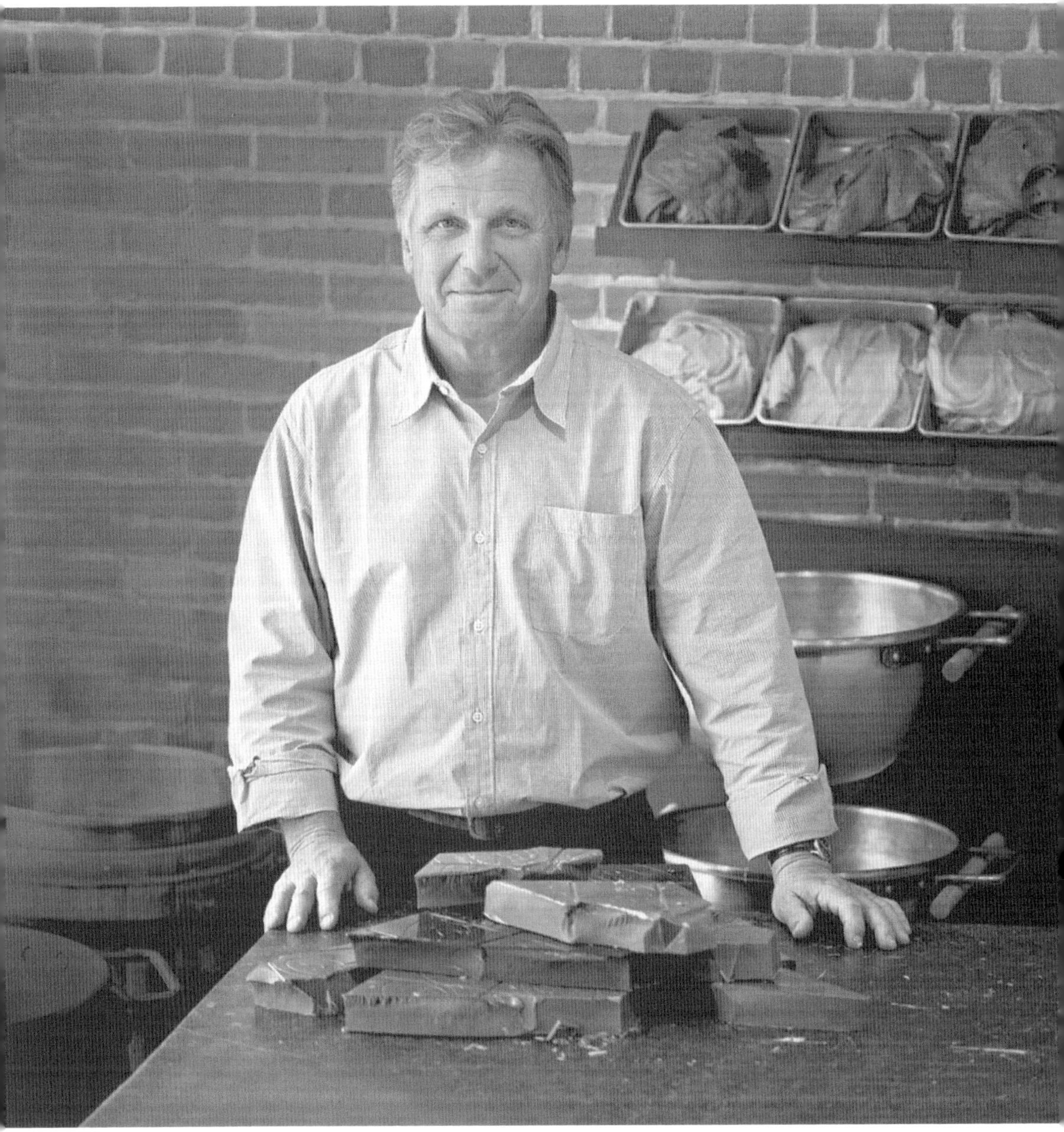

**Jim Lampman and Lake Champlain Chocolates**
Burlington's own gourmet chocolate company got its start in 1983 when Jim Lampman, then owner of the popular Ice House Restaurant on Burlington's waterfront, started serving hand-rolled chocolate truffles as a special treat for Sunday customers. The demand for these truffles, originally created by one of the Ice House's pastry chefs, inspired Lampman to expand production. Lake Champlain Chocolates is still headquartered in Burlington and has two retail stores in town. Jim Lampman takes pride in the fact that the company only uses cacao produced in environmentally and socially responsible ways, and that Lake Champlain Chocolates contributes 10 percent of its annual pretax profits to local nonprofit organizations and programs. Lampman's chocolates, by the way, are extraordinarily delicious. (Courtesy of Lake Champlain Chocolates.)

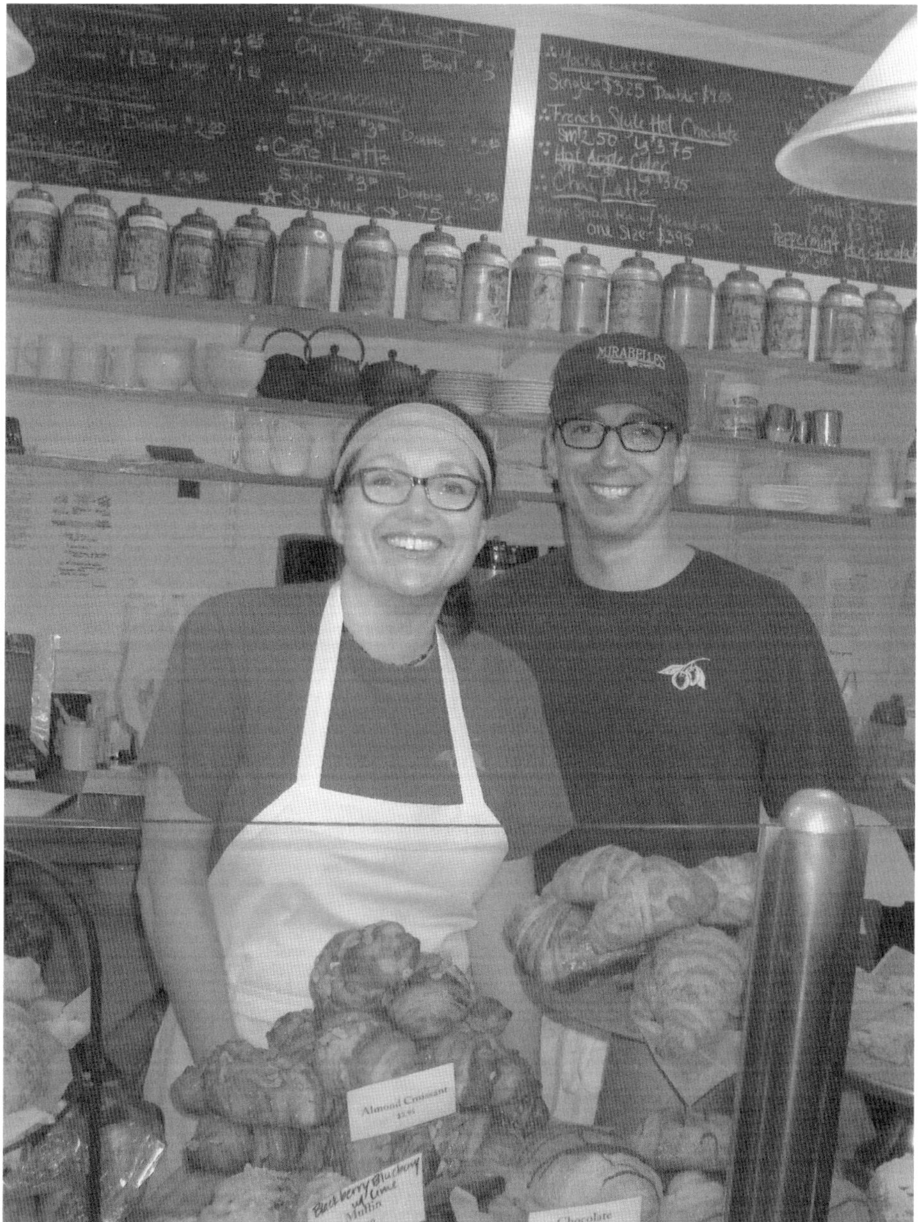


**Mirabelles**

As is the case with many restaurateurs in the Burlington area, chefs Alison Lane and Andrew Silva have connections to the New England Culinary Institute in Montpelier, where they met and taught courses after graduating. Lane and Silva decided to open what has become one of Burlington's most popular pastry shops and cafés. Today, 20 years later, Lane still specializes in pastries (she interned in a French patisserie in England), and Silva supervises prepared foods. Mirabelles is a local favorite for breakfast (hot popovers!) and for snacking (salted caramels and infamously rich brownies). Both chefs can often be found, after all these years, still cooking in the café's busy kitchen. "It's what we love to do," says Alison Lane. (Photograph by the author.)

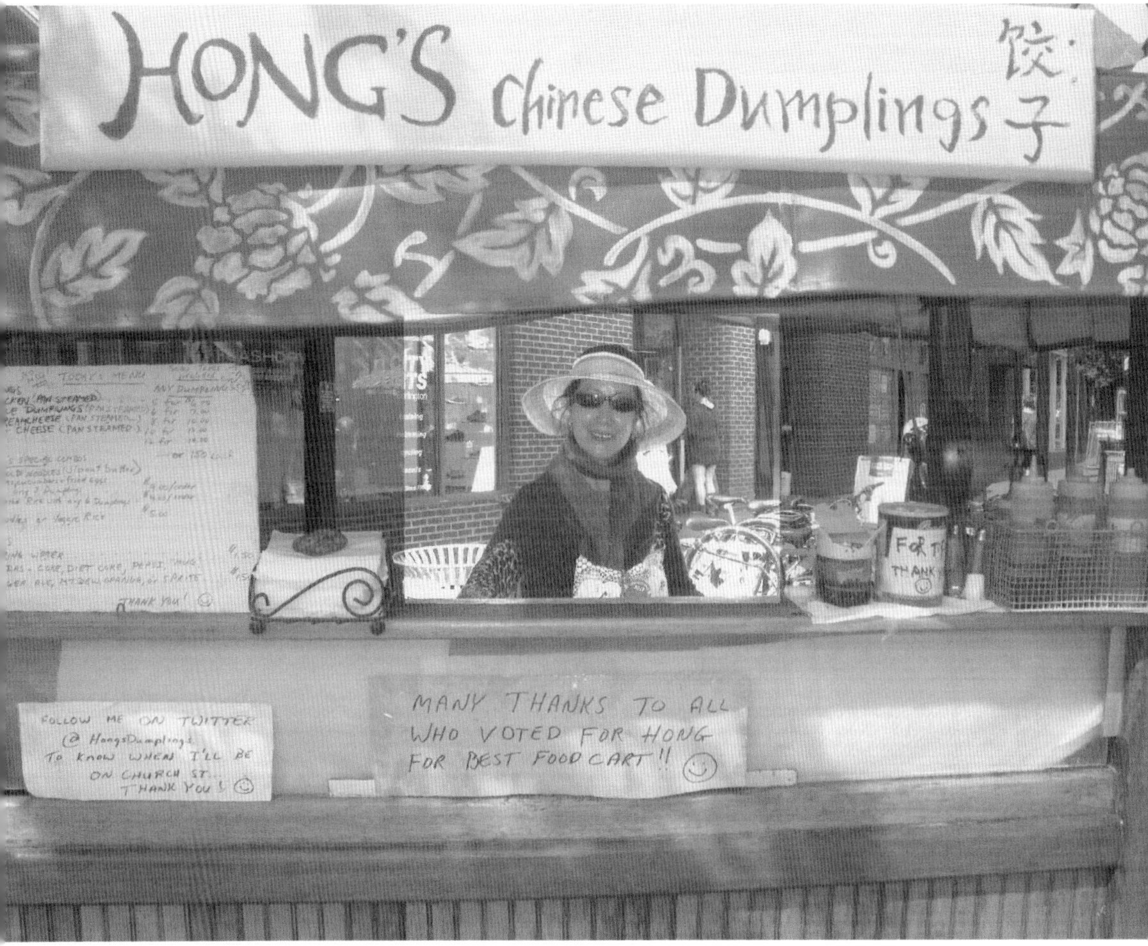


**The Dumpling Lady**

Hong Yu makes some of the world's best Chinese dumplings. A native of Liao Ning province in northeastern China, she has been selling the homemade meat and vegetable dumplings, which she learned to make from her mother's recipe, on the upper block of Church Street since 2000. Hong's brightly colored food cart is a one-woman operation. She makes the dough, rolls the dumplings, takes the orders, and does it all with a smile. Hong's dumplings have been a regular winner of the Seven Daysies "Best Street Eats" award, a respected local "best of" poll taken each year by *Seven Days* weekly newspaper. (Photograph by the author.)

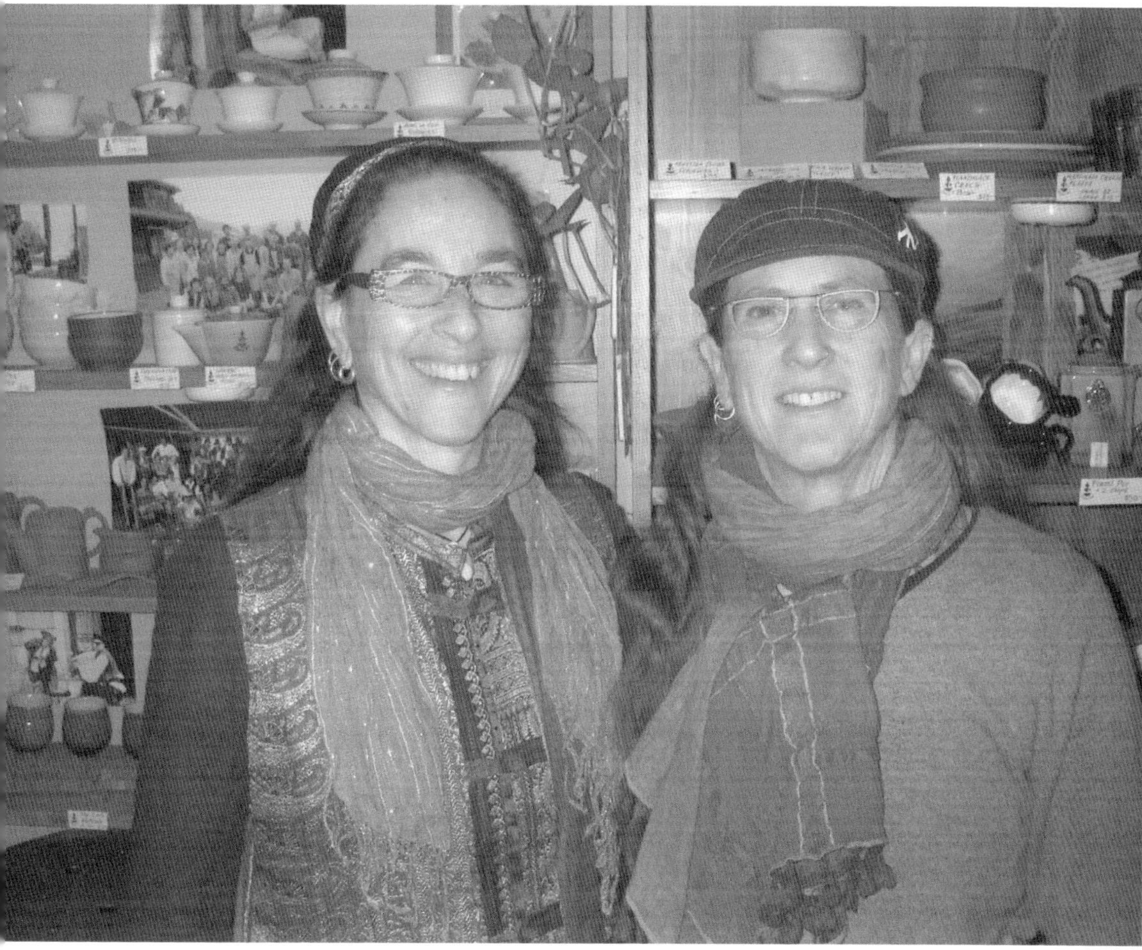

**Magical Tea Room**

Nina Beck (left) and Stacey Jolles are the owners and operators of one of Burlington's treasures. Near the corner of Bank and Church Streets in the middle of downtown Burlington is a surprising oasis from the cacophony of daily life. Dobra Tea, the first North American version of a series of Bohemian-style tearooms originating in Prague, features an encyclopedic selection of teas and other drinks from around the world. The soft lights, handmade teacups, and cushioned alcoves add to the exotic and relaxed atmosphere. With a shop concept designed in Eastern Europe and with teas that mostly originate in Asia, Beck and Jolles are local champions of multiculturalism and have been named the company's representatives for opening other Dobra locations in the United States during the next few years. (Photograph by the author.)

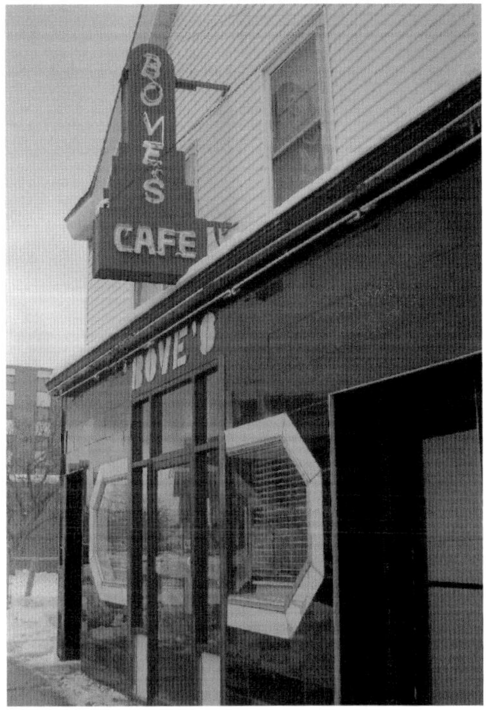


### Bove's Café

There's only one longtime Burlington restaurant that looks and feels almost exactly as it did the day it opened. Louis and Victoria Bove opened their eponymous café in December 1941 and, three generations later, Rick and Mark Bove (pictured below) continue to serve manicotti, lasagna, and other classic Italian dishes with sauce made from their grandparents' original recipe. The Boves have also launched a successful business selling eight varieties of their pasta sauce by mail and in supermarkets. But for Burlingtonians old and young, it is a visit to the café at 68 Pearl Street that will always be a special treat. (Above, photograph by the author; below, courtesy of Mark Bove.)

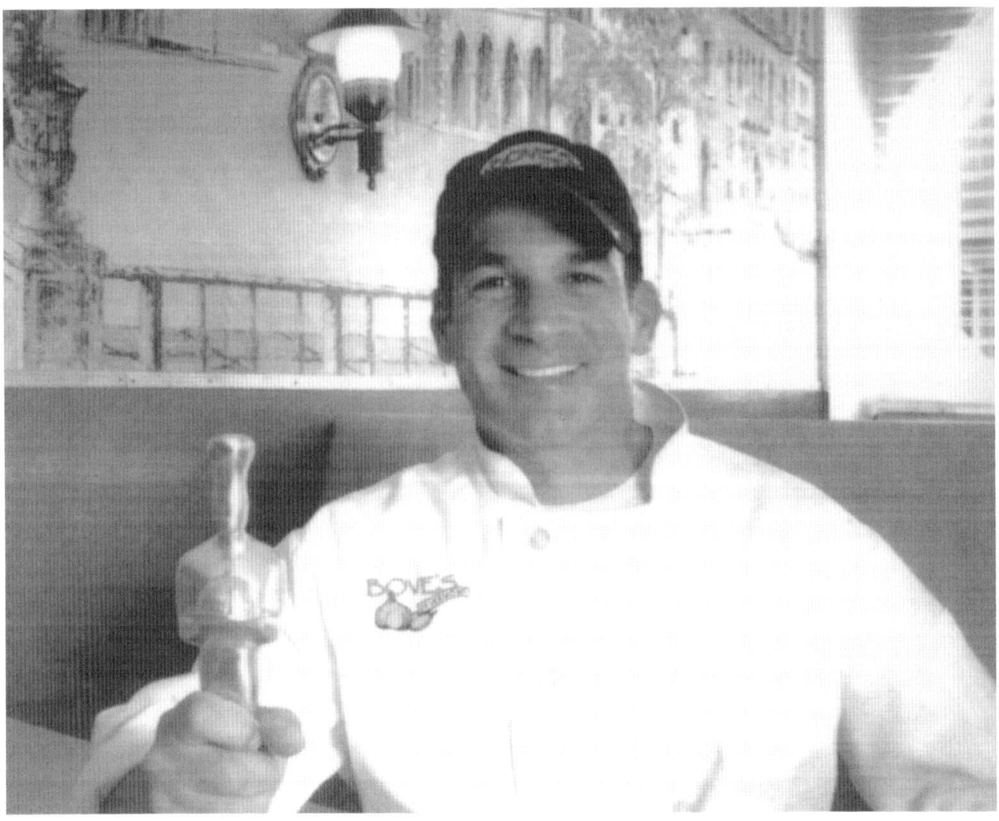

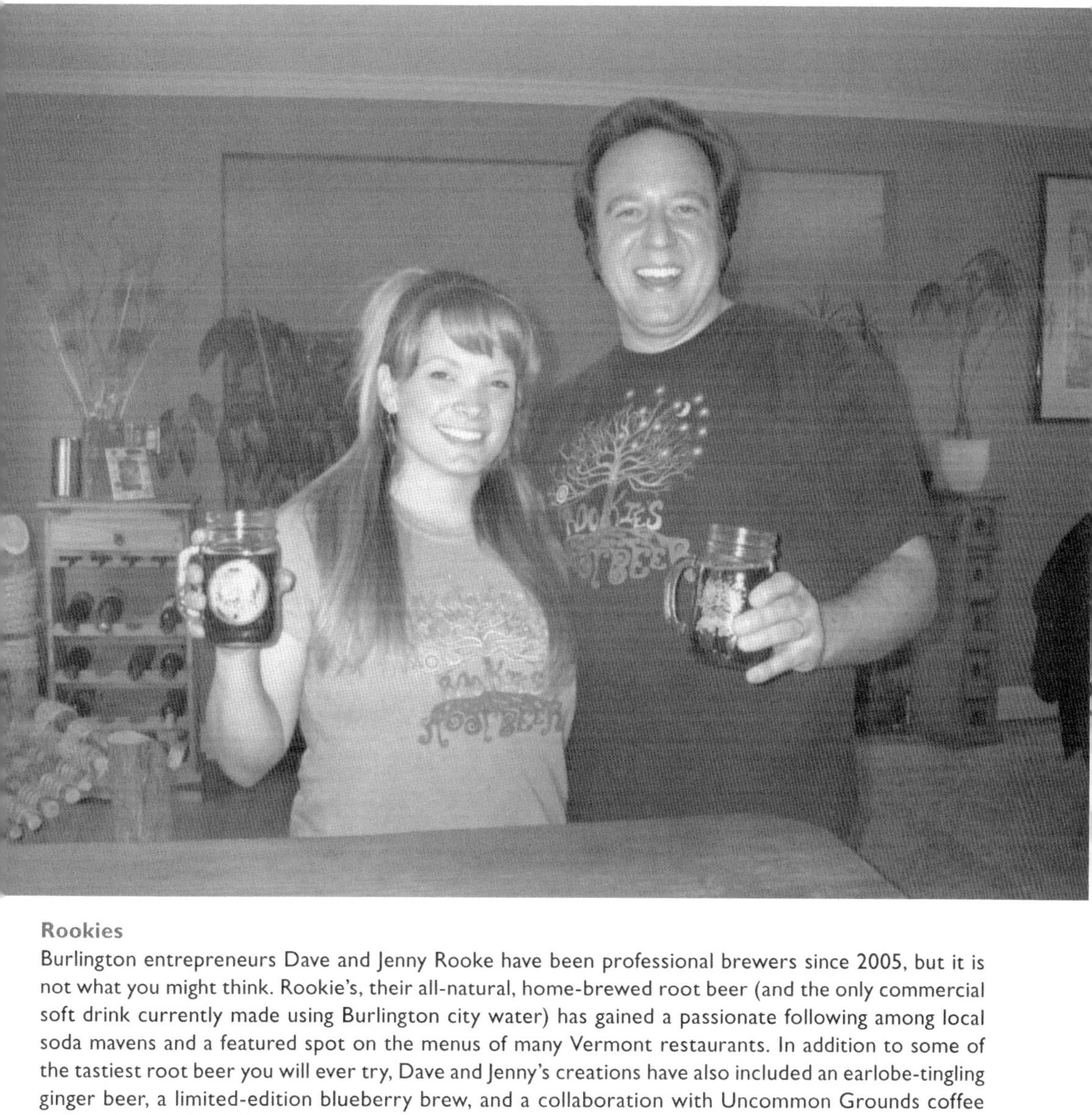

**Rookies**

Burlington entrepreneurs Dave and Jenny Rooke have been professional brewers since 2005, but it is not what you might think. Rookie's, their all-natural, home-brewed root beer (and the only commercial soft drink currently made using Burlington city water) has gained a passionate following among local soda mavens and a featured spot on the menus of many Vermont restaurants. In addition to some of the tastiest root beer you will ever try, Dave and Jenny's creations have also included an earlobe-tingling ginger beer, a limited-edition blueberry brew, and a collaboration with Uncommon Grounds coffee shop called The Dark Side: root beer infused with espresso and topped with a vanilla molasses whipped cream. (Photograph by the author.)

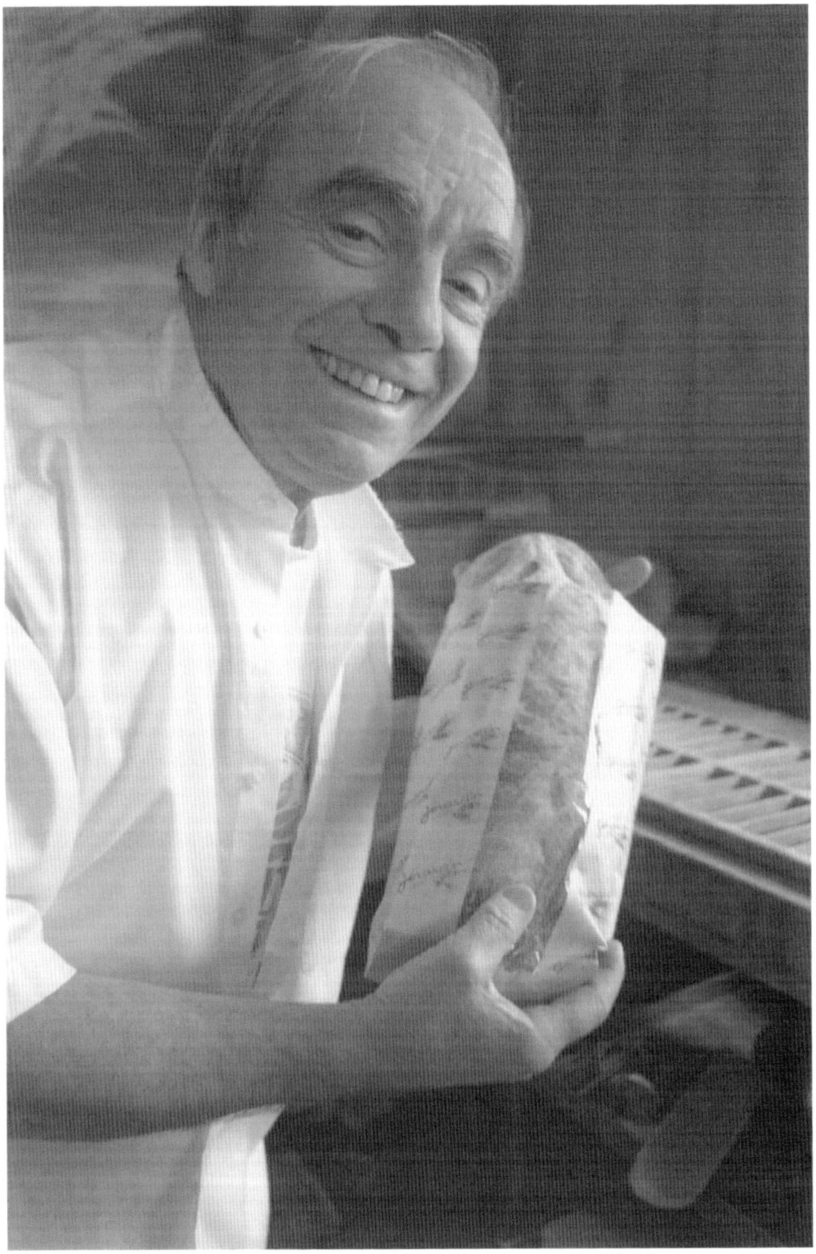

**Gerard's Bread**
Gerard Rubaud makes delicious bread, and it is not easy to get. There's a fixed schedule of delivery days and times. In Burlington, the precious loaves, still slightly warm, arrive at City Market, the downtown grocery store and co-op, at around 3:30 in the afternoon every Wednesday and Sunday. It is definitely worth the wait. Gerard only makes one type of sourdough bread, created out of white flour with rye and spelt that he mills himself, leavened with wild yeasts, and baked in a hand-built brick-and-clay oven. Before suffering a serious stroke in 2004, Rubaud used to produce more than 1,200 loaves each week. After a long recovery, Gerard is still very much in business, but has been forced to slow down, making his marvelous bread a bit rarer, and even more of a treat than ever before. (Courtesy of Matt Thorsen.)

# CHAPTER FIVE

# Artists of Every Sort

Many talented painters, photographers, musicians, authors, graphic artists, and performers have called Burlington home over the past 250 years, particularly since a cultural renaissance began in Chittenden County in the late 1970s. It makes sense that Vermont's largest city and the largest population center between Boston and Montreal would be a destination for artists of every kind.

Burlington's music scene has run the gamut, from rock 'n' roll to jazz to Americana. A few Burlington musicians have become quite famous, including Eugene Hütz, the frontman and founder of Gogol Bordello, a world-renowned gypsy punk band. Jam band Phish worked out its onstage performing style in downtown bars. Louis Beaudoin, who serviced car radiators in his south end garage during the day and played and shared music the rest of the time, is still considered one of the best French-Canadian fiddlers ever. Pine Island, a talented quintet of acoustic musicians who were local favorites in the 1970s, was one of the first bands ever to meld bluegrass and jazz. "Big Joe" Burrell became a standard-bearer for the growing Burlington jazz and blues scene. He was often accompanied by guitarist Paul Asbell, who moved to the Queen City after playing with blues legends Muddy Waters and Howlin' Wolf as a youngster in Chicago.

Burlington has also been a mecca for photographers and other visual artists. Marion Ettlinger, well known around town for beautiful hand-colored portraits, has become famous as a photographer of authors. Lyn Severance is responsible for the light-hearted graphics and lettering that are so familiar to fans of Ben & Jerry's ice cream. Wes Disney made headlines and caused controversy in the 1980s with his "Wall" project, in which a huge downtown brick wall was covered with a glued-on image of a rock face. For 60 years, Louis L. McAllister took photographs of everything from Burlington graduating classes to street scenes, documenting Burlington history for a good part of the 20th century with a unique panoramic camera. Photographer Matt Thorsen is also a documentarian whose specialty is memorable portraits of the area's famous and potentially famous.

And then, defying all categories, there are the "multitaskers," those rare individuals who make a name for themselves in many varieties of artistic endeavors. James Kochalka, the "cartoon laureate" of Vermont, is also a talented songwriter. Creston Lea is a published author who also builds beautiful electric guitars. Marc Awodey positioned himself as a political artist and as an organizer of Burlington's art community. Outsider artist, greeting card executive, and cultural icon Dug Nap does it all.

From the murals on downtown walls, to poetry jams in the FlynnSpace, art and artists can be found just about everywhere in town.

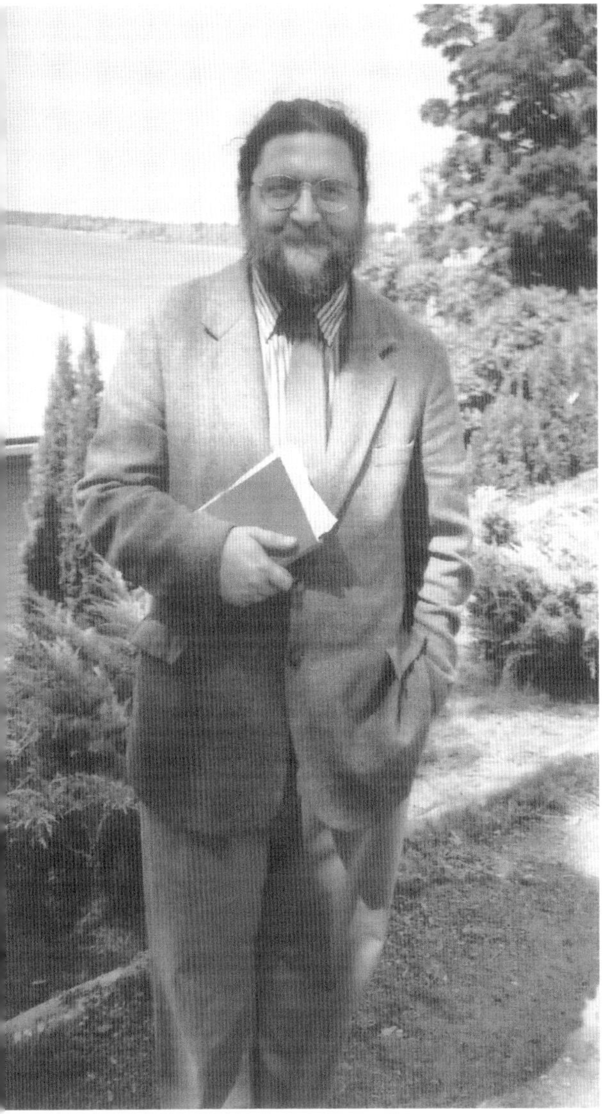

**Marc Awodey**
Local artist and provocateur Marc Awodey (1960–2012) did so many things that helped support Burlington's arts scene that it was hard to keep track of them all. Awodey was a respected art critic for the Burlington weekly *Seven Days*; the winner of the 2000 Haiku Poetry Championship at the National Poetry Slam; the founder, in 1997, of Burlington's Rhombus Gallery as an independent, nonprofit community arts center; and the originator of the Poetry Vending Machine, the idea of converting decommissioned cigarette machines so that they would distribute small books of poetry. On top of all this, Awodey was a gifted painter in his own right. Marc's sudden death from a heart attack at the age of 51 left Burlington's arts community surprised and saddened. (Courtesy of Matt Thorsen.)

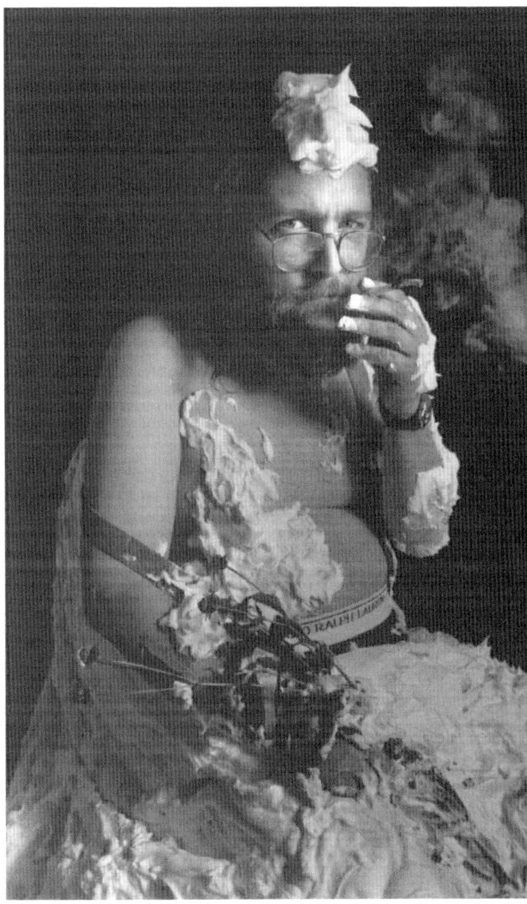

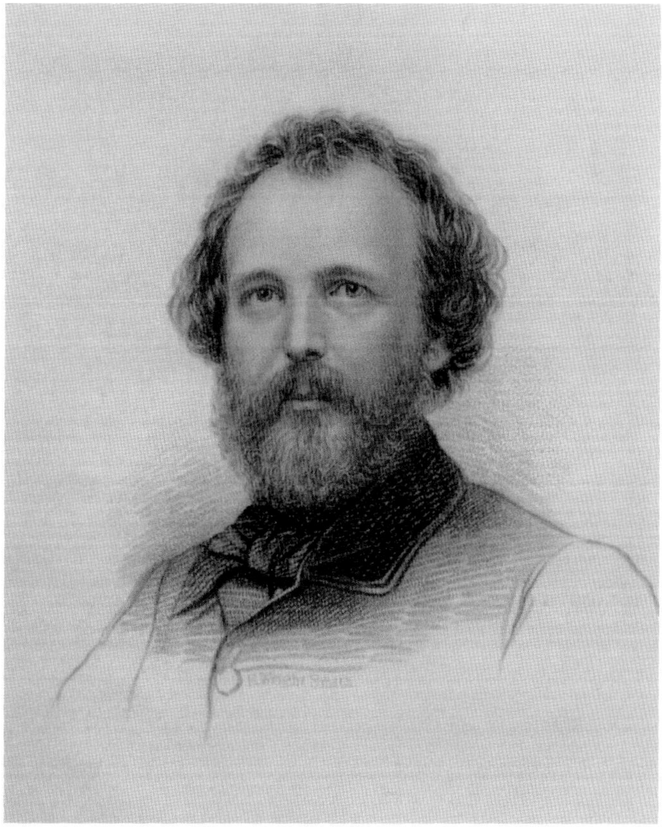

### John Godfrey Saxe

Vermont attorney general John Godfrey Saxe (1816–1887) was also one of the state's favorite poets. His specialty was lighthearted and satirical verse. Saxe's first collection of poems was popular enough to warrant 10 reprintings and was said to have outsold contemporary works by Nathaniel Hawthorne and Alfred, Lord Tennyson. Saxe lived in Burlington from 1835 to 1855 at 177 South Union Street, a building described as "an architectural gem" in the guidebook *Look Around Burlington, Vermont*. Saxe's name occupies a place of honor in the stained-glass memorial window in the Fletcher Free Library's Carnegie building. (Courtesy of the Fletcher Free Library.)

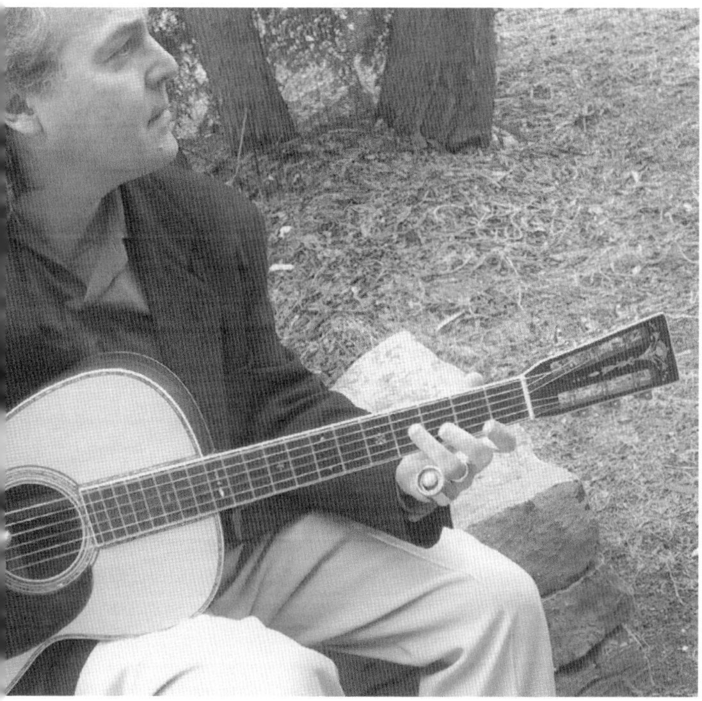

### Burlington's Lead Guitarist

Acoustic and electric guitarist Paul Asbell has been a central player in Burlington's live music scene since moving to town from Chicago in 1971. Asbell was one of the founders of Kilimanjaro, a popular fusion jazz combo, and also the Unknown Blues Band, which featured "Big Joe" Burrell (see page 90). During the past 40 years, Asbell has taught lessons privately and at many local universities, inspiring hundreds of guitar students. One of those students, Trey Anastasio, rose to fame as the lead guitarist for the band Phish (see page 83). (Photograph by Rose Lucas.)

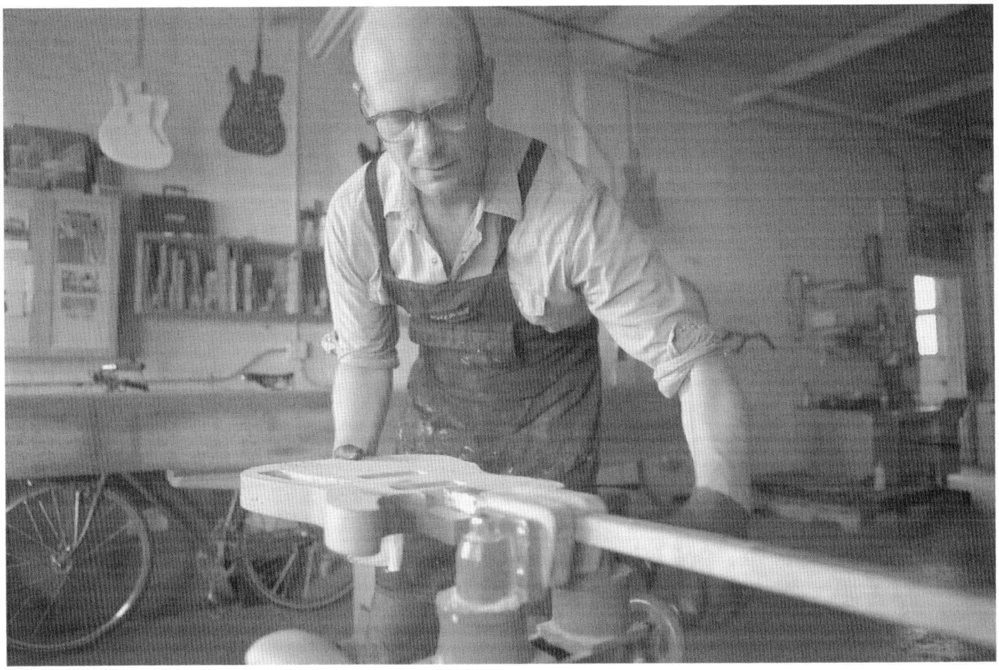

**A True Renaissance Man**

Creston Lea is one of Burlington's quiet geniuses. A line of custom-made electric guitars that he builds in his Pine Street workshop is generating excitement among professional and amateur guitarists in Vermont and beyond. He is also a well-respected author – his first book of short stories, *Wild Punch*, was published by Turtle Point Press in 2010. As if that wasn't enough, Creston Lea is the daddy of two young children, served until recently as the board chair of Planned Parenthood of Northern New England, and plays guitar in many local bands. (Photograph by Amanda Kowalski, courtesy of Creston Lea.)

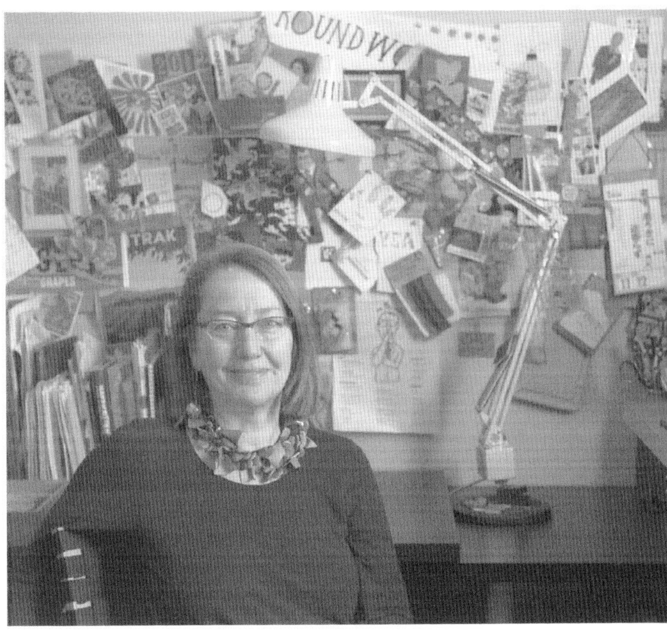

**Happy Cows and Puffy Clouds**

Burlington graphic artist Lyn Severance served as creative director and one of the lead designers for Ben & Jerry's during the company's first 18 years. The puffy clouds, perpetually blue skies, and bright colors that immediately identify many of Ben & Jerry's flavors can be traced back to Severance's influence. From 1978 on, all visual materials at Ben & Jerry's were hand-lettered in multiple styles developed by Severance. In 1988, one font, called "Chunky," and another, called "Severance," were formalized in order to give the company's products a unique and homemade look. (Photograph by Ben Resnik.)

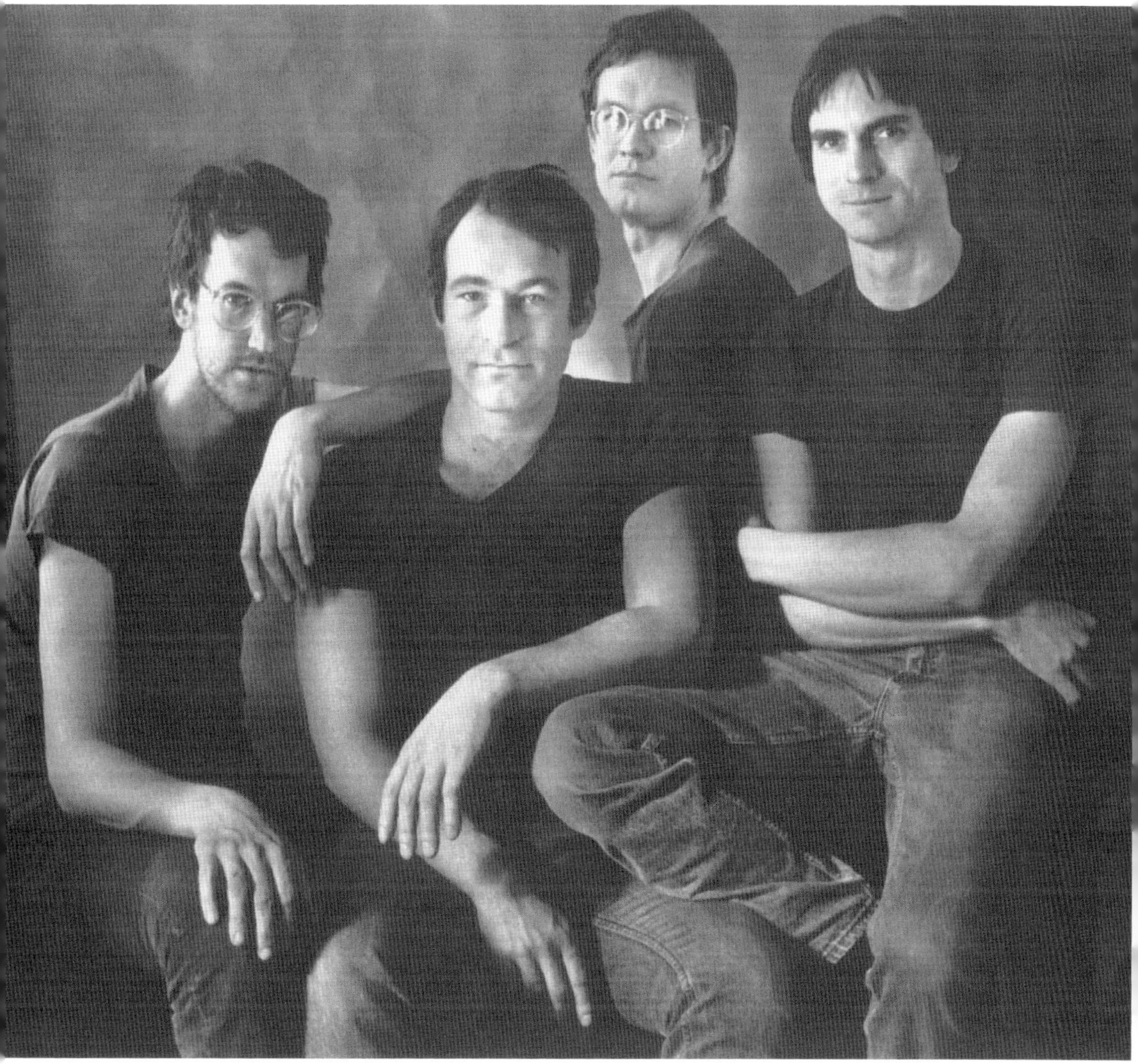

**Zoot Wilson with the N-Zones**
Long before Phish and Eugene Hütz rose to stardom, Burlington had the N-Zones, a legendary bar band fronted for most of its history in the 1970s and 1980s by Richard "Zoot" Wilson. Zoot was a musical force to be reckoned with, singing, strutting, and sweating onstage with the best of them. Zoot played blues and rock in many local Burlington bands, including the Fabulous Dogtones, Ham and Cheese, and the Tremendous Johnson Blues Band; and at legendary downtown venues Nectar's, Hunts, and Warehouse Hall. Some of these stages, like Zoot himself, are no longer with us. Zoot Wilson took his own life in June 1997. He lives on in the music he created and in the fond memories of the many area musicians who were inspired by him. The members of the N-Zones, shown here in 1983, are, from left to right, Don Sidney, Zoot Wilson, Mark Ransom, and Bruce McKenzie. (Photograph by Marion Ettlinger; from the collection of the author.)

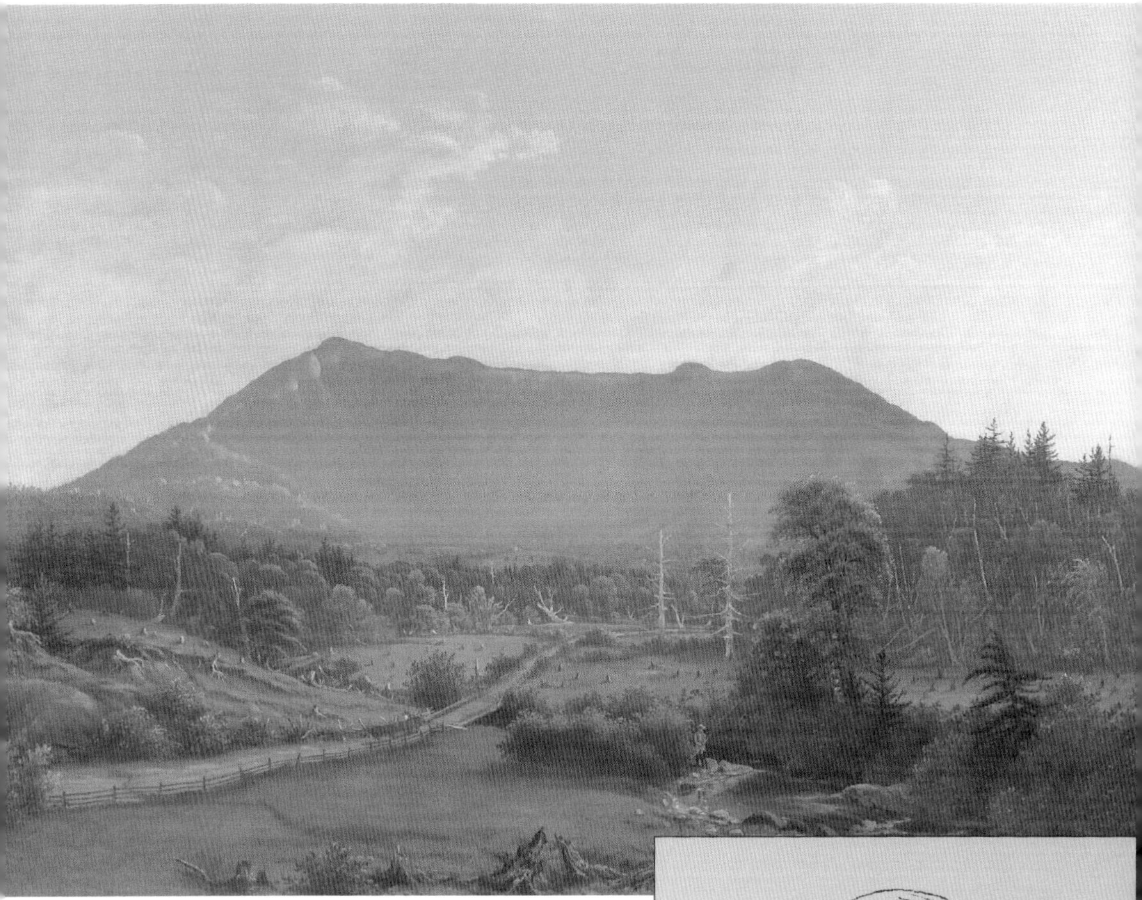

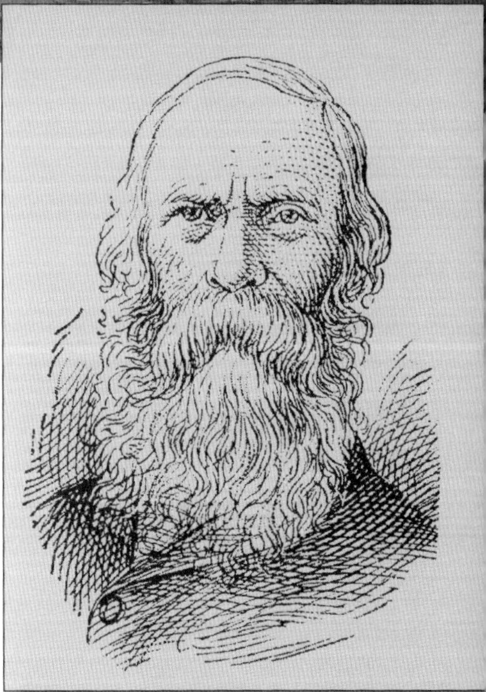

**Charles Louis Heyde**

Landscape painter Charles Louis Heyde (1822–1892) first visited Vermont in 1852, then moved to Burlington in 1856. For more than 30 years, some of Heyde's favorite subjects were Mount Mansfield (Vermont's highest mountain, clearly visible from Burlington), Lake Champlain, the Winooski River, and Otter Creek. There are 154 known paintings by Heyde in existence, and many of these are a testimony to his talent and to the natural beauty of the Burlington area and the surrounding Champlain Valley in the 19th century. Shown above is the c. 1857 painting *Mount Mansfield.* (Above, courtesy of the Fleming Museum of Art, University of Vermont. Gift of Mrs. Guy Bailey, 1944.3; right, courtesy of Special Collections, University of Vermont Libraries.)

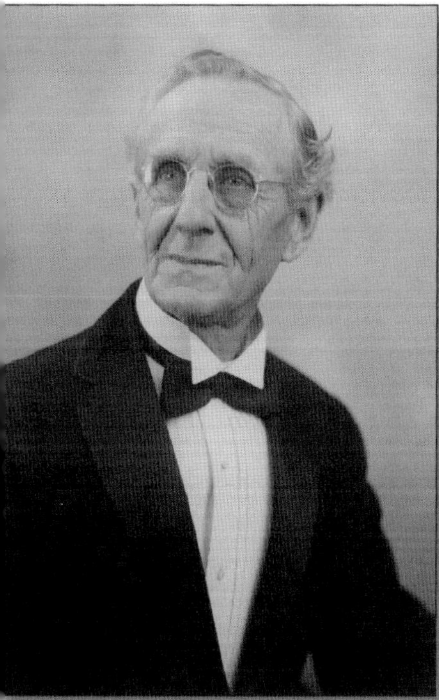

**The Man with the Panoramic Camera**
Louis L. McAllister (1876–1963), one of Burlington's best-known photographers, clicked away at people and places around the city for almost 60 years. McAllister was already a professional photographer when he moved to the Burlington area from Thomasville, Georgia, in 1910. He became well known for his wide-angle panorama camera, which he used to photograph everything from class pictures to crowds at community picnics. In some of his class photographs, the same children can be spotted at both ends of the picture if they were fast enough to run behind the camera and beat the motor that moved the lens from one end of the frame to the other! McAllister's entire collection of prints and negatives, a priceless archive of 20th-century Burlington, is now maintained by the Special Collections at the University of Vermont's Bailey-Howe Library and can be enjoyed online. (Courtesy of Special Collections, University of Vermont Libraries.)

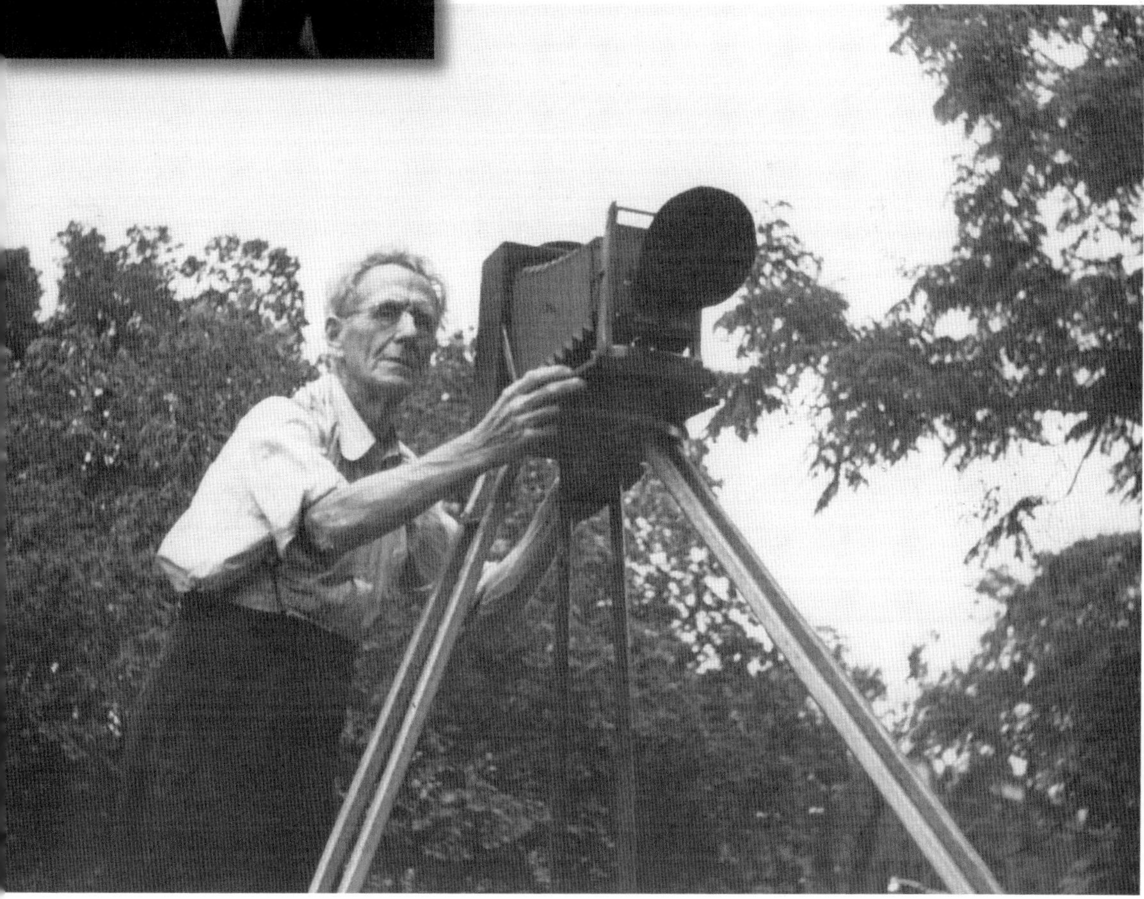

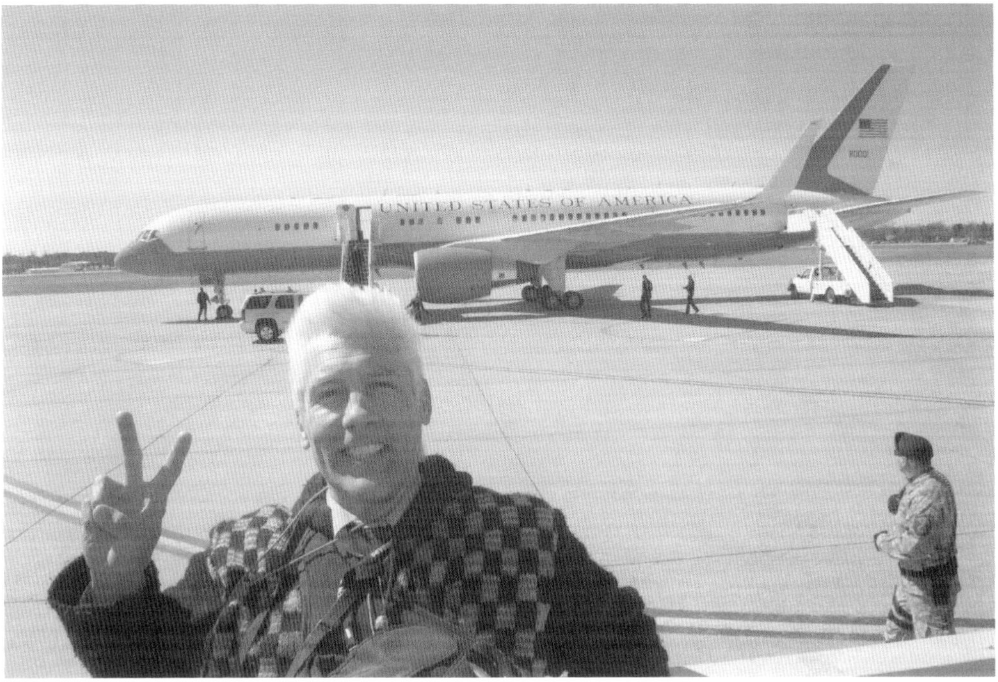


**Matthew Thorsen**

Matt Thorsen is one of *the* local photographic journalists. He has been capturing people, places, and things in the Burlington area for almost 20 years. His self-portraits are numerous and amazing. Thorsen is also famous for his photographs of local musicians, and he has recently published the first in a series of books of his music photographs. This is a self-portrait, with *Air Force I* at the Burlington Airport. (Courtesy of Matt Thorsen.)

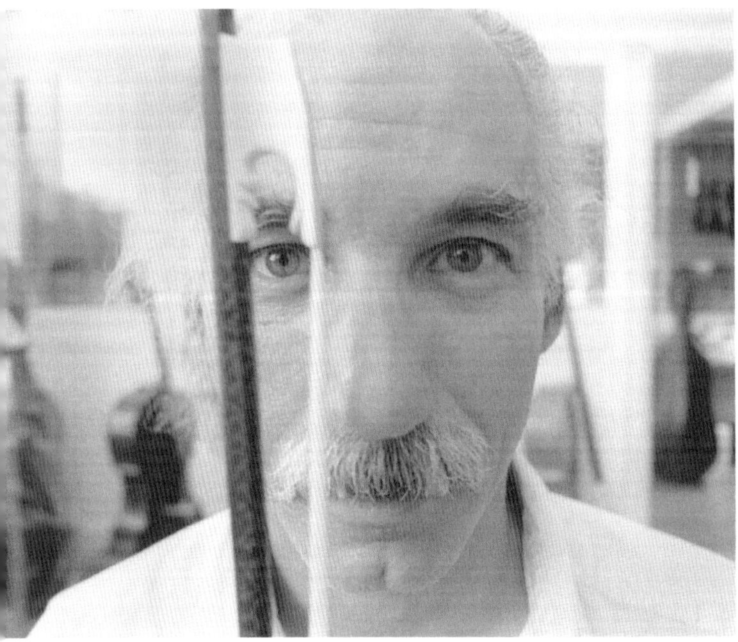

**Wood and Sound**

Harry Grabenstein began building musical instruments after moving to Burlington in the early 1970s. After two years at Time Guitars, a guitar factory in Waltham, Vermont, Grabenstein studied bow-making at the University of New Hampshire and spent the next seven years at Tourin Musica, a company that built viola de gambas and other historical stringed instruments. Grabenstein is now is one of only a few full-time bow makers in the United States and has earned an international reputation for his handcrafted bows. (Photograph by Matt Thorsen.)

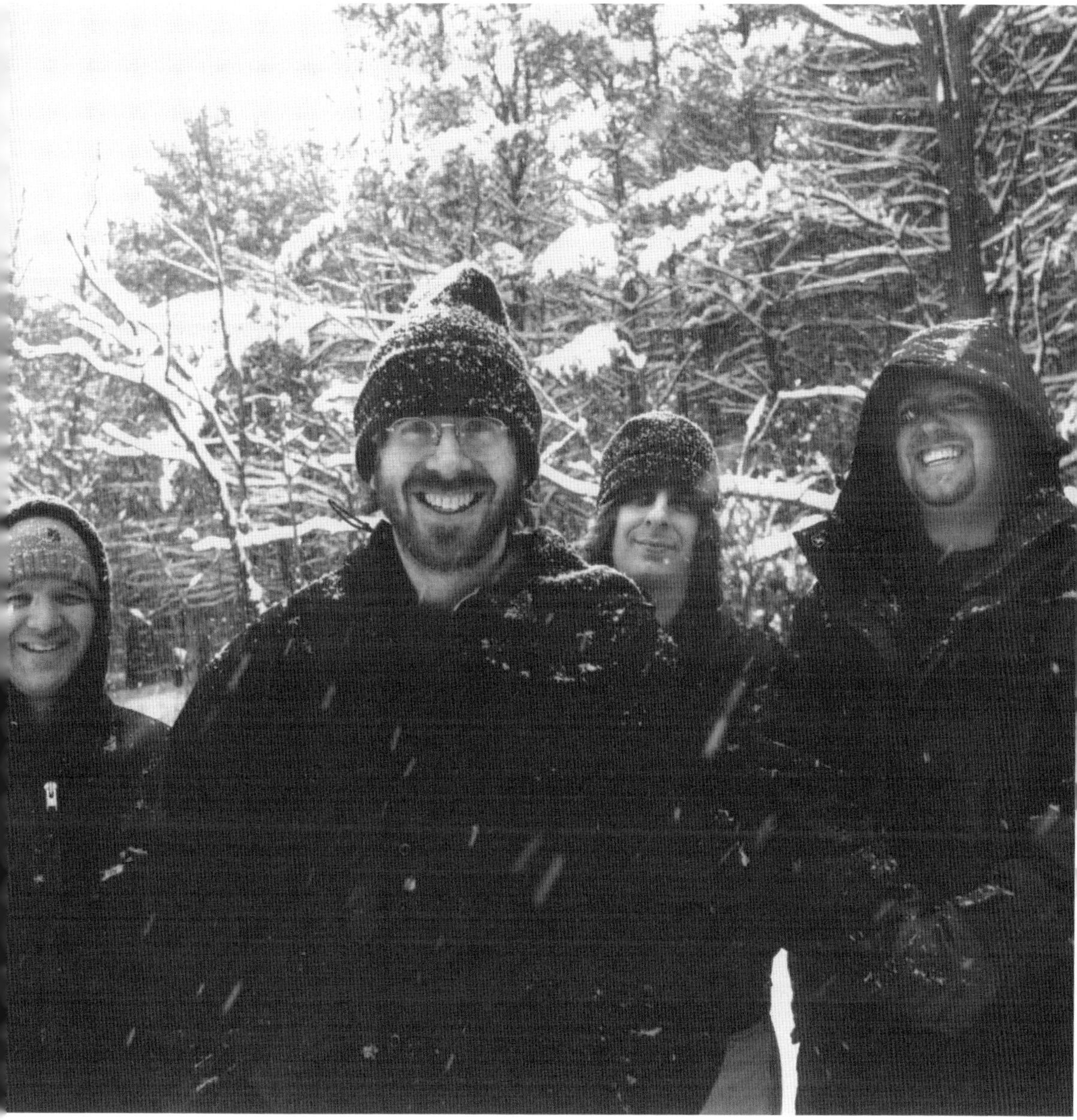

**Phish**

Phish, one of the world's most famous quartets, is a true Burlington band. The members, shown here from left to right, are Jon Fishman, Trey Anastasio, Mike Gordon, and Paige McConnell. They met at UVM and, by the late 1980s, were performing regularly at Nectar's on Main Street. The band's third album, *A Picture of Nectar,* is dedicated to that now-legendary performance venue. In the 1990s, at the peak of the band's fame, many fans would come to town just to see Nectar's. In 1997, Ben & Jerry's released an ice-cream flavor called "Phish Food." To celebrate the release, the band held a concert at Flynn Theatre and donated its share of the profits from the show and from the new flavor's sales to help clean up Lake Champlain. Band members still own homes in the Burlington area and can sometimes be spotted downtown when they aren't performing all over the world. (Photograph by Danny Clinch, courtesy of Phish, Inc.)

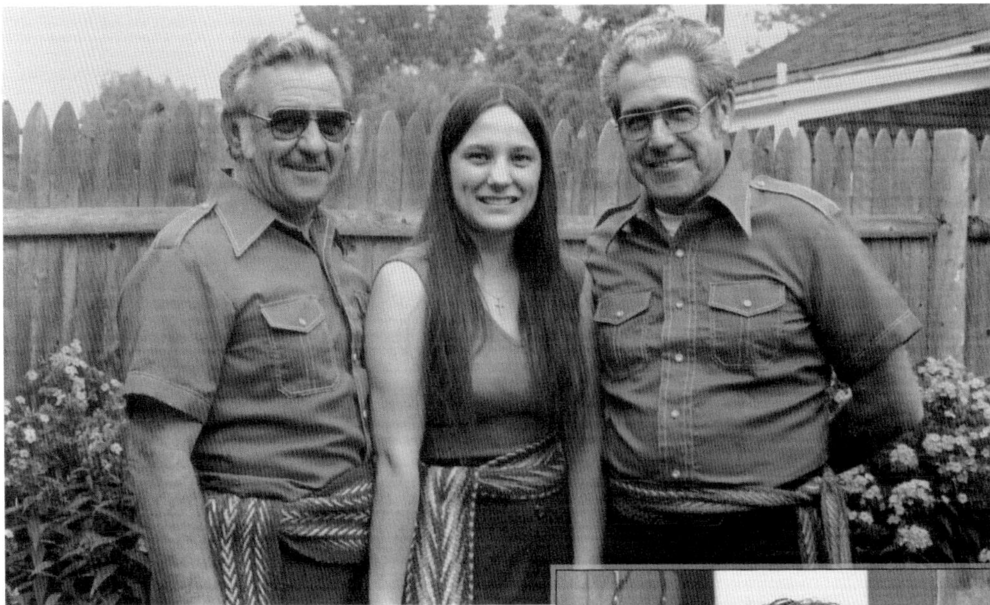

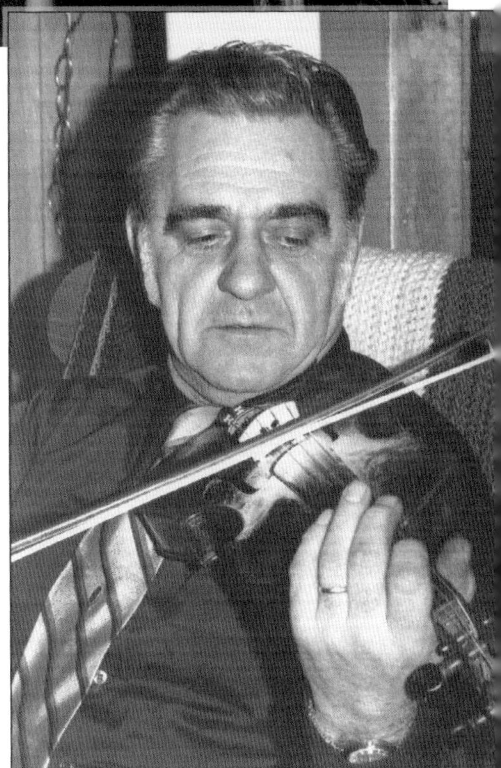

## The Beaudoin Family's Legacy

More than 30 years after his death, Louis Beaudoin's reputation is secure: He is still considered one of the great Quebecois fiddlers, even though he lived in Burlington for most of his life. In the classic French-Canadian tradition, Louis (pictured above on the left) and his brother Willie (a fiddler and guitarist) learned much of their repertoire from their parents, who played and sang traditional French music at soirees and parties in Lowell, Massachusetts, where the brothers grew up. The Beaudoins moved to Vermont in 1937, and in 1964, after serving for 11 years as a Burlington policeman, Louis opened an automobile radiator repair shop in Burlington's south end that, not surprisingly, also served as a popular meeting place for local fiddlers.

Louis (above, left) and Willie (above, right) with Louis's daughter Lisa Beaudoin (above, center) were selected to play at the Smithsonian Institution for a square dance on the eve of Pres. Jimmy Carter's inauguration. Louis also recorded a number of influential recordings at Vermont's Philo Records. Although by all accounts Louis Beaudoin was an entertaining and lively performer, he chose to spend most of his musical energy continuing the family traditions by sharing French-Canadian music with others, including his own family members, who still perform on special occasions as The Beaudoin Legacy, and with Northeast fiddlers Pete Sutherland, Donna Hebert, and George Wilson, who carry the torch and teach the next generation about the musical genius of the Beaudoins. (Photographs by Ann Meuer, courtesy of Bill Schubart.)

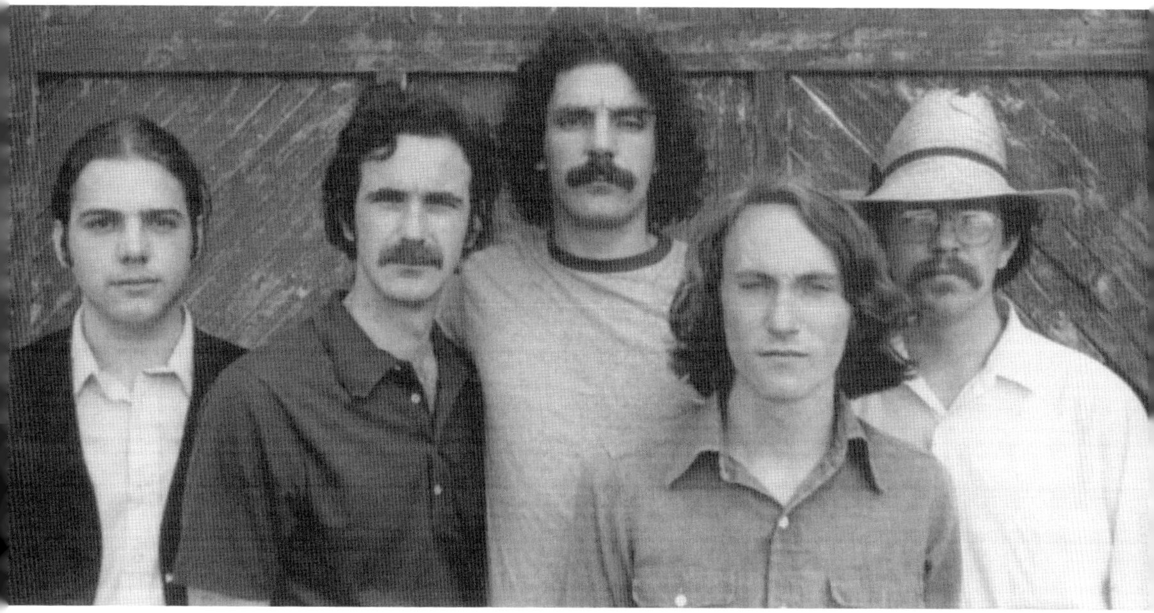

**Pine Island**

Pine Island, named after a dry spot in the middle of the swampy Burlington Intervale, was one of the first bluegrass bands in Vermont and one of the first "jazzgrass" bands anywhere. The group began as a trio in 1973 with Burlington natives Tim McKenzie and Jim McGinniss joined by banjo prodigy Gordon Stone, originally from Connecticut. Within the next few years, fiddler David Gusakov and mandolinist Jim Ryan joined the band. Pine Island was a regular at Tut's, a small and often crowded bar on North Street, and at the R.W. Hunt Mill & Mining Co., a much-loved downtown music venue. Four of the five original bandmates can still be found playing everything from Irish traditional music to gypsy jazz in a variety of musical combinations in the Burlington area. The memory of Pine Island is a shining star in the town's musical memory: a 30th-anniversary reunion concert at Burlington's Flynn Theatre in 2003 was a joyous and sentimental party for many of their old fans, proof to everyone that Pine Island was every bit as brilliant musically as everyone remembered. Pine Island members, shown here in 1977, are, from left to right, Gordon Stone, Tim McKenzie, David Gusakov, Jim Ryan, and Jim McGinniss. (Photograph by Marion Ettlinger, courtesy of Jim McGinniss.)

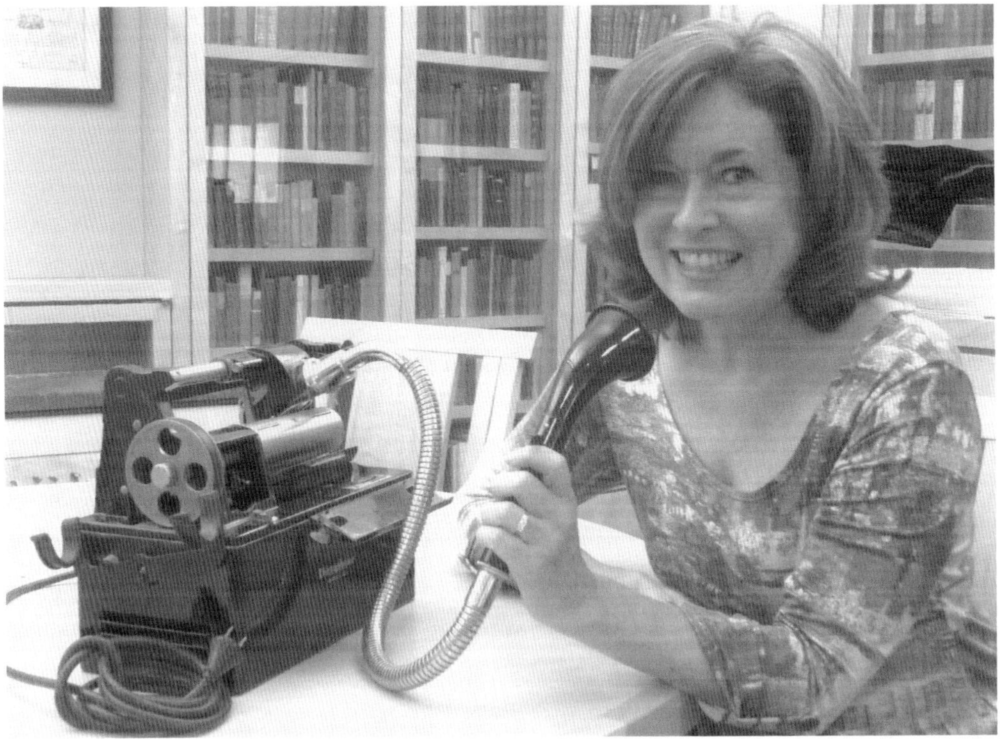

**Continuing the Tradition**
Burlington vocalist Deb Flanders is on a mission. She is the great-niece of Helen Hartness Flanders (1890–1972), one of the Vermont's premier "song catchers," who traveled around New England recording and transcribing traditional songs and tunes. Deb Flanders has made two recordings of songs learned from Helen Flanders' collections. The profits from these projects will help support Deb's campaign to digitize more than 4,000 field recordings and transcriptions housed at Middlebury College in order to make them easier for everyone to use and appreciate. (Photograph by Vikki Day, courtesy of Deb Flanders.)

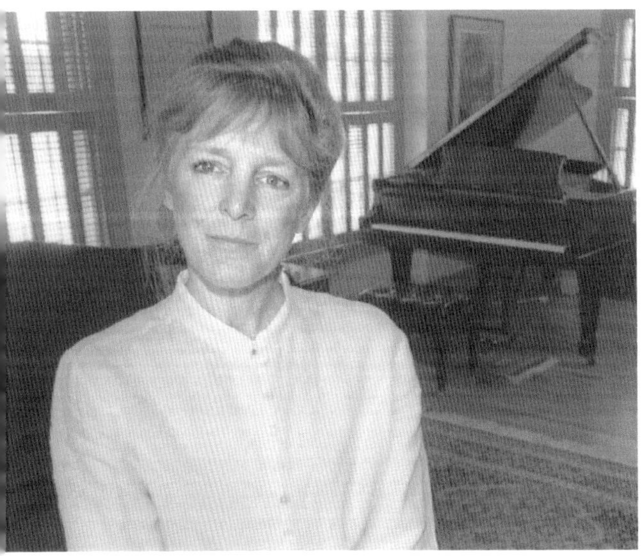

**Elaine Greenfield**
Local pianist and teacher Elaine Greenfield is one of the Burlington area's most respected classical musicians. She is a founding performer of the Vermont Contemporary Music Ensemble, an organization dedicated to performing and recording rarely heard works of living 20th- and 21st-century composers. In 2004, Greenfield made a historic recording of the 24 preludes by Claude Debussy on a 1907 German piano that is virtually identical to Debussy's piano of choice when he composed the works. (Photograph by Matt Thorsen.)

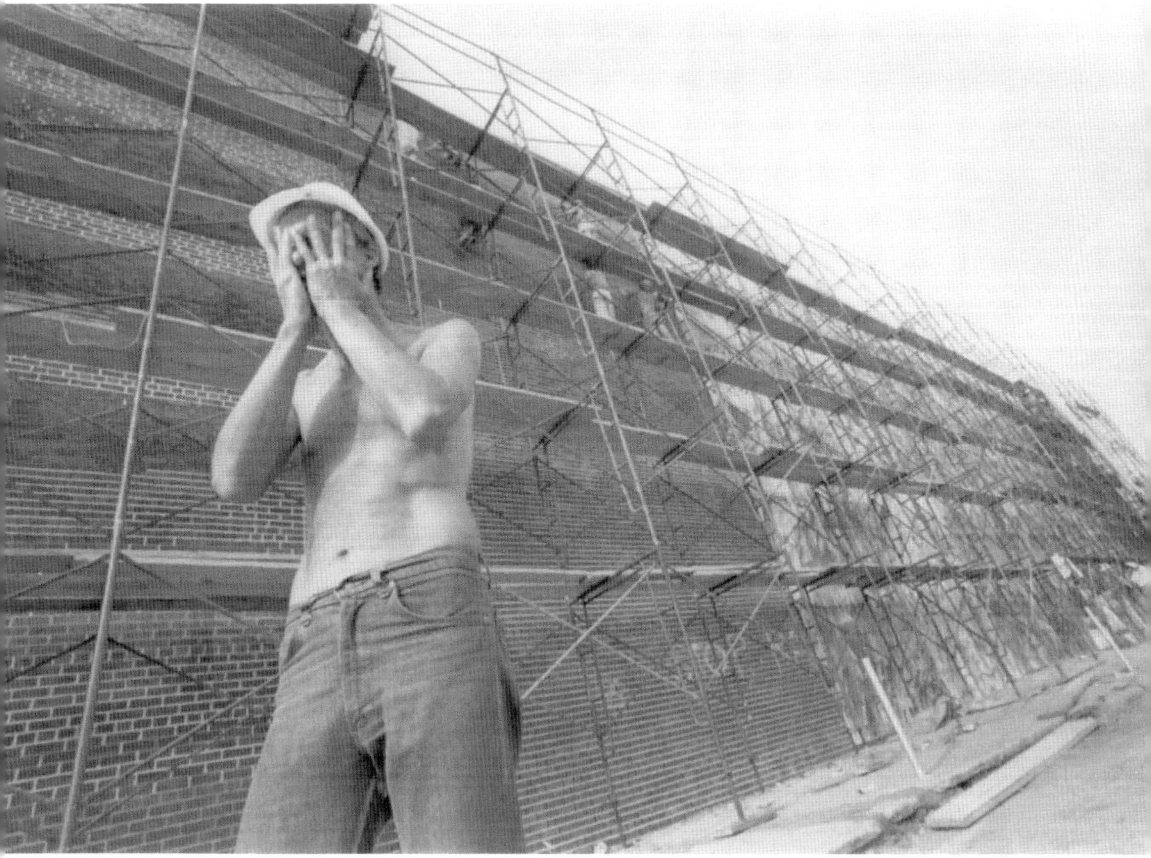

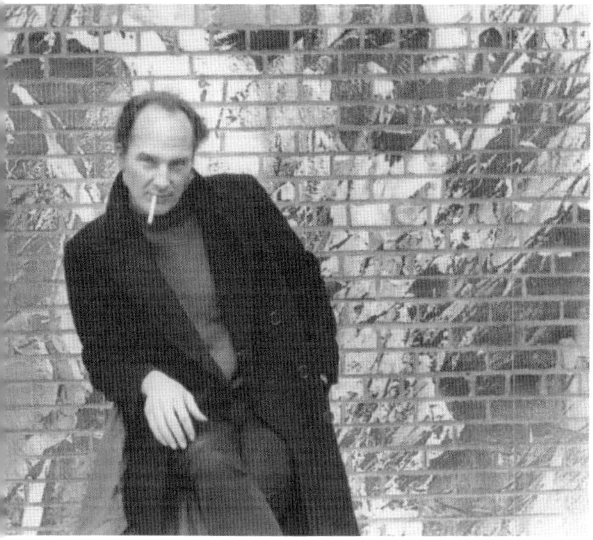

**Wes's Wall**

Burlington artist Wes Disney (1943–2000) took thousands of pictures, but it was for photographs of a 1981 project that he is best remembered in Burlington. For "The Wall," Disney photographed a rock face on Interstate 89 that was then transformed into 3,561 feet of Xerox wallpaper. The image of the rock was then glued to the 35,000 bricks on the south side of the J.C. Penney building in downtown Burlington by a team of volunteers, who then cut the image to expose the mortar. The resulting installation only lasted a few years, as the sealed paper did not stand up well to Burlington's weather. If successful art is meant to provoke, Disney's wall was a huge success. Some observers dismissed it as a complete waste of time and money; others marveled at the scale of the project or puzzled over its meaning. Few ignored it. (Courtesy of the W.E.D. Art Trust.)

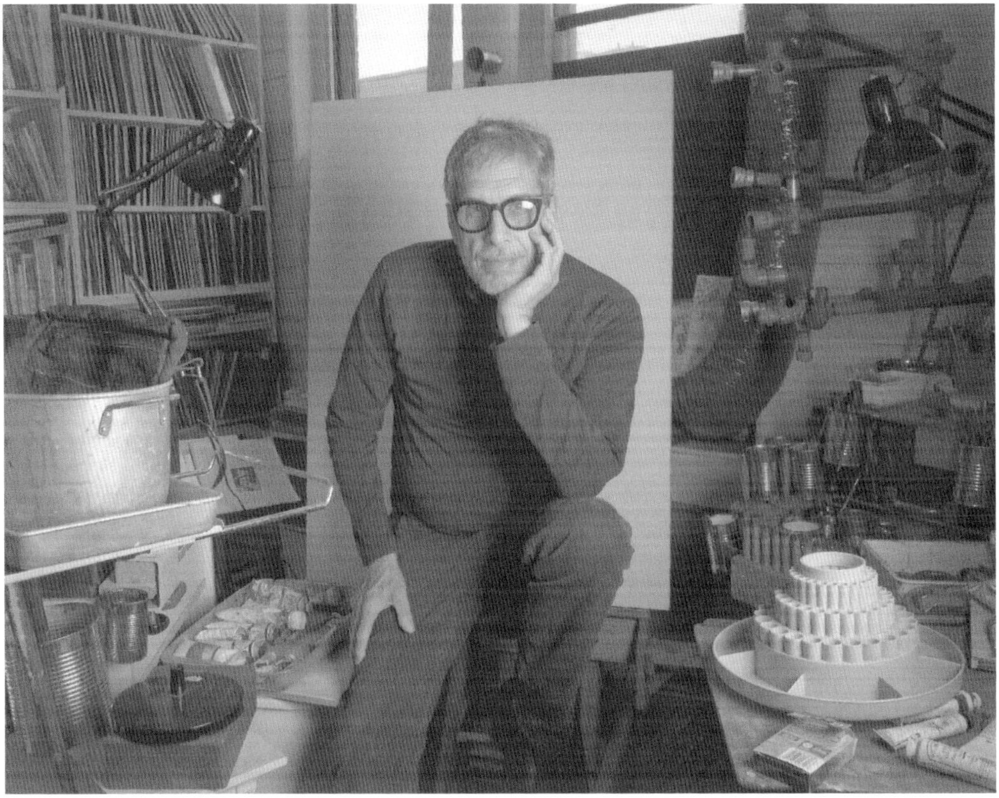

**Dug Nap**

Burlington icon and self-taught artist Dug Nap has been a source of boundless energy for the city's cultural scene over the past 30 years. Nap moved to Burlington in 1982 when he was the lead singer and songwriter for Pinhead, one of Vermont's first and most famous punk-rock combos. Since that time he has become well-known for his many artistic endeavors, including outdoor poetry readings downtown on warm summer nights, pet portraits, gloriously self-centered one-man multimedia performances, and, most famously, for his humorous greeting-card art. (Photograph by Ben Resnik.)

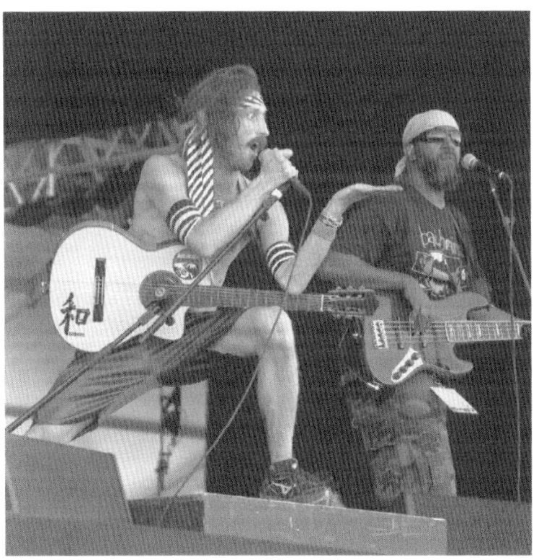

**Eugene Hütz**

In 1992, Eugene Nikolaev and his family settled in Burlington after leaving Kiev a few years earlier in the wake of the Chernobyl nuclear disaster. After playing for years in local bars with a celebrated punk band called The Fags, Nikolaev moved to New York City, changed his name to Eugene Hütz, and started Gogol Bordello, one of the world's most popular and outrageous gypsy punk bands. Even though he is now an international star, Hütz can sometimes be spotted around town. He comes back to Burlington regularly to visit old friends. (Courtesy of Kadellar.)

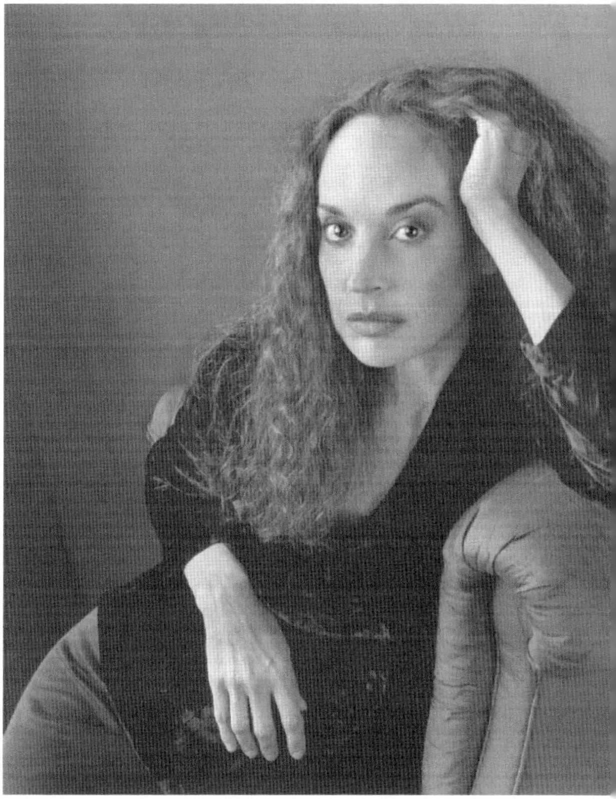

**The Author's Photographer**
In the 1970s, Burlington photographer Marion Ettlinger was well known around town for creating hauntingly beautiful black-and-white and hand-tinted portraits of musicians and other local luminaries. In 1983, Ettlinger was commissioned by *Esquire* magazine to photograph 50 authors as part of its 50th-anniversary issue, and she soon became known as one of the nation's leading author photographers. Shooting with the same camera that she has been using since 1968, Ettlinger creates her unique results using only natural light. (Courtesy of Marion Ettlinger.)

**Vermont's Cartoonist Laureate**
Burlington resident James Kochalka is a celebrated comic-book author, the creator of a popular syndicated comic strip, a regular visiting artist and faculty member at the Center for Cartoon Studies in White River Junction, Vermont, and a rock musician. On March 10, 2011, Kochalka was officially declared the first Cartoonist Laureate of the State of Vermont, a position that he will hold for three years. (Courtesy of Matt Thorsen.)

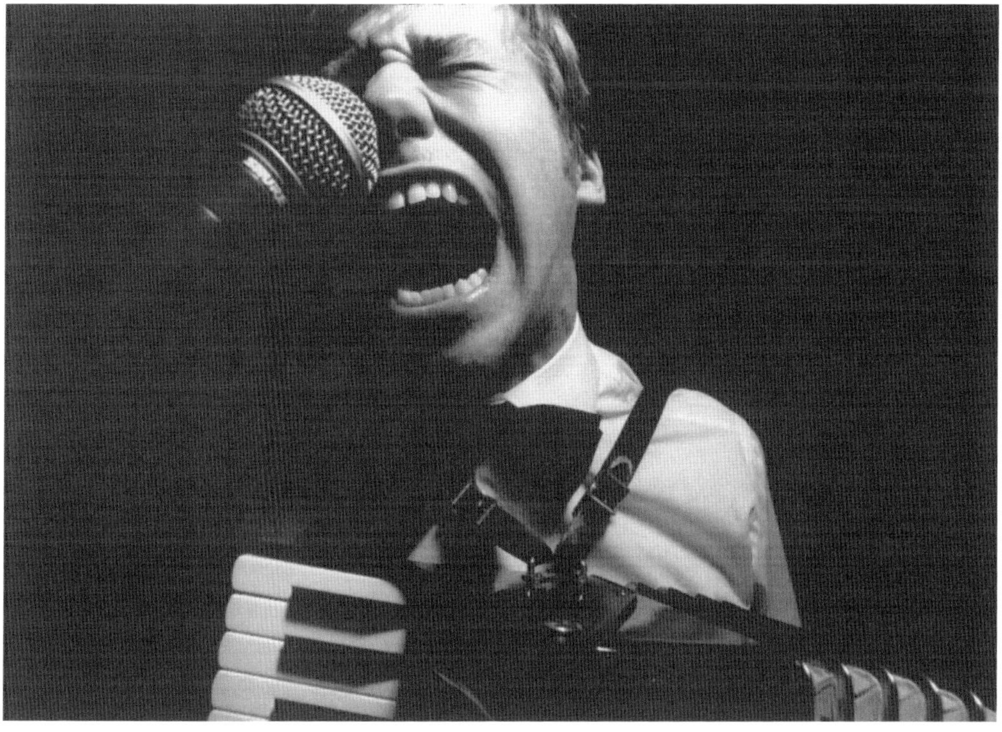

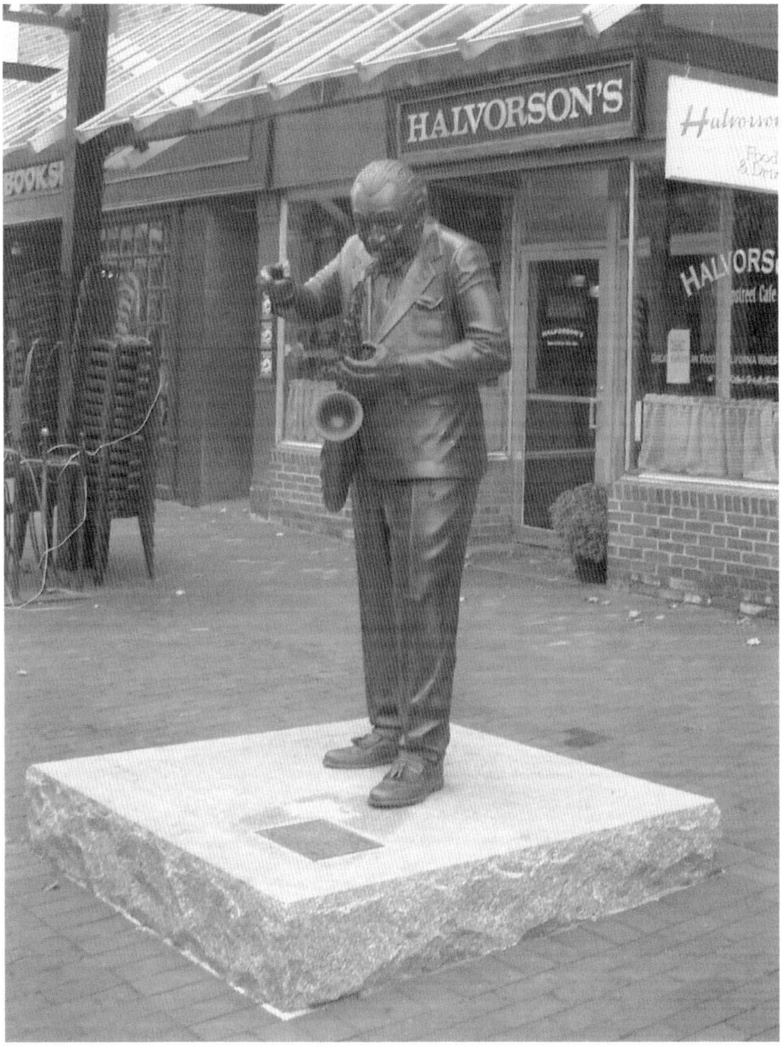


**Joseph Henry "Big Joe" Burrell**

As a young man, saxophonist "Big Joe" Burrell (1924–2005) played with a number of different combos, including the B.B. King Orchestra, and even got a chance to play with his hero, Count Basie, in New York City. After years of touring with bands in Canada, Big Joe moved to Burlington in 1976, started playing with a popular Vermont band called Just Jazz, and soon formed the Unknown Blues Band with Burlington guitarist Paul Asbell. For the next 20 years, Big Joe and the Unknown Blues Band were local favorites, playing regular appearances at Halverson's Bar and Restaurant on Church Street, and headlining everything from the city's Independence Day parties to the Burlington Discover Jazz Festival (see page 54). The Unknown Blues band called it quits in 2002, but Burrell still performed regularly at Halverson's until a short time before his death.

In 2007, a life-sized statue of Burrell, created by local metal artist Chris Sharp, was dedicated on the upper block of Church Street, directly in front of Halverson's, the site of many of Big Joe's gigs. The statue's inscription reads: "The people of Burlington wish to express our genuine gratitude to 'Big' Joe Burrell for sharing his passion for life and for inspiring our city's love of all music, especially Jazz and the Blues. Big Joe is our giant in 'America's greatest contribution to world culture,' and we are proud to be patrons of this evolving expression known as . . . 'JAZZ.' " (Photograph by the author.)

# CHAPTER SIX

# Local Heroes

There are many things that can make a person a "hero" in the eyes of their neighbors. The Burlington community has many heroes.

Philanthropists like Antonio Pomerleau, who has donated millions of dollars to nonprofit social service organizations, and Mary Martha Fletcher, whose donations founded the Fletcher Free Library and Mary Fletcher Hospital, have directly helped thousands of local people with their generosity.

Many in Burlington have become heroes simply for doing what they love. Artist Bonnie Acker has personally managed the planting of public flower gardens downtown for years. Local businessman Ray Pecor is the champion of Burlington baseball, the owner of the Lake Monsters ball club, and the guardian of Centennial Field, the stadium where the team plays. Star of the 1946 Burlington High School baseball team, Merle Glasston, made it to one of the St. Louis Cardinals' farm teams after graduating from BHS. Jazz aficionado Ed Bemis paved the way for local jazz radio programming and successfully campaigned for a degree program in jazz studies at the University of Vermont. Brewmaster Greg Noonan spent years lobbying the state for permission to open Vermont's first brew pub. Emily Anderson created the Awareness Theater Company to provide a creative outlet for adults with disabilities. Michael and Valerie Wood-Lewis developed the Front Porch Forum, a hugely successful online bulletin board for neighborhoods, in an effort to strengthen their own community. Rabbi Max Wall dedicated his life to building connections between Burlington's Jewish community and other local organizations. Chapin Spencer directs Local Motion, a Burlington organization dedicated to alternative transportation and to the preservation of bike paths. Gardener and social activist Ron Krupp founded Recycle North, a nonprofit business that reduces waste and provides training for the homeless. Tommy Thompson successfully negotiated for a permanent community garden plot in Burlington's Intervale and, in the process, rekindled a wide interest in gardening throughout the city. City arborist Warren Spinner managed the replanting of the entire city after most of its trees were killed by Dutch elm disease. Singer-songwriter Rachel Bissex started the Burlington Coffeehouse to create additional local venues for acoustic musicians. Andrea Rogers was the guiding light behind transforming the Flynn Theatre from a broken-down Art Deco movie house into Burlington's performance center, and Dr. Lewis First has become a local media star as a result of his desire to support responsible parenting and healthy children.

Finally, some Burlington heroes are famous for one specific thing. Marcella Chapman was instrumental in saving the Fletcher Free Library's Carnegie building from the bulldozers when structural problems arose in the 1970s. Madeleine Kunin served as Vermont's first female governor. Patrick Brown is a tireless campaigner for racial equality, and Sara Holbrook was a UVM professor best remembered for the community center founded to aid new arrivals to Burlington that still bears her name.

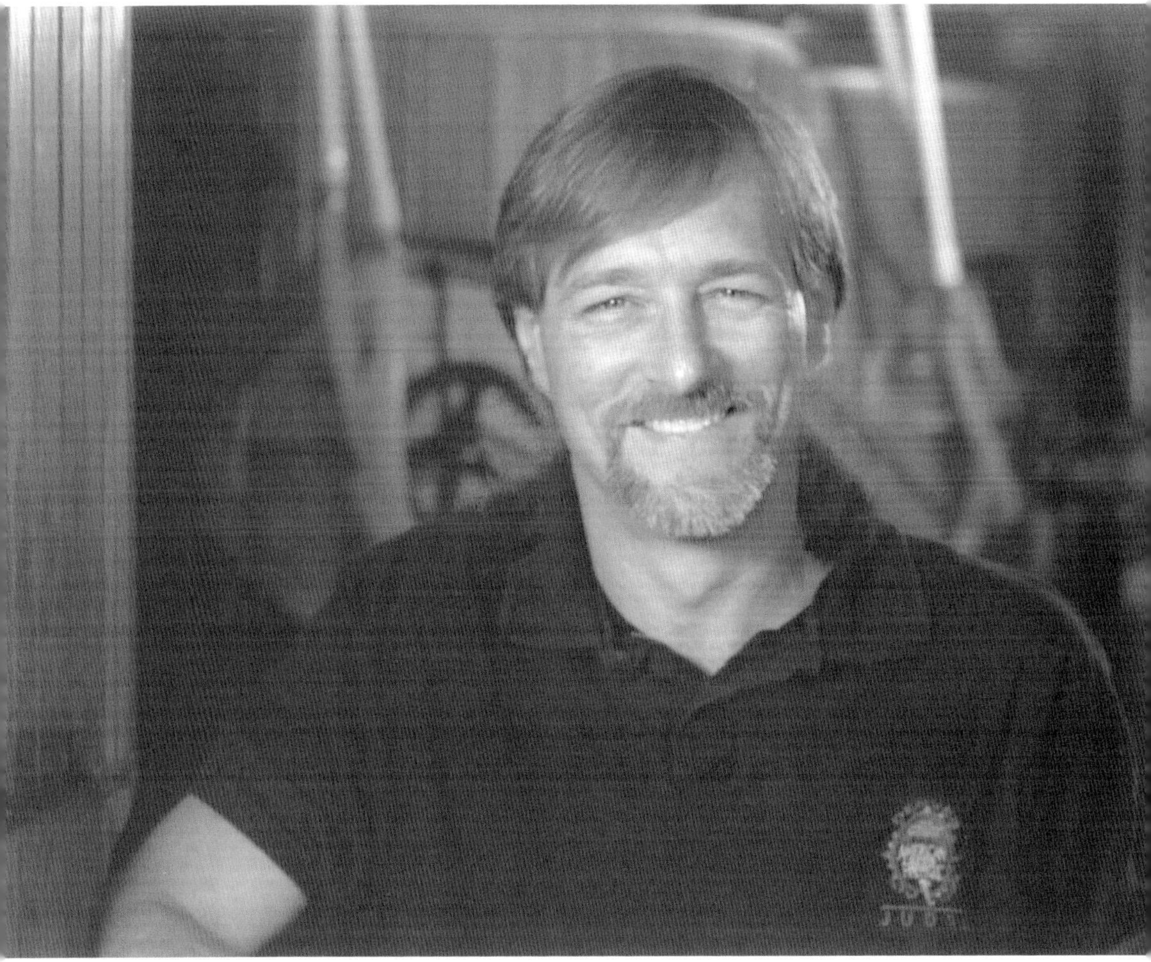

**The Home Brewer's Godfather**

Greg Noonan was one of the pioneers of craft beer brewing in the United States. In Burlington, Noonan opened the Vermont Pub & Brewery in 1988, the first business in Vermont to served beer that was brewed on the premises. Noonan inspired all comers, amateur home beer makers and fledgling brewers alike, with his willingness to share information and for his brews that were jazzed up with innovative flavorings like herbs or maple syrup. Before opening his pub, Greg spent three years lobbying the Vermont legislature to legalize brewpubs. The fruits of his labors include the establishment of craft breweries all over the state, with at least seven brewpubs or breweries in the Burlington area alone. Greg Noonan died in 2009 of lung cancer, which was undetected until shortly before his death. The books and articles that he authored are still considered essential reading. (Courtesy of Vermont Pub & Brewery.)

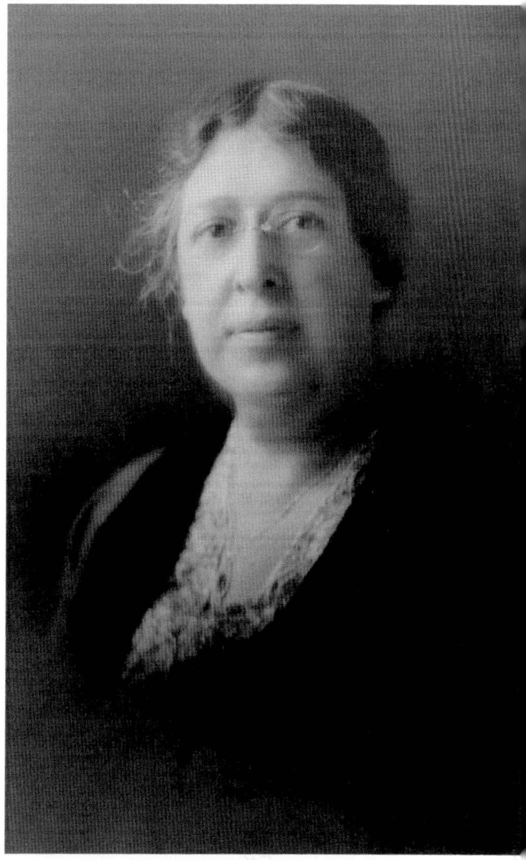

**Sara Holbrook**

Sara M. Holbrook (1878–1958) worked as a clinical psychologist in Burlington and as a professor of education at UVM, but she is best remembered for the Burlington Community Center, founded in 1937 with funds raised by Holbrook and her close friend, Dr. Bertha Terrill (see page 35). The center was a place for Burlington's Irish, Italian, and French-Canadian immigrants to learn to speak English, study for citizenship tests, and take cooking and sewing classes. The organization was renamed the Sara Holbrook Community Center in 1958 in honor of its founder. (Courtesy of the Sara Holbrook Community Center.)

**A Very Special Artist**

Emily Anderson is a talented musician, videographer, puppeteer, and playwright. She is also the creator of VSA Vermont's Awareness Theater Company, a dramatic troupe made up of adults with developmental disabilities who perform original works on a variety of themes in live performances and on public access television. Anderson is well known in the Burlington area for a recent collaboration with Mark Utter, a Vermonter who cannot speak because of a neurological condition. They have created a documentary film titled *I Am In Here: A View of My Daily Life, With Good Suggestions From My Intelligent Mind.* (Photograph by S.J. Kariko, courtesy of Very Special Arts Vermont.)

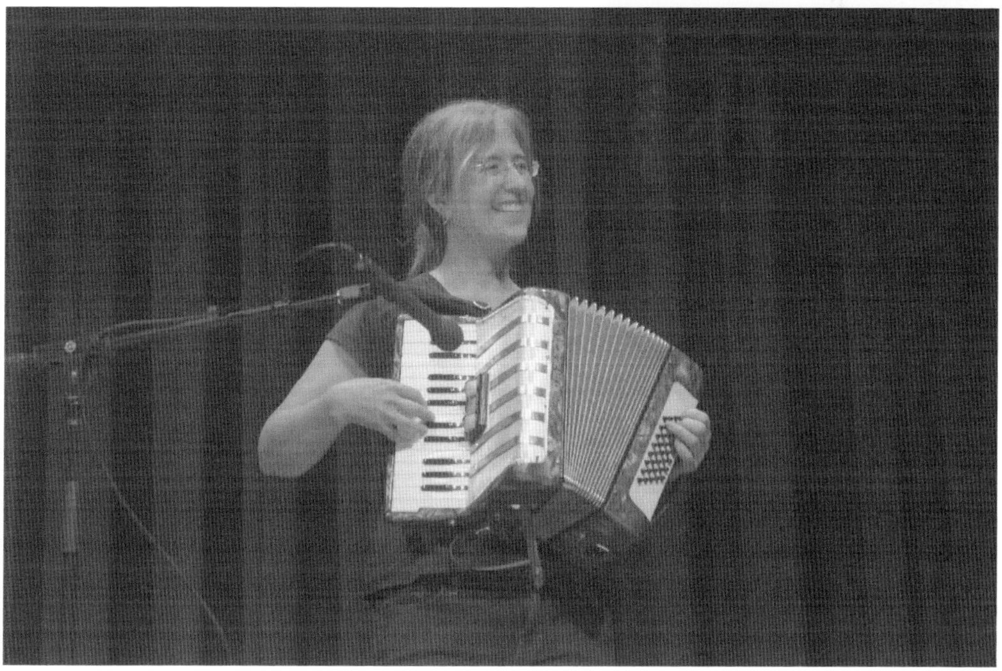

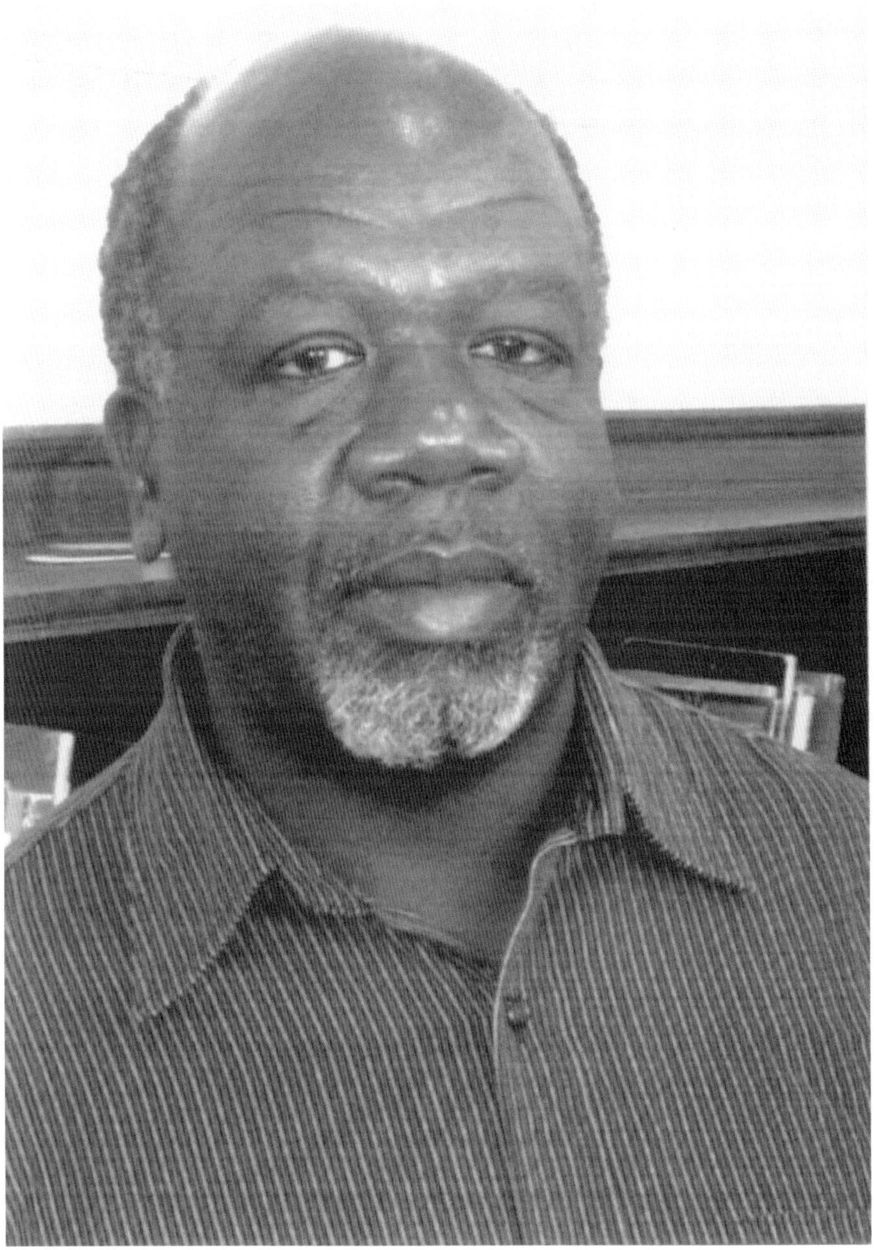

**The Organizer**

Patrick Brown, the director of the Greater Burlington Multicultural Resource Center, is a quiet man who gets a lot done. In 1990, Brown starting organizing events to commemorate Martin Luther King Day. Since then, Burlington has been treated to an impressive series of speakers who have come to Vermont each January to honor Dr. King's memory, including Angela Davis, Dick Gregory, Anita Hill, the Reverend Al Sharpton, and Bishop Desmond Tutu. For all of his work supporting diversity in Burlington, and for promoting the recruitment and retention of people of color in the city's school system, Patrick Brown was honored with a United Way Community Impact Award in 2005 and a Lifetime Achievement award at Burlington's first Champions of Diversity and Equity conference in 2009. (Photograph by the author.)

### Andrea's Theater

In June 2010, Andrea Rogers finally passed the baton and retired from her position as the first and only executive director of Burlington's Flynn Center for the Performing Arts. During the previous 30 years, Rogers had worked nonstop, serving as chief fundraiser, head accountant, public ambassador, and prime visionary for an organization that undertook a prize-winning renovation of a worn-out 1930s Art Deco movie house and created a mutifaceted performance center and one of Burlington's cultural gems.

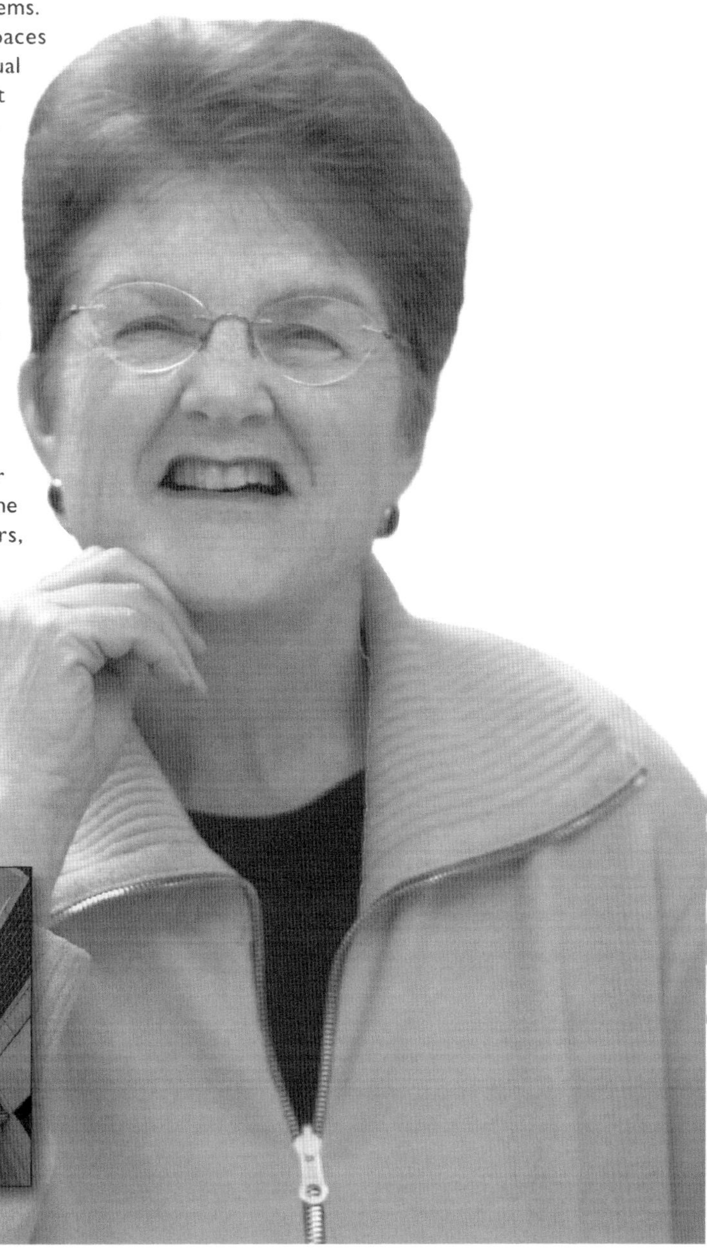

The Flynn Theatre's performance spaces are an integral part of Burlington's annual Discover Jazz Festival and First Night Burlington, and the main stage serves as the home of the Vermont Stage Company and Lyric Theatre, the amateur stage troupe that provided some of the original impetus to save and renovate the theater. The main stage is also Burlington's ritziest venue, the place to see the likes of Mikhail Barishnikov and Tony Bennett. The Flynn complex also includes smaller performance and lecture spaces and an art gallery. Today, close to 200,000 people annually attend performances on the Flynn main stage and in the FlynnSpace, a smaller venue next door to the original theater. One of those 200,000 is often Andrea Rogers, still keeping a seasoned eye on things, but now able to sit in the audience and enjoy the show. (Inset, photograph by Frederic Silberman, courtesy of Andrea Rogers; center, photograph by the author.)

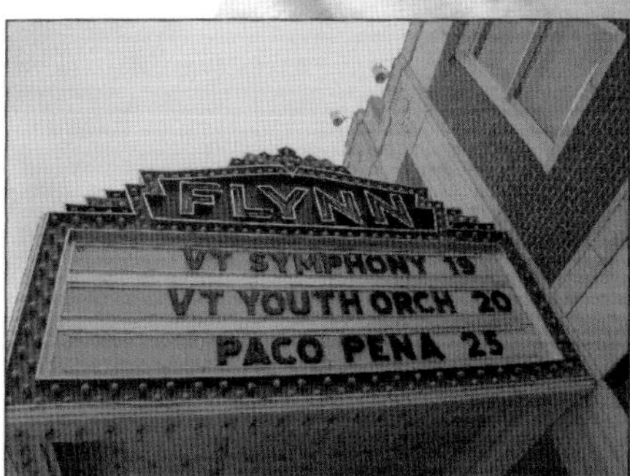

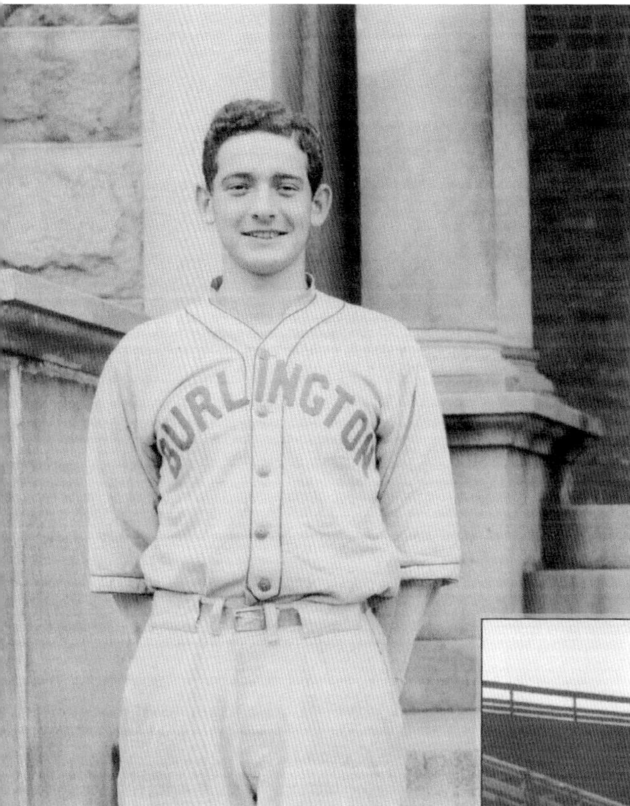


### The Ballplayer

Merle Glasston (1929–1975), called "Sonny" by his family and known by many of his teammates and fans as "Moe," played all varieties of sports at Burlington High School from 1943 to 1947, including varsity football and basketball. But it is for his career as a catcher on the BHS baseball team that he is best remembered. Glasston caught for ace pitcher Doc Newton in the Burlington Legion state championship win over Rutland in 1946. In 1947, Glasston was drafted to play for the Columbus Red Birds in Ohio, one of the St. Louis Cardinals' minor league teams. Even though he was never called up to play in the majors, Merle Glasston still remains a hero to Burlingtonians who remember and loved local baseball in the 1940s. (Courtesy of the Glasston family.)

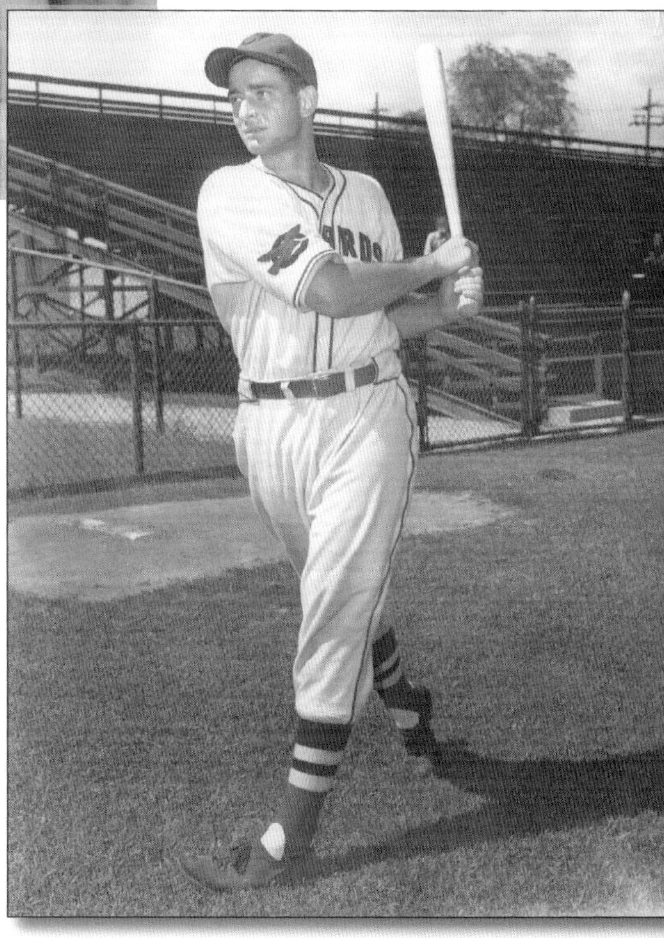

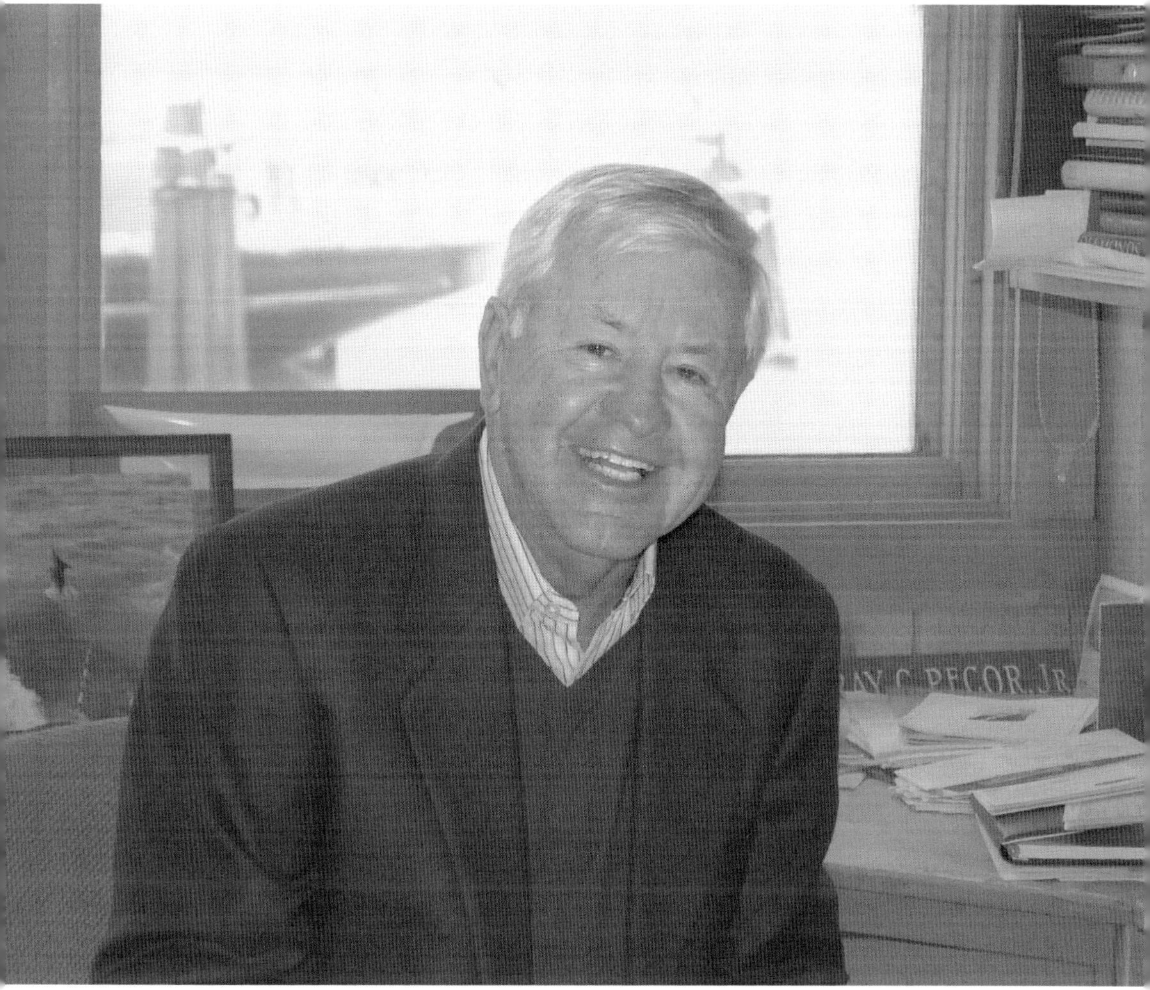

**Baseball Hero**

Ray Pecor, a lifetime fan of the Boston Red Sox, loves presenting baseball games in Burlington. Pecor, past president of the Lake Champlain Transportation Company (the firm that operates most of the ferryboats on the lake), purchased the Jamestown Expos, an AA New York state team, in 1993, and renamed them the Vermont Expos. The Expos became the Lake Monsters in 2006. All of their home games continue to be played at Centennial Field, a ballpark that has been operated by the University of Vermont since 1906. In exchange for an agreement with UVM granting him a 20-year lease for just $1 per year, Pecor invested over $1 million to improve Centennial Field prior to the 2012 season, a promise to Burlington fans of many more ball games to come. (Courtesy of Lake Champlain Transportation Company.)

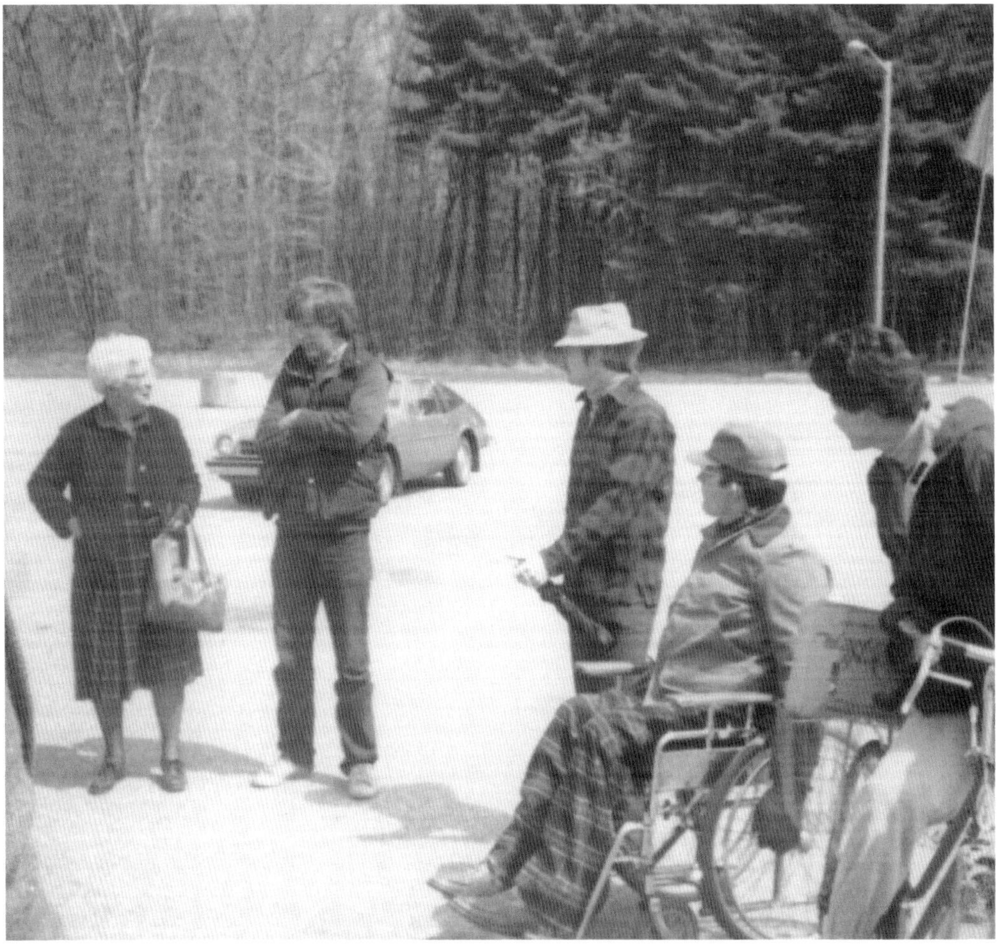

**Citizens Waterfront Group**

Local attorney Rick Sharp has been a champion of public access to Burlington's waterfront for more than 30 years. Sharp, along with local physician Howard Dean (later a six-term governor of Vermont) and UVM environmental studies professor Tom Hudspeth, laid the groundwork for Burlington's waterfront bike path. The men formed a citizens' group that eventually overcame political and legal challenges to public access to a disused railroad right-of-way along the lakefront. Burlington's 7.5-mile-long bike path is one of the city's treasures and a favorite destination for residents and visitors alike. Sharp was also one of the few voices opposing the Alden Plan, a 1983 development scheme backed by many at city hall that could have resulted in a 200-room hotel, 300 condos, and a large parking garage located directly on the waterfront. The Alden Plan was defeated by Burlington voters in December 1985. Rick Sharp feels that his contribution to the evolution of the waterfront is his greatest gift to posterity. Many other locals agree. Shown here are, from left to right, Citizens Waterfront Group members Dorothy Hunt, Rick Sharp, unidentified, Alderman Alan Gear, and unidentified. They are gathered at Burlington's Leddy Park just before the "chain saw party" in 1985 that celebrated the defeat of legal challenges to the waterfront bike path. (Courtesy of Rick Sharp.)

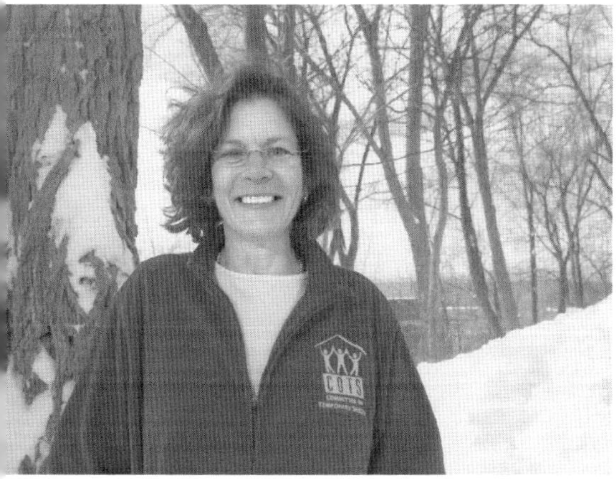

**Rita Markley**
Rita Markley is the longtime executive director of the Committee on Temporary Shelter, known around Burlington as COTS. The nonprofit organization helps prevent homelessness and aids homeless individuals and families to find immediate shelter and to connect with resources to give them a fresh start. Markley's belief that "everyone deserves a chance" has become the motto for COTS. She was honored in 2000 as "Vermonter of the Year" by the *Burlington Free Press*. (Photograph by Alison Redlich, courtesy of COTS Vermont.)

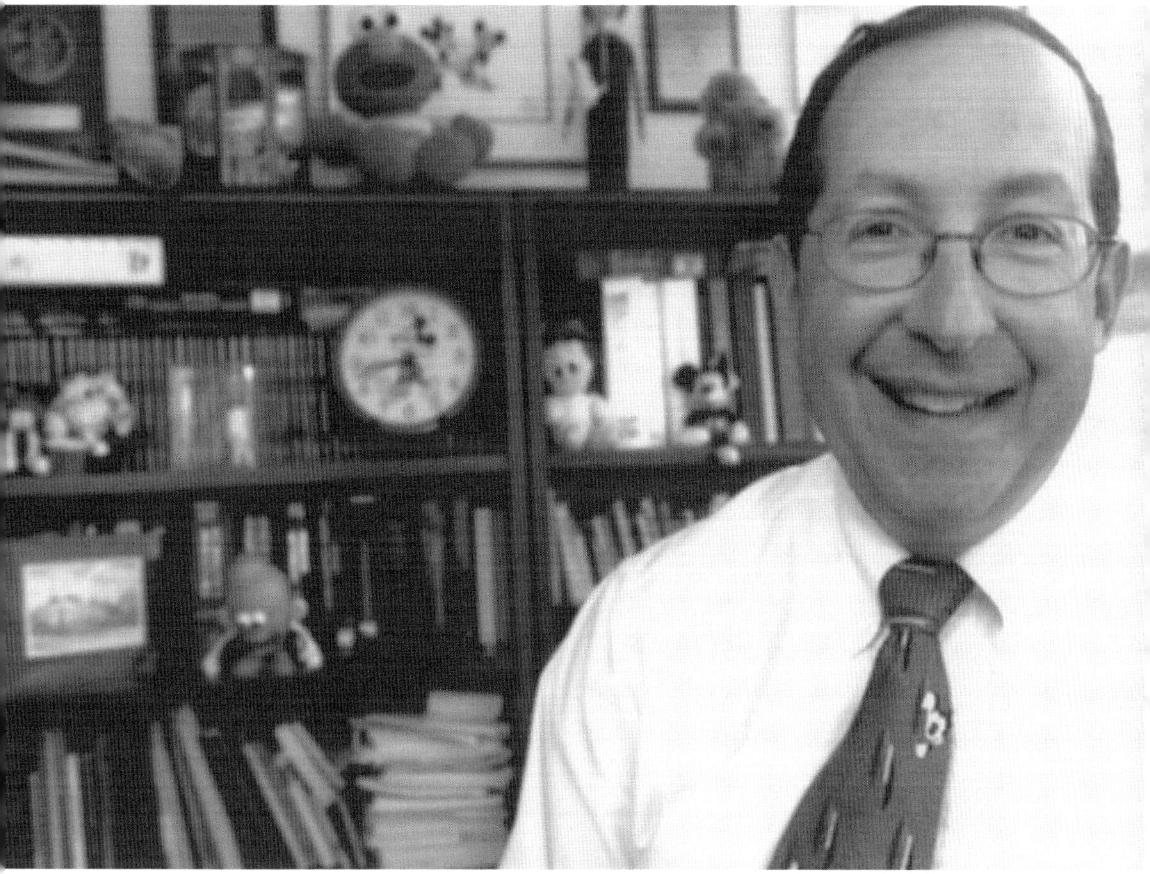

**First with Kids**
Dr. Lewis First is much more than a dedicated pediatrician. He came to Burlington in 1994 to become the chief of pediatrics at the Vermont Children's Hospital at Fletcher Allen and the chairman of the department of pediatrics at the UVM College of Medicine. Dr. First is the editor-in-chief of *Pediatrics* magazine and one of Vermont's most visible advocates for child wellness. He is the host of a popular weekly television and radio program, *First with Kids*, that provides parents with the latest advice for keeping children and adolescents healthy and happy. (Courtesy of Fletcher Allen Heathcare.)

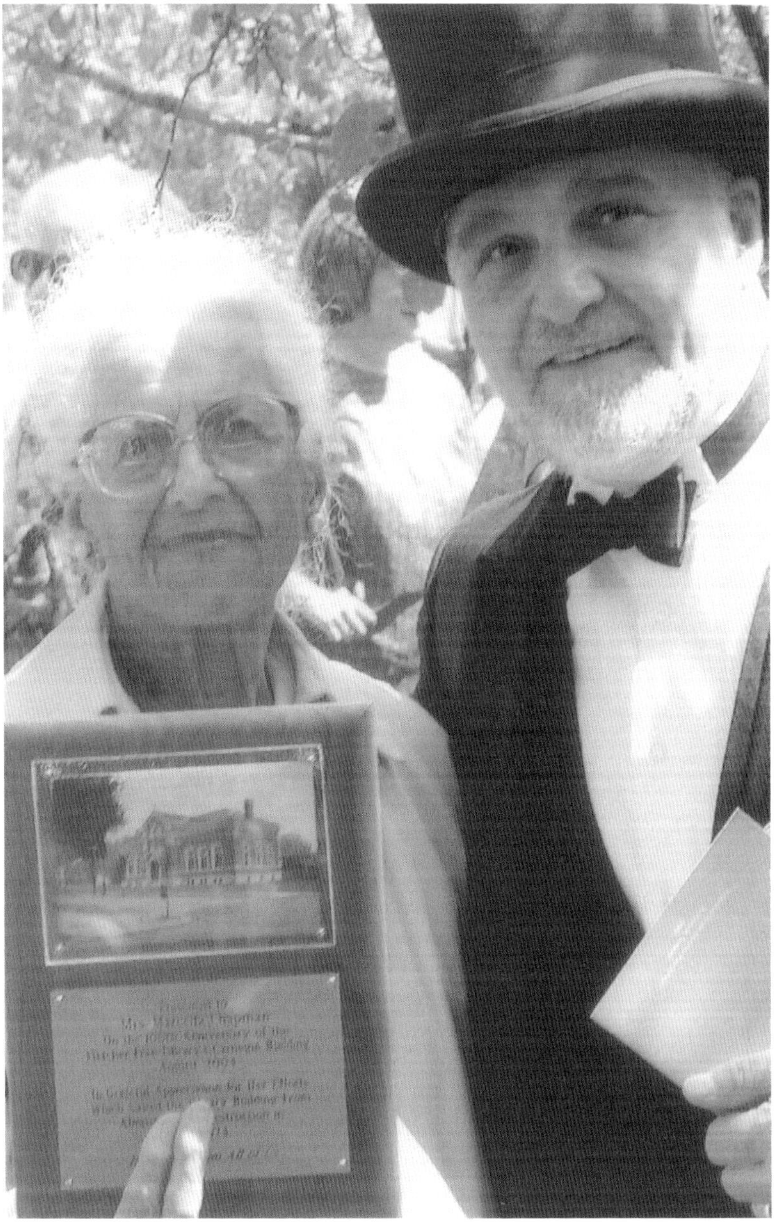

**Marcella Chapman**
When Marcella Chapman passed on at the age of 100 in October 2008, she left Burlington with much more than fond memories. Without her drive and dedication, the Fletcher Free Library's ailing Carnegie building, which had developed serious cracks in its foundation, almost certainly would have been demolished in early 1974. Chapman and other library friends worked nonstop, circulating petitions and writing letters until the building was entered into the National Register of Historic Places in August 1974. In the midst of the fray, Chapman was quoted as saying, "those bulldozers will have to roll over me before they touch that building!" She is pictured here, at the age of 96, celebrating the 100th anniversary of Burlington's Carnegie Library. This book's author is on the right. (Photograph by Lilian Baker Carlisle, courtesy of the Fletcher Free Library.)

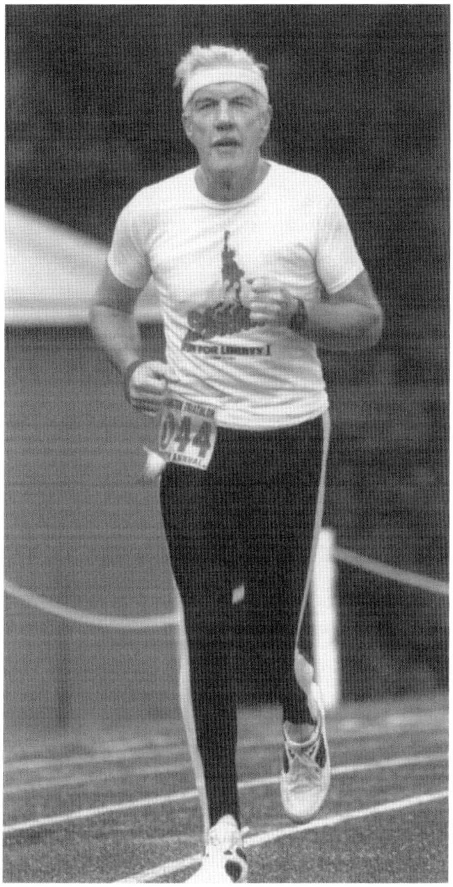

**The "Townie"**
In 2012, at the age of 81, Burlington native William Keogh "retired" from the Burlington City Council after serving for 16 years, a term that included three years as council president. In addition to his career in city hall and a lifelong avocation as a baseball umpire, basketball referee, and athlete (he ran a marathon to celebrate his 60th birthday), Keogh spent eight years representing Burlington in the Vermont House of Representatives, seven years on the city's planning commission, and most of the 1960s as the superintendent of the city's parks and recreation department (during which time he built a new bathhouse and made other lasting improvements at North Beach, Burlington's most popular sandy beach). (Courtesy of Bill Keogh.)

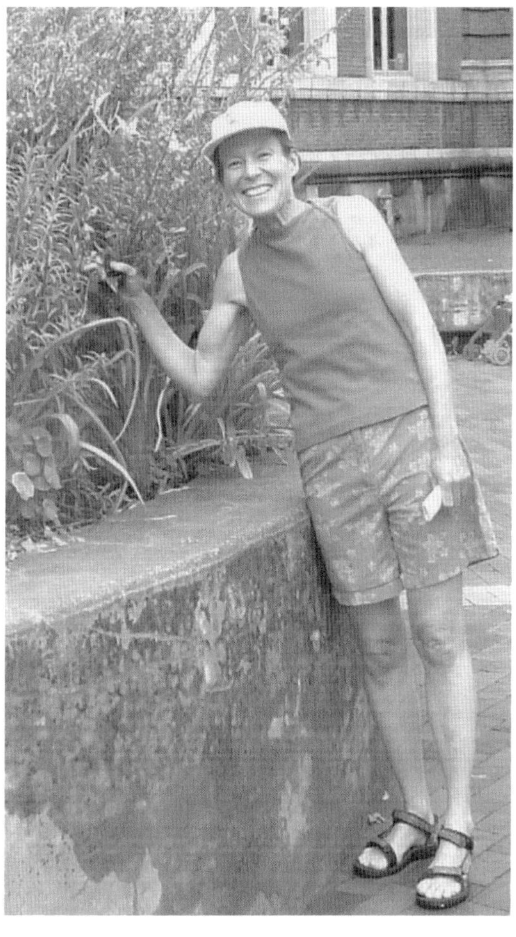

**A Very Public Secret Gardener**
Burlington artist Bonnie Acker is known around town for her colorful pastels and oil paintings and as an advocate for locally grown food in Burlington's public school cafeterias. Acker volunteers her time to create the lovely and endlessly changing flower gardens that seem to spring up like magic each year in front of City Market (Burlington's downtown food co-op) and in the raised beds along College Street in front of the Fletcher Free Library. (Courtesy of the Fletcher Free Library.)

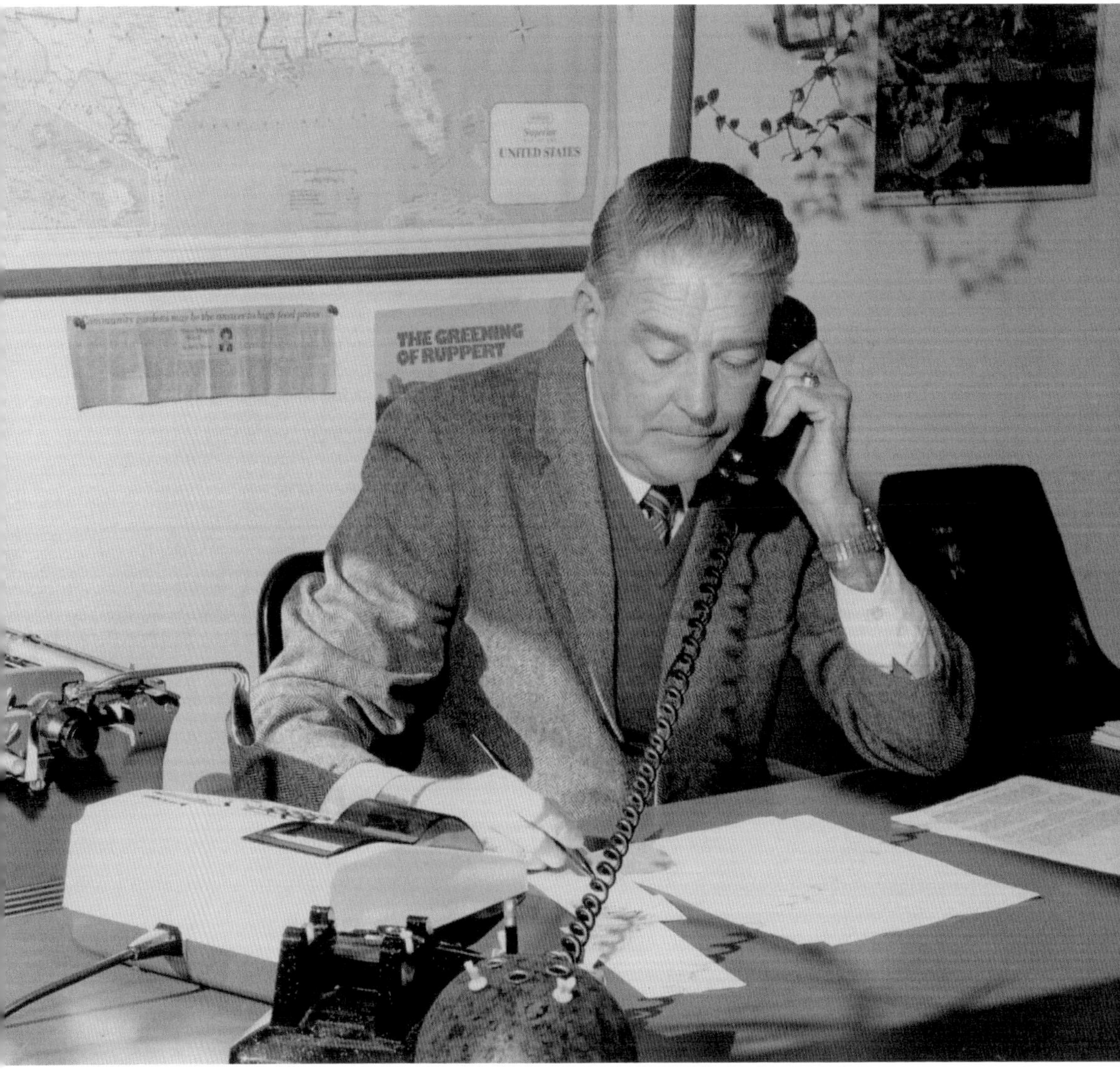


**Community Gardener**

In 1973, Gardens for All, an organization formed to promote community gardening, hired Tommy Thompson, a retired restaurateur from Ascutney, Vermont, as its director of community gardens. Thompson made things happen right away: 14 community garden sites were established in Burlington and neighboring towns within the next year. To provide a permanent community gardening site in Burlington, Thompson made a deal with the Burlington Electric Department and eventually obtained a 20-year lease that established the Intervale Community Garden, which contains 20 organic gardening plots. Thompson died suddenly in 1983, but his gardens live on: the garden plots he established in the Intervale were renamed the Tommy Thompson Community Garden in his honor. (Courtesy of Marilyn Neagley.)

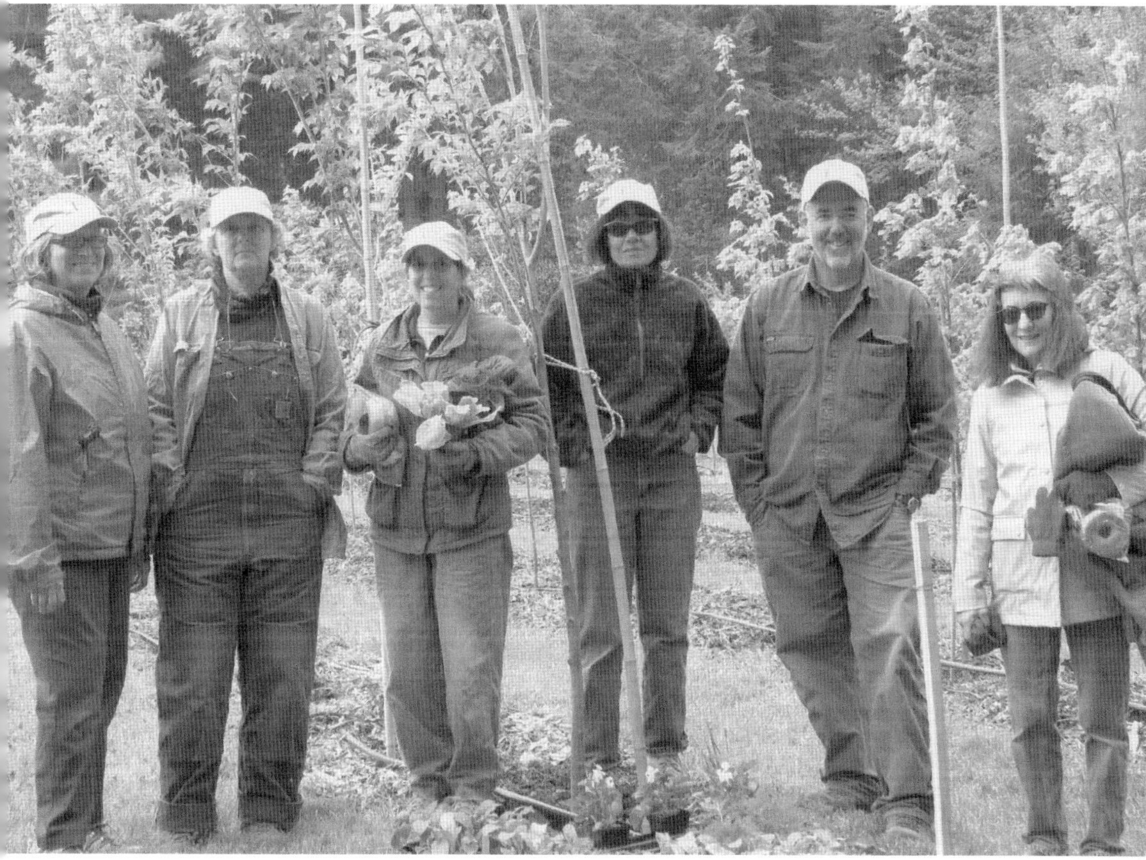

**Warren Spinner**

Warren Spinner has been the city's arborist for 32 years, managing Burlington's "urban forest" of more than 10,000 trees. Spinner supervises the removal of old and damaged trees along Burlington's streets and directs the planting of young trees to ensure a healthy diversity of species. He is also the point person when disaster strikes the local tree population, as when Dutch elm disease killed the majority of the city's trees in the 1960s and when an ice storm destroyed about 20 percent of Burlington's trees in two terrible days in 1998. Spinner also works closely with Branch Out Burlington, a group of dedicated volunteers formed in 1996 to help supply young trees for replanting on Burlington's streets and to inform the residents about nurturing the city's trees. Spinner (second from right) is pictured with members of Branch Out Burlington at the UVM Horticulture Farm in the spring of 2012. (Courtesy of Warren Spinner.)

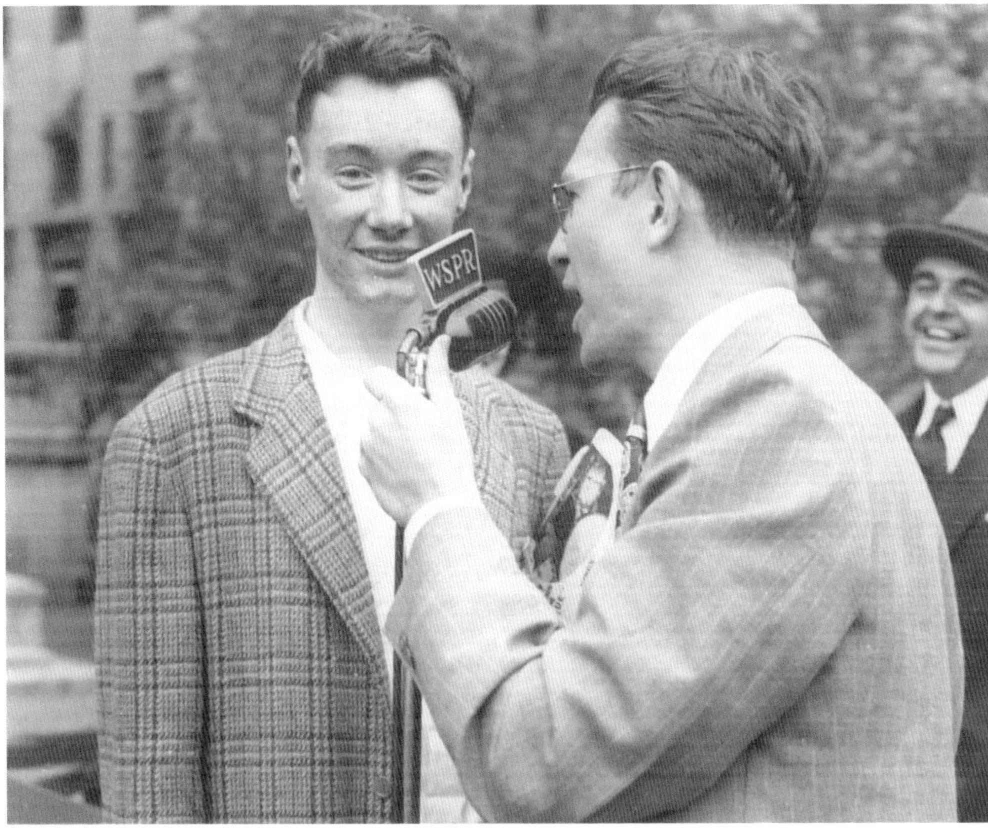
WSPR

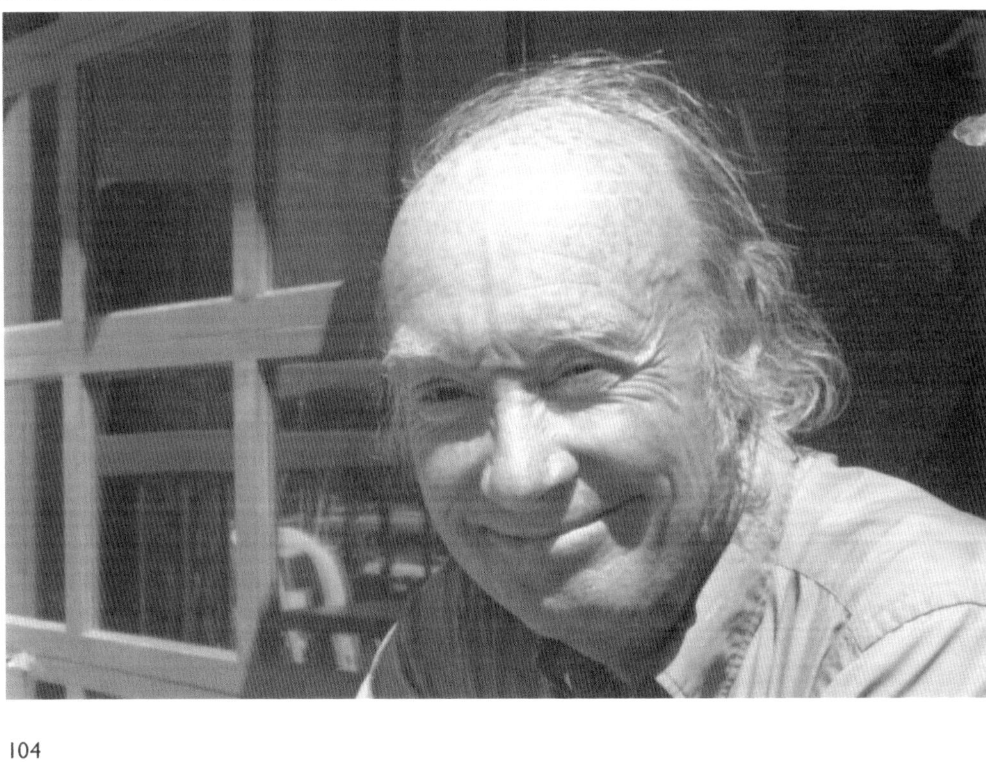

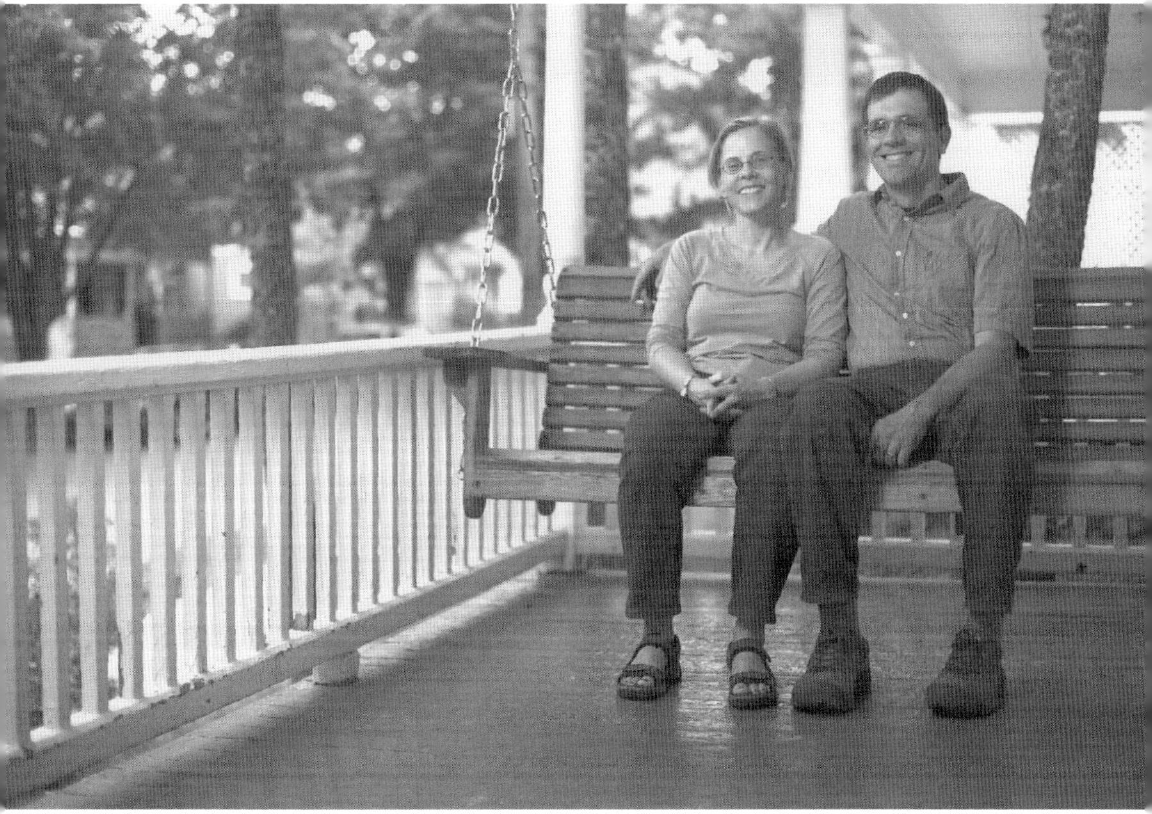

**Michael and Valerie Wood-Lewis**
Burlington residents Michael and Valerie Wood-Lewis are hi-tech community builders. They are the originators of the Front Porch Forum, a free network of online neighborhood discussion groups. Subscribing members can recommend reliable car-repair shops, report lost pets, announce upcoming garage sales, or comment on other subjects of shared interest with their neighbors. The Front Porch Forum has grown from a pilot project in 2006 serving a single south end Burlington neighborhood to a network of 140 forums serving 25 towns in northwestern Vermont. An increased sense of community has grown with expansion of the network: According to Michael Wood-Lewis, many forum users report that they feel more connected to neighbors, more tuned in to local goings-on, and more a part of their community. (Courtesy of Front Porch Forum.)

**The Jazz Guy** (OPPOSITE PAGE)
Ed Bemis (1928–2012) loved jazz. He also loved introducing jazz to others. After moving to Burlington from New York, where he hosted a jazz program on WBAI (a famous "free-form" radio station), Bemis produced Vermont's first jazz radio show on WRUV at the University of Vermont and spent almost 20 years broadcasting on WWPV-FM in Winooski. When not on the air or working his day job at the college bookstore, Bemis lectured and taught and campaigned for a jazz music curriculum at the University of Vermont. It was a hard road; many thought that jazz wasn't a worthy college-level topic. Thanks largely to Bemis, the UVM music department now offers a bachelor of arts program with a jazz concentration and has a faculty that includes noted jazz trumpeter Ray Vega. Somewhere up in jazz heaven, Ed Bemis is surely smiling. He is seen at left in 1946 in the above photograph and in 1994 in the photograph below. (Courtesy of the Bemis family.)

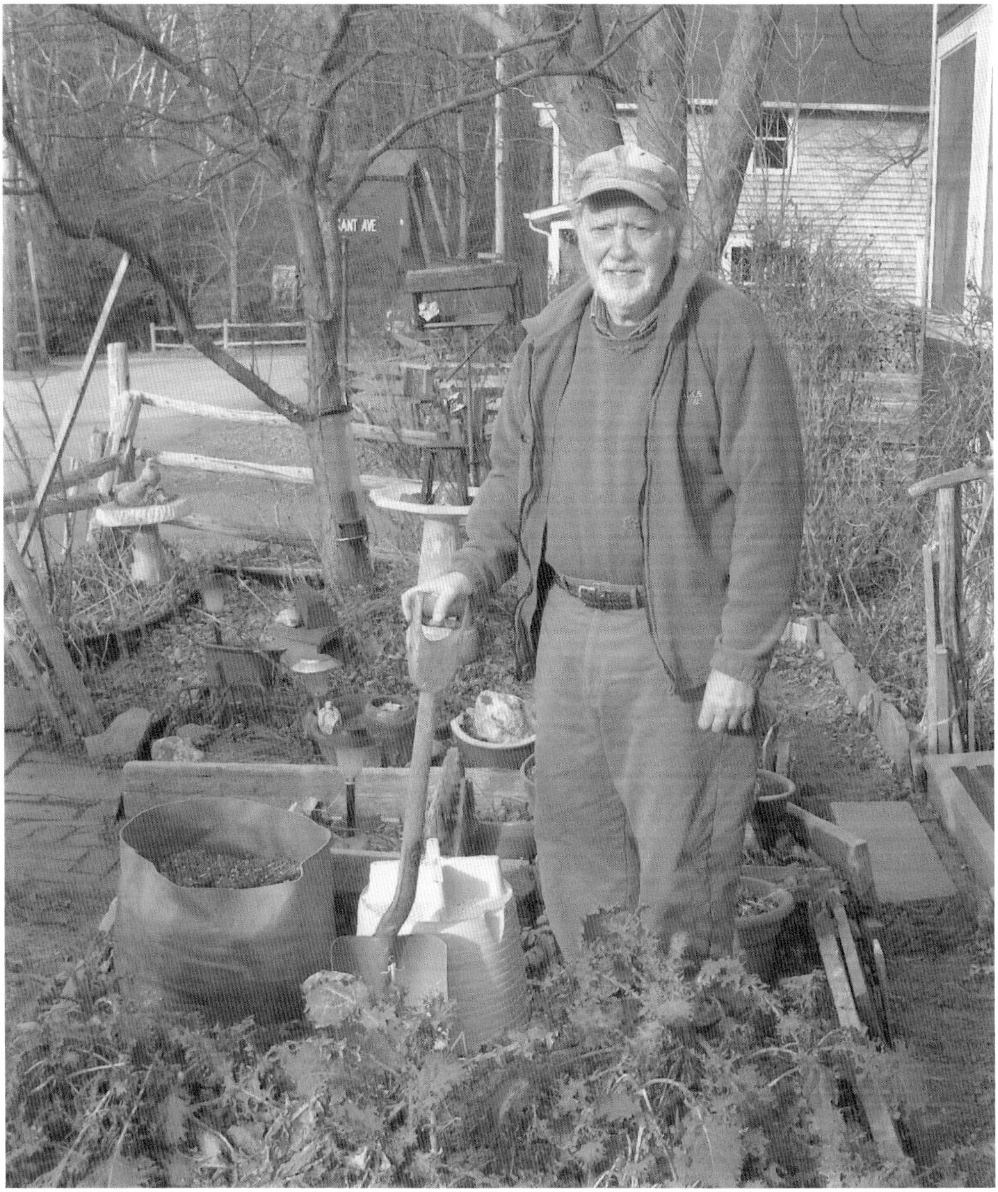

**Ron Krupp**

Author and localvore champion Ron Krupp loves to grow things. He also likes to start projects that support local commerce and community. The fruits of his labors include one of the first organic farms in Vermont (in Putney), the first farmer's market in the state (in Brattleboro), the largest community garden in Vermont (in Burlington's Intervale), and Burlington's ReCycle North, now called ReSource. The latter is a nonprofit business that repairs and resells items that would otherwise be discarded, at the same time offering job training in repair and retail sales for homeless and other at-risk community members. Since its launch in 1991, ReSource has expanded its operations to include the reuse of building materials and computer and appliance repair services. Krupp's original vision continues to grow and prosper, with partner organizations in Montpelier, Barre, and Morrisville. Krupp is pictured in his garden in 2012. (Photograph by the author.)

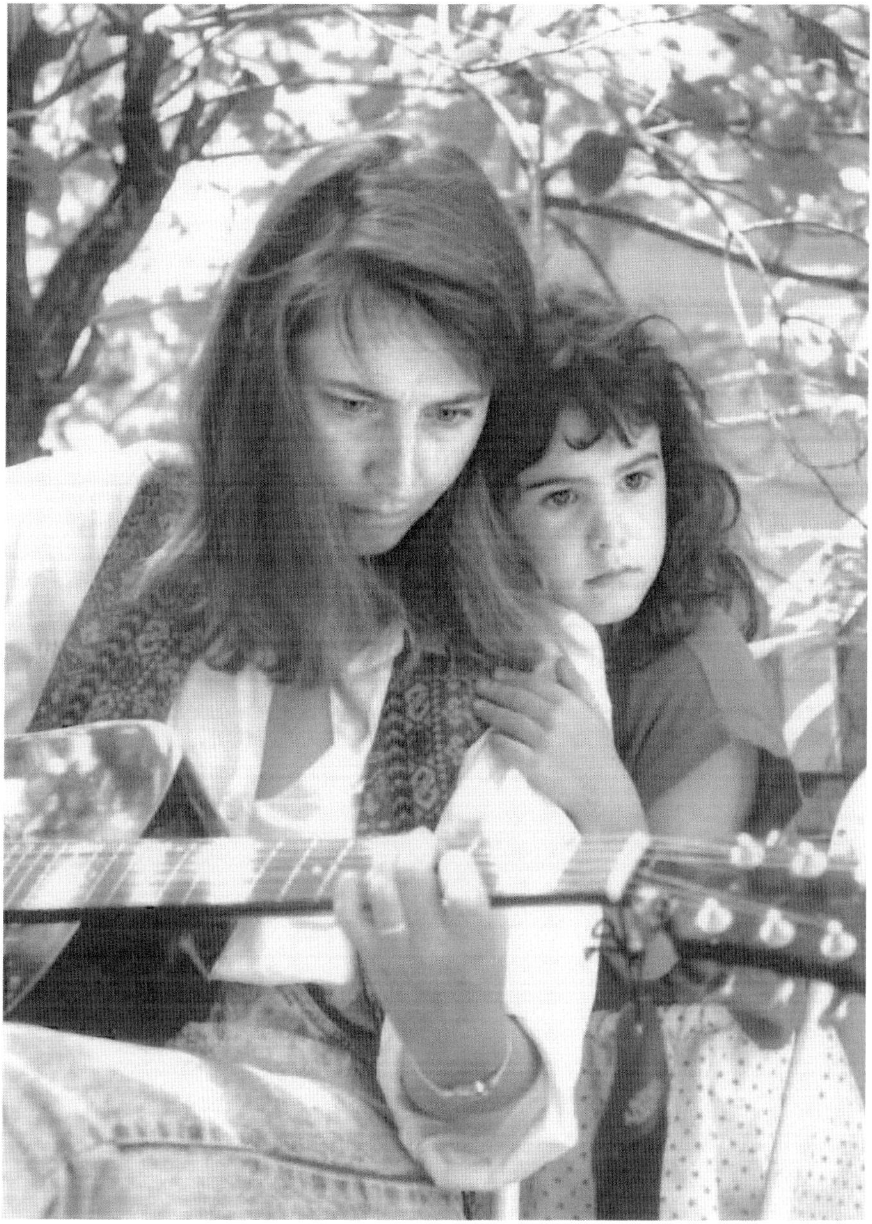

**Rachel Bissex**

Burlington singer-songwriter Rachel Bissex died in 2005 at the age of 48 after a long battle with cancer, but her musical legacy is being continued by friends, family, and fans. Bissex created the Burlington Coffeehouse in 1989 to provide a regular performance space for local musicians and to give touring acoustic performers a venue to play in town. More than 2,000 local performances later, through changing times (Burlington now has many places that feature live acoustic music), the Coffeehouse is still an essential part of First Night Burlington, the city's New Year's celebration. Rachel Bissex was also well known for her support of local musicians. The White Light Fund, named after her final recording, continues to provide funding opportunities for aspiring performers and recording artists. Bissex is pictured with her daughter Emma. (Photograph by and courtesy of Stephen Goldberg.)

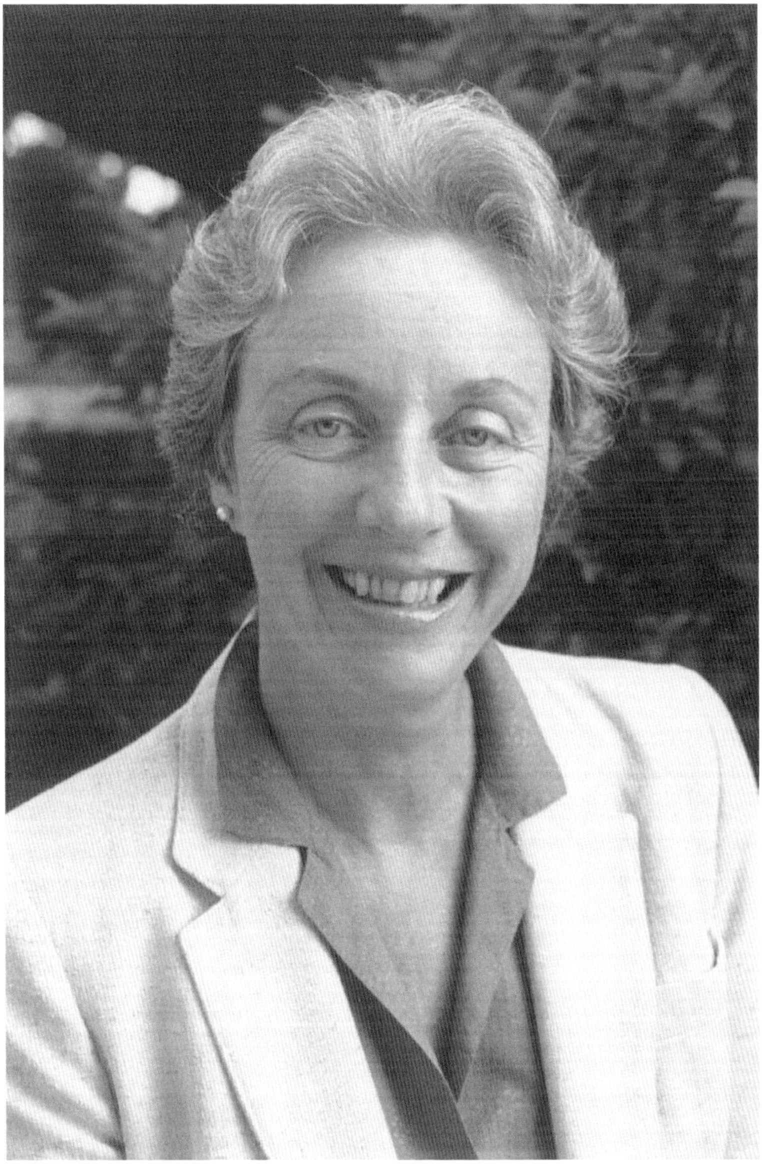

**Gov. Madeleine Kunin, 1988**

Madeleine Kunin is not the only Vermont governor to have called Burlington home, but she is noteworthy for a variety of reasons. Vermont's first and, so far, only female governor has been a political pioneer, the US ambassador to Switzerland, an outspoken feminist, and an inspiration for all women who consider entering politics. Kunin, currently a Marsh Scholar Professor-at-Large at the University of Vermont, still gives regular guest lectures, including a seminar on "Women, Politics, and Leadership" for UVM's history and women's studies departments. She is also an outspoken advocate for "active parenting." In a 2009 response to a story by President Obama, who told of his mother waking him up to do schoolwork at 4:30 a.m., Governor Kunin (herself a mother and grandmother) sums it all up: "It's time that parents, communities, states and the nation recognize that improving our children's chances to fulfill their own great potential will only be possible if we make sacrifices for them, and that will be no picnic either." (Courtesy of Vermont Historical Society.)

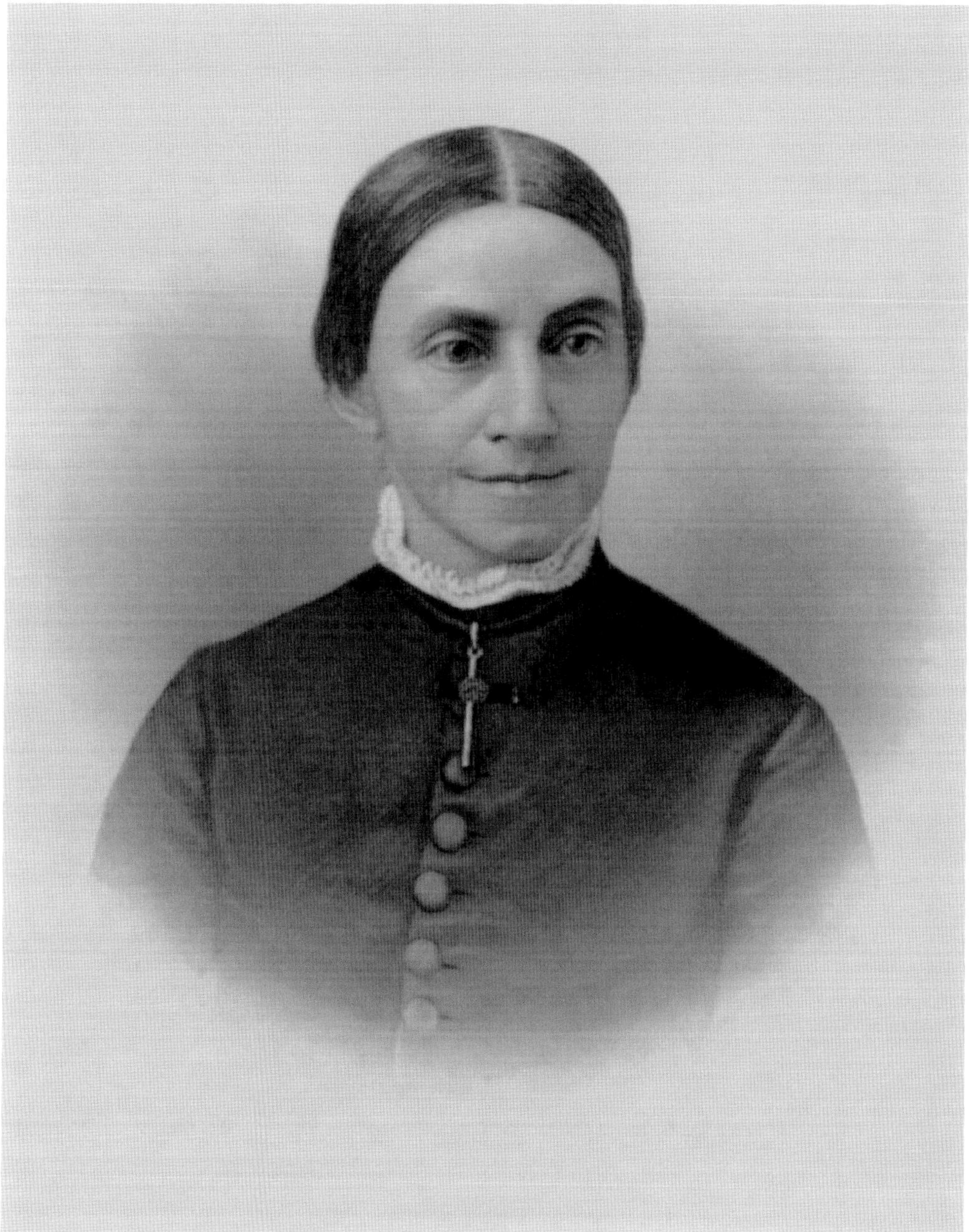

**Mary Martha Fletcher**

Mary Fletcher (1830–1885) was one of Burlington's first and most visible philanthropists, responsible for the founding of the Fletcher Free Library in 1873 and the Mary Fletcher Hospital in 1879. Mary's mother, Mary L. Fletcher, died in 1876, leaving Mary as the heir to a $400,000 fortune, most of which was given as a gift to finance the hospital in honor of her parents. In February 1885, Fletcher, reportedly suffering from a severe cold, was told by her doctor that she had hours to live. At her request, she was bundled into a sleigh and died later that day in a room in her beloved hospital. (Courtesy of Fletcher Allen Healthcare.)

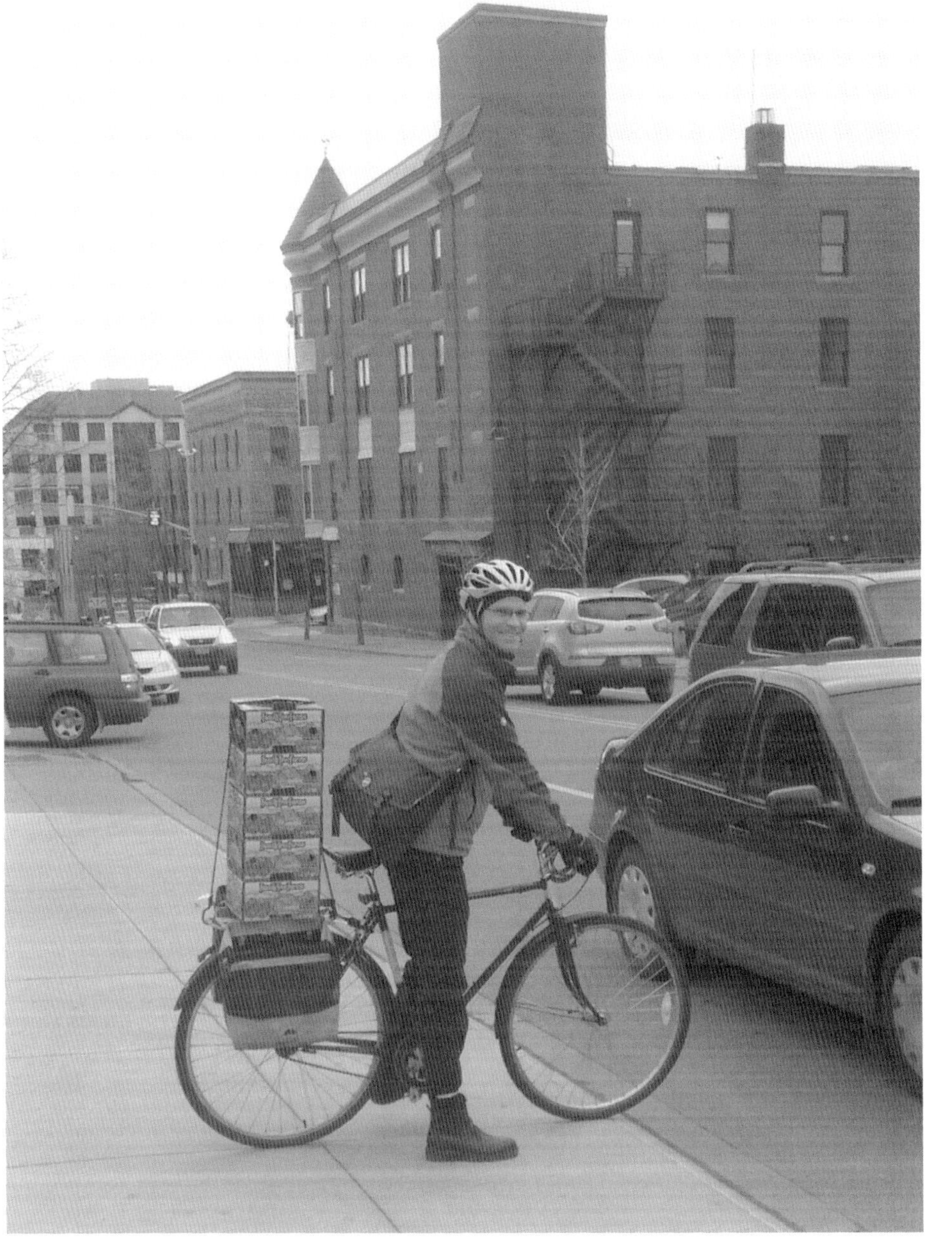

**Rolling Along**

Chapin Spencer can be spotted all over town, but almost never in a car. Spencer is the "big wheel" of Local Motion, a Burlington nonprofit organization organized in 1998 that promotes bicycling, walking, and other nonmotorized travel in the Queen City. The group also promotes the development of routes to make all kinds of "alternative" travel safer and easier. Spencer is one of the guardians of the bike path, Burlington's 7.5-mile treasure that runs close to and along the shores of Lake Champlain. A "bike ferry," one of Spencer's pet projects, connects Burlington's bike path with trails in the Champlain Islands and points north, making it possible to bike safely from Burlington all the way into Canada. (Photograph by Dan Cahill, courtesy of Chapin Spencer.)

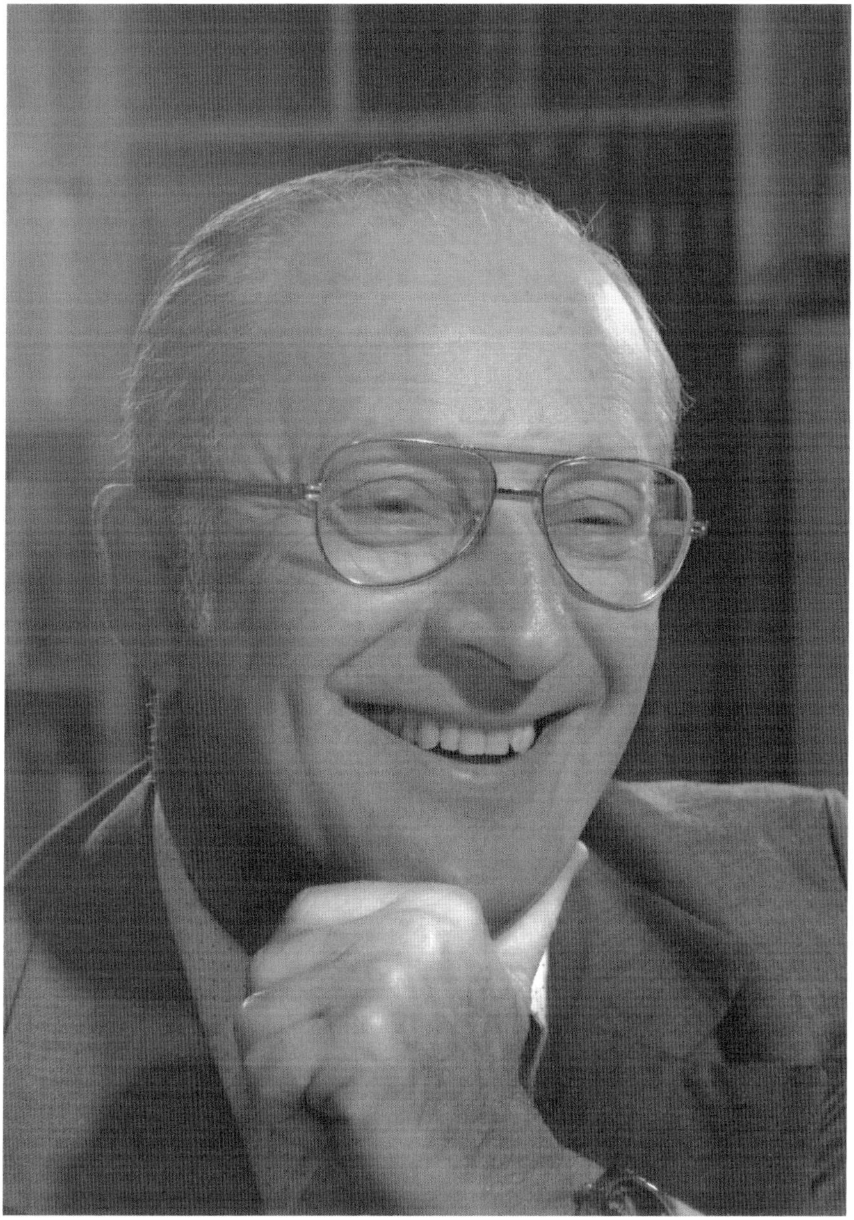

**A Teacher and a Mensch**

Rabbi Max Wall (1915–2009) was much more than the beloved leader of Burlington's Ohavi Zedek synagogue. He was a real community builder. Rabbi Wall dedicated his life to serving as a bridge between the local Jewish community and other religious, educational, and cultural organizations in the Burlington area. After serving as a US Army chaplain during the Battle of the Bulge and during the liberation of the concentration camps, Max Wall moved to Burlington in 1946 to be Ohavi Zedek's rabbi. He spent the next 60 years teaching and counseling, serving as a faculty member at St. Michaels and Champlain Colleges, participating in pulpit exchanges with local churches, giving guest lectures at the University of Vermont and Norwich University, and inspiring his own congregation to establish dialogues with others in Burlington's increasingly diverse community. (Photograph by Frank Star, courtesy of Mindy Evnin.)

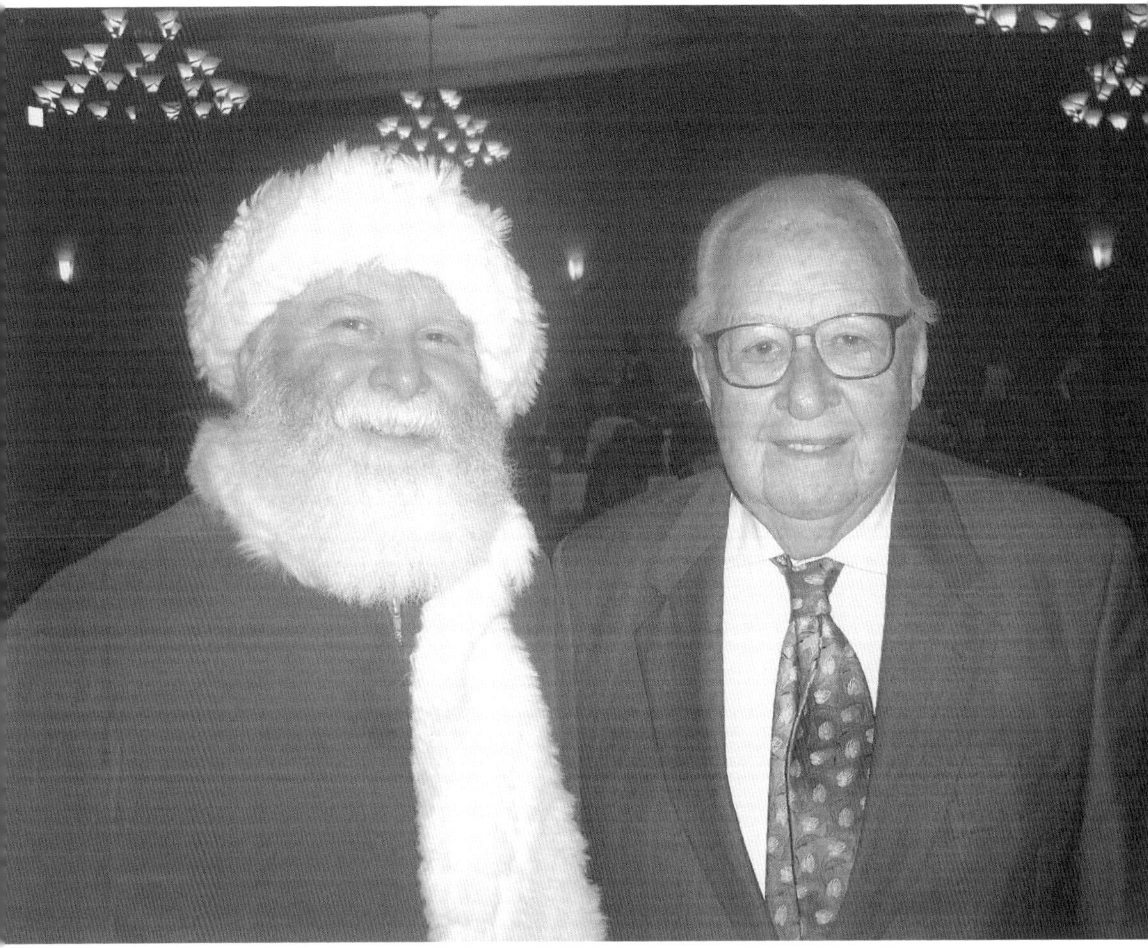

**Tony Pomerleau**

Antonio Pomerleau, the founder and chairman of one of Burlington's most successful real estate companies, is also one of the area's most generous philanthropists. Some of the many local gifts that Tony Pomerleau has given in recent years include million-dollar donations each to Saint Michael's College in Winooski, the Greater Burlington YMCA, and the Hurricane Irene Recovery Fund. Pomerleau (who is celebrating his 90th birthday this year) has been selected as the 2012 Citizen of the Year by the Vermont Chamber of Commerce for "work that has bettered the state through self-sacrifice, service, and volunteerism."

Pomerleau's most-remembered contribution to the Burlington area, however, may be the annual holiday party with "all the fixings" that he throws for needy families, a tradition that he began 30 years ago and that he promises will continue even after he passes on. For some of the attendees, this is the only holiday dinner they will have. "I get a real pleasure in seeing these little kids eating, getting their presents, and having a good time," Pomerleau is quoted as saying. Santa Claus (Tom Hudspeth) poses with the real Santa Claus (Pomerleau) in December 2011. (Courtesy of the *North Avenue News.*)

# CHAPTER SEVEN

# One of a Kind

The legendary locals of Burlington included in this chapter are all marvelously unique. This can be said about practically everyone, of course, but the uniqueness in the case of these individuals makes them nearly impossible to classify. Some of them are well known for accomplishing something that has had a lasting influence on Burlington, and some are local celebrities, famous for simply being themselves.

The list includes: Ethan Allen, one of Burlington's most famous citizens, who lived in town for only two years, but made a lasting impression; former Burlington mayor and current Vermont senator Bernie Sanders, a declared socialist whose term as mayor launched decades of political dominance by his liberal Progressive Party in Burlington; Lois Bodoky, commonly known as "The Hotdog Lady," a beloved vendor on Church Street for decades; Bob Conlon, the maitre d' and one of the owners of Leunig's, a restaurant at the corner of Church and College Streets, one of Burlington's best-known characters, and the city's greatest joke archivist, who is told at least once a week, "You should run for Mayor!"; Grace Coolidge, a Burlington woman who married the future president of the United States, and who then became the "life of the party" in the White House and a perfect foil for her notoriously reserved husband; Rev. Roger Anthony "Yolanda" Mapes, a talented and dynamic drag queen who helped found Burlington's "Winter is a Drag" ball, one of the social highlights of the city's winter season; H. Nelson Jackson, a wealthy Burlingtonian who, to win a bet, became the first person to drive an automobile across the continental United States; Herb Bloomenthal, a local television personality and one of the greatest authorities on Burlington trivia; Phil Bowler Jr., one of the "most-traveled" residents of Burlington; Richard Haupt, also known as the "clarinet man," Burlington's most unforgettable street musician; Peter Bridge, bon vivant, college dean, Dixieland jazz drummer, inveterate jokester, and possessor of endless joie de vivre; Joe Citro, a Burlington author and folklorist who has made his mark collecting and reporting on weird and spooky happenings in Burlington and around Vermont; and Rena Calkins, Burlington's last dairy farmer, who led her cattle through the corn in Burlington's Intervale until the age of 91.

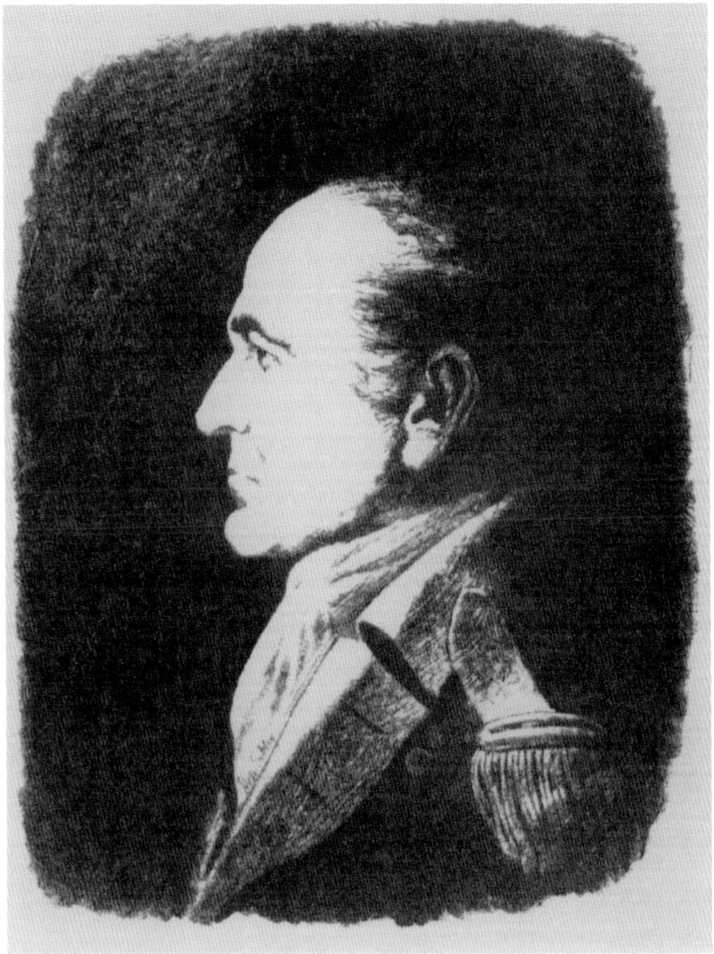

## Ethan Allen

Ethan Allen, the state's most famous Revolutionary War hero and the namesake for everything from Vermont furniture companies to tour boats, only lived in Burlington during the final two years of his life. Allen had apparently been planning to settle in the Burlington area, however. In 1778, he purchased 150 acres along the Winooski River in Burlington's north end from Col. James Claghorn, an officer with the revealing title "Commissioner for the confiscation and sale of the estates of the enemies of Vermont and the United States." Allen's adventures with the Green Mountain Boys and his fabled capture and imprisonment by the British were far behind him in 1787 when he built a house on 40 cleared acres near the Winooski River, adjacent to the woods now known as Ethan Allen Park. He settled in to a life of farming at the age of 50 with his second wife, Fanny, age 29. Allen died in February 1789 after suffering from a "fit," possibly a stroke, while returning on an oxcart from a journey to South Hero to pick up hay from his cousin Ebenezer Allen. Ethan Allen's farmhouse and outbuildings have been restored by Burlington's parks and recreation department, and an 1858 monument near his gravesite in the city's Greenmount Cemetery (a replacement for the grave's original marker, which had been stolen years earlier) is topped by a statue created by Vermont sculptor Larkin Mead that is the most common image of Ethan Allen. No contemporary painting or other bona fide image of him seems to have survived. The image shown here is adapted from a picture of Ethan's grandson Ethan Allen Hitchcock, a Union general in the Civil War who, the family claimed, bore an uncanny resemblance to his grandfather. (Courtesy of the Ethan Allen Homestead.)

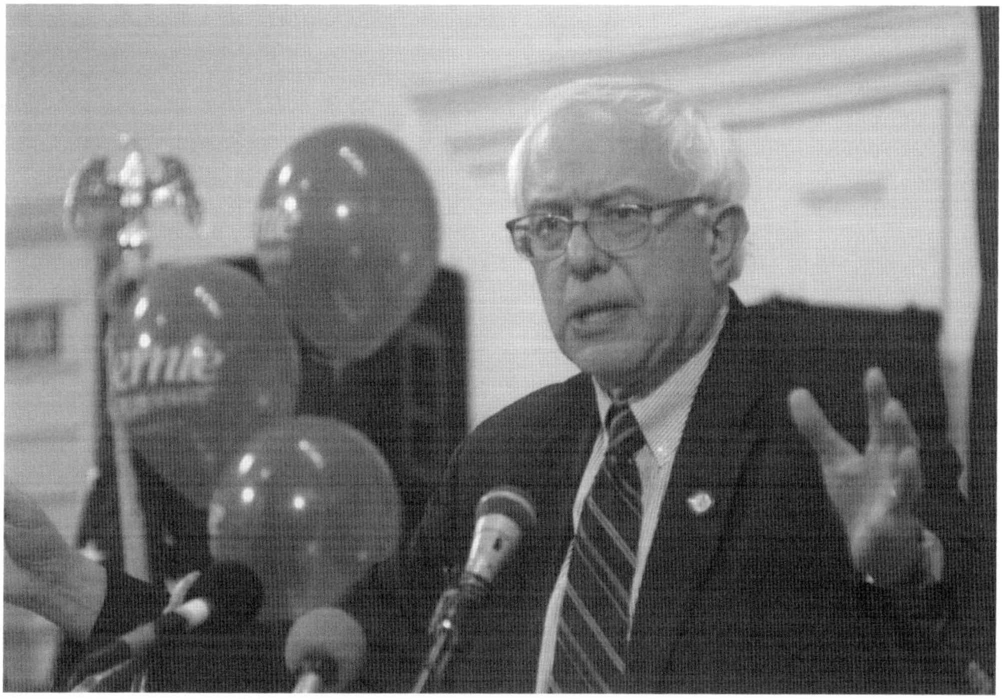


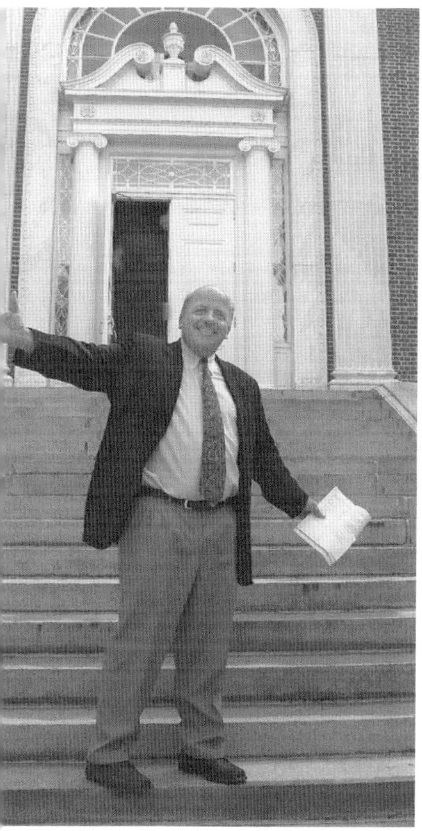

**Bernie Sanders**

In 1981, long before he made history as the one of the nation's first socialist members of the House of Representatives, Bernard Sanders was elected mayor of Burlington, eking out a victory over Democratic incumbent Gordon Paquette by only 10 votes in a four-way race. During his four terms as mayor, Sanders saw the birth and development of Burlington's Progressive Party, a liberal and community-centered group of activists who were to dominate city hall and Burlington politics for almost 30 years. A few of Mayor Sanders's many lasting contributions include his dedication to "re-foresting" the city after many of Burlington's trees had been killed by Dutch elm disease and his support for the waterfront bike path that has now become one of Burlington's most popular attractions. (Photograph by and courtesy of Matt Thorsen.)

**Peter Clavelle**

Progressive mayor Peter Clavelle, one of Burlington's most successful politicians, holds the distinction of serving as the city's chief executive for longer than anyone else. His seven terms in city hall lasted from 1989 through 2006, interrupted by one-term mayor Peter Brownell, who surprised everyone when he was elected in 1993. Clavelle has recently moved to Albania, where he is working under a five-year contract with the US Agency for International Development. (Courtesy of Matt Thorsen.)

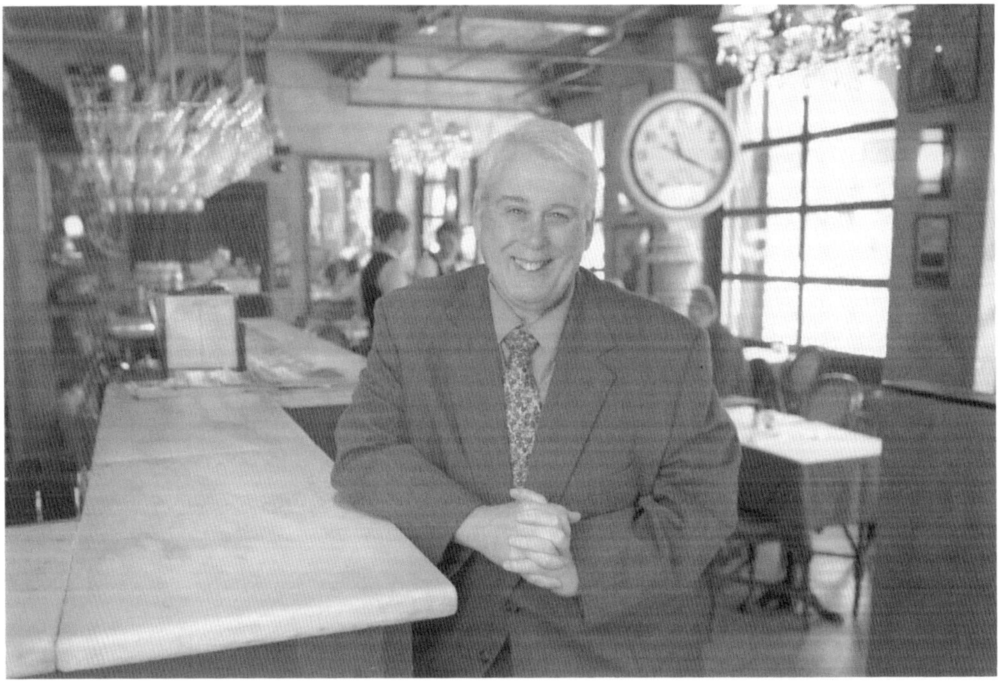

**The Mayor of Church Street**

For 30 years, Bob Conlon has held court at Leunigs, a Parisian-style bistro at the corner of Church and College Streets in the center of downtown Burlington. Conlon found his ideal job at Leunigs as the morning bartender, dispensing jokes and Bloody Marys to a regular clientele. He has become a part owner of the restaurant and the maitre'd. Conlon knows and is known by everyone in town, and is urged to run for mayor of Burlington by customers at least once a week. Even if he wanted to, he could not do it: He lives in Winooski! (Photograph by Ben Resnik.)

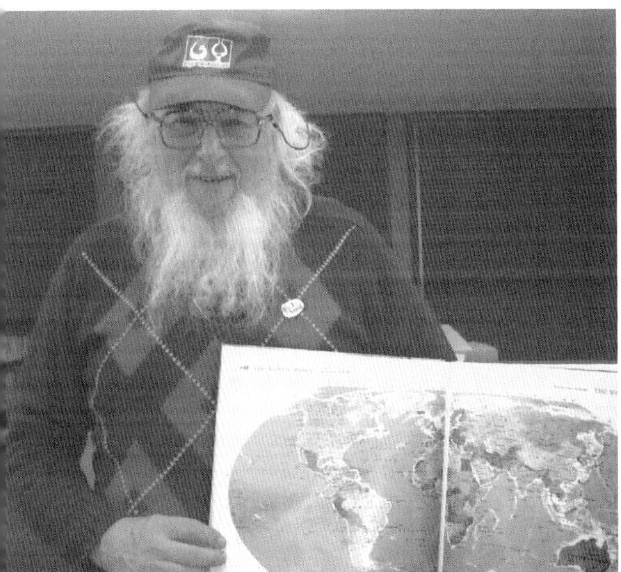

**The Traveler**

Phil Bowler Sr. loves being one of the most-traveled people in Burlington. Bowler has journeyed to each of the 3,143 counties in the United States; has visited every continent on earth, including Antarctica; traveled the entire length of the Lewis and Clark trail, from Virginia to Oregon; and has visited at least 70 countries. Bowler has undertaken most of his traveling since retiring from IBM and from his subsequent career as a landlord in the Burlington area. Between trips, Phil Bowler can often be found at the Fletcher Free Library, working on his extensive travel journals or planning his next adventure. (Photograph by the author.)

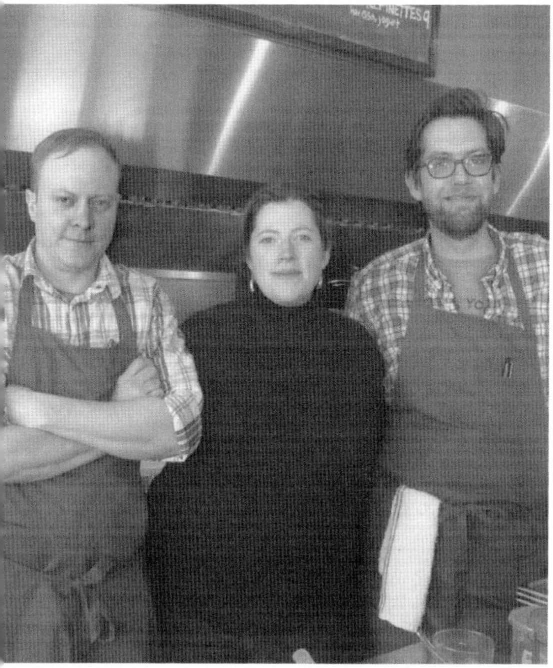

**The Delicious Misery of Laura, Nathaniel, and Aaron**
During the summer of 2012, hungry residents of the Burlington area kept their eyes out for "Big Red," a 1976 Winnebago that has been converted into a mobile kitchen. The vehicle's veteran chefs are, shown above from left to right, Nathaniel Wade,Laura Wade, and Aaron Josinsky. "Misery Loves Company," the name of their "pop-up" gourmet fast-food business, appeared just in time for lunch at Burlington parking lots. Tremulous potential eaters checked Misery's Facebook page for places, times, and daily menus. Misery's memorable sandwiches and herb-dusted fries are not for the calorie-conscious but are yummy beyond description. The Wades and Josinsky have recently opened a "real" restaurant in downtown Winooski but have promised their many fans that "Big Red" will roll again in the Queen City in the spring. (Photographs by the author.)

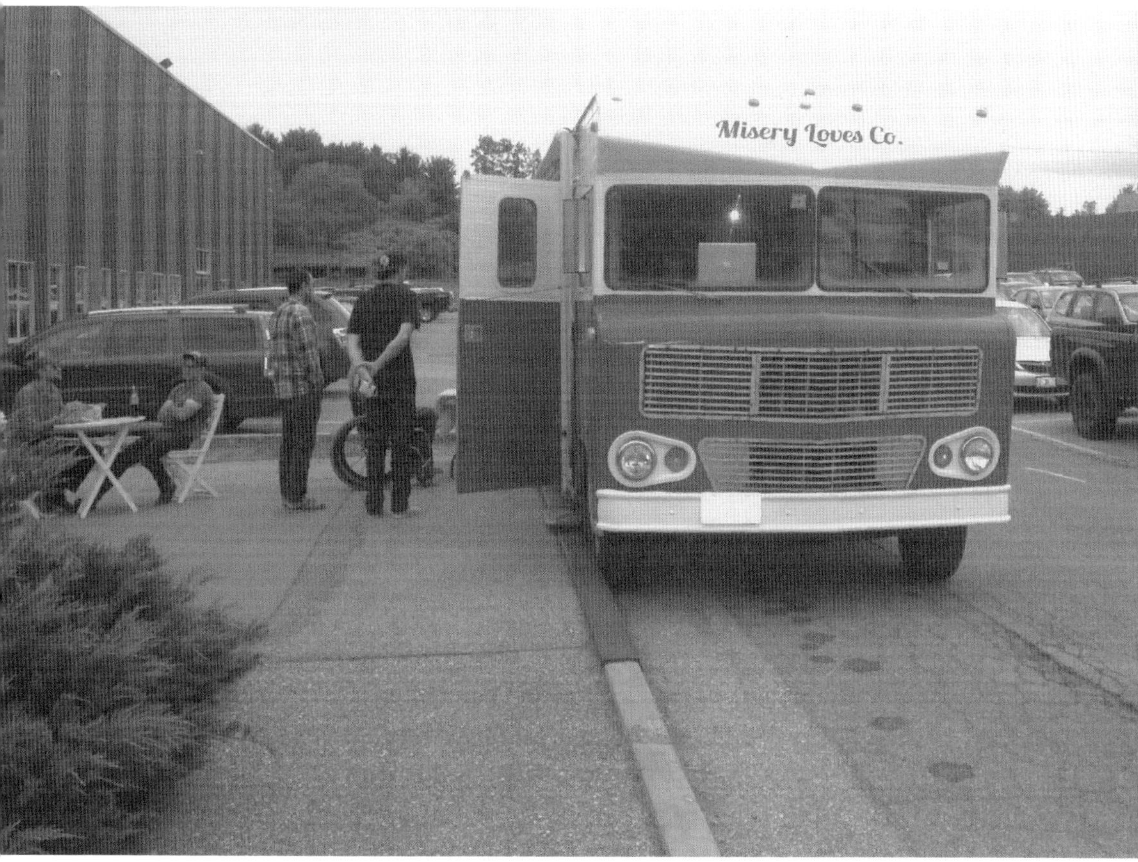

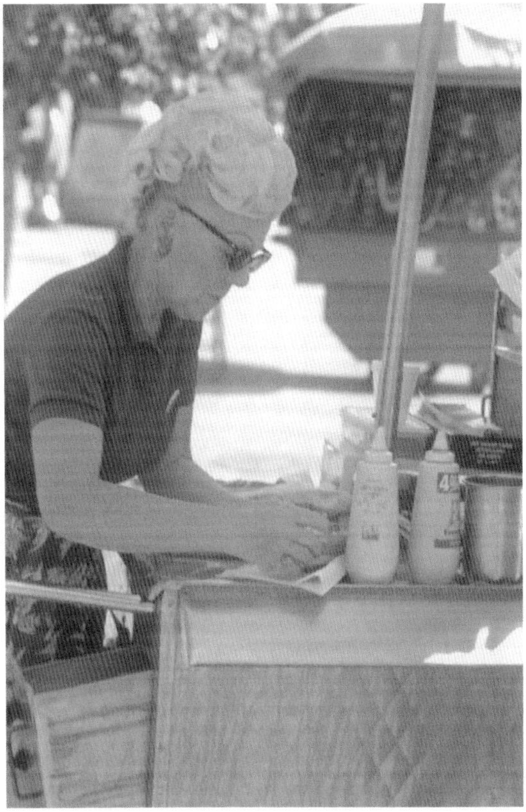

**The Hot Dog Lady**

Lois Bodoky, also known as "the hot dog lady," was a beloved downtown fixture on Church Street, Burlington's main pedestrian thoroughfare, for almost 30 years. In addition to reliably delicious hot dogs, Lois also specialized in friendliness, providing smiles to passersby and crumbs for nearby birds. After a fast-food career full of awards, appreciation, and thousands of satisfied customers, the "hot dog lady" moved to Santa Cruz, California, to be closer to her family in spring 2012, just short of her 90th birthday. In a farewell interview with a local food columnist, Bodoky shared her philosophy: "My motto is to put one foot in front of the other and don't go backward." (Courtesy of the Church Street Marketplace.)

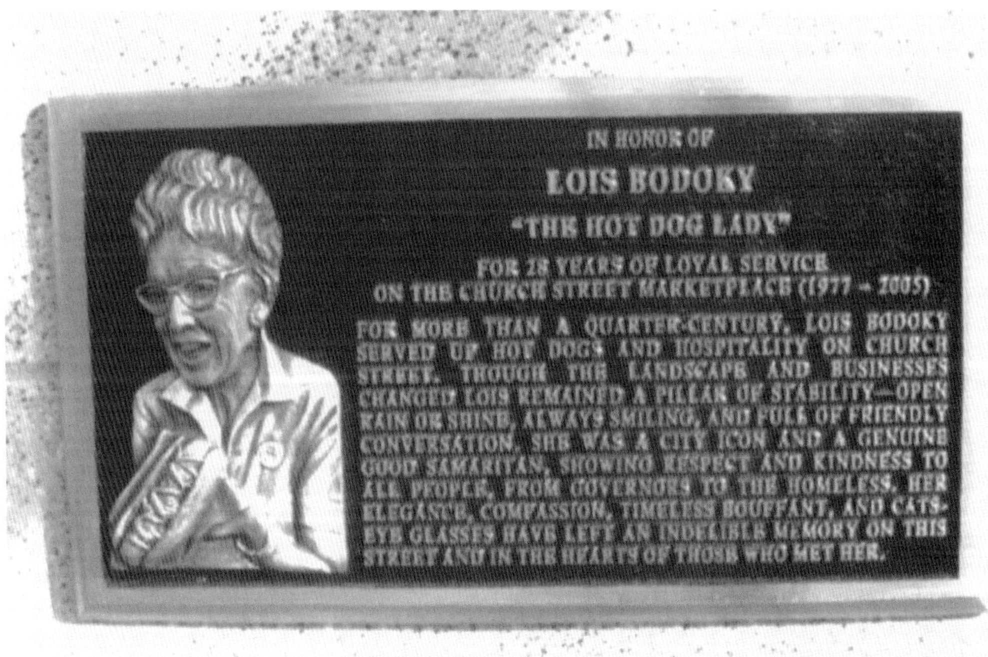

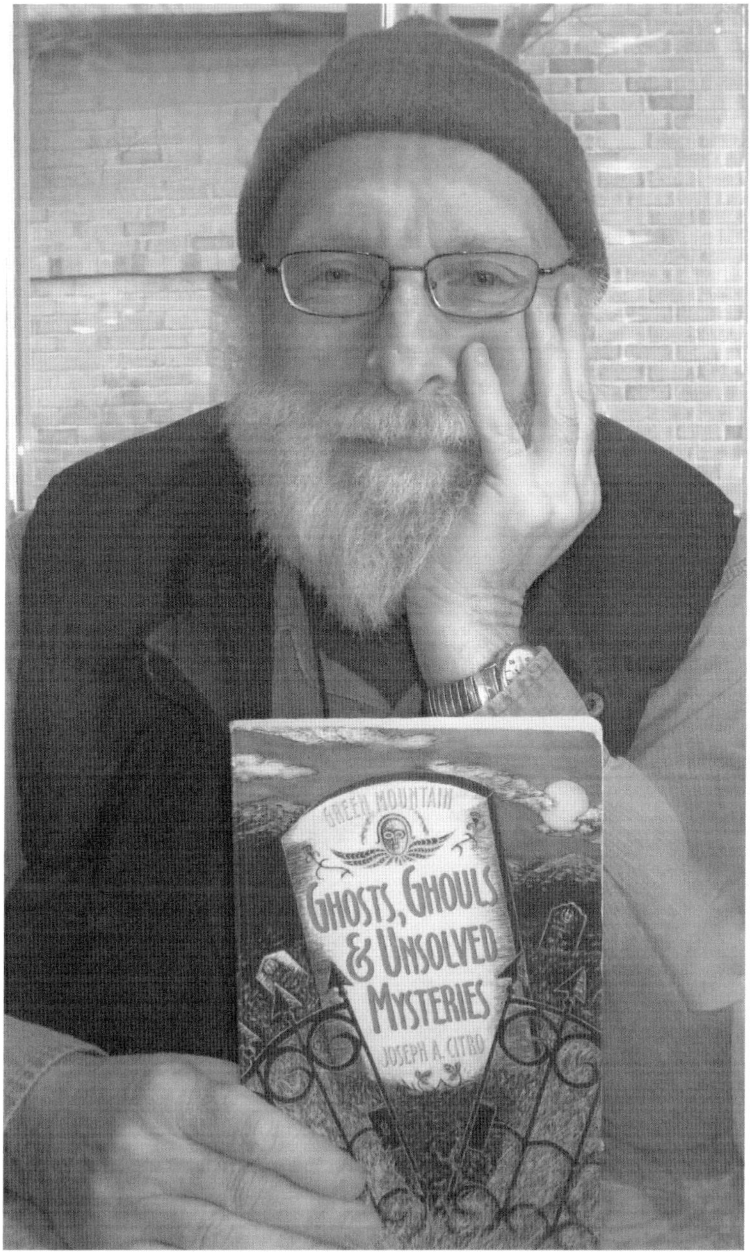


**Joe Citro**

Joe Citro is Burlington's "Master Chronicler of the Macabre." Folklorist, lecturer, and public radio commentator, Citro revels in documenting mysterious local lore—the creepier, the better. Citro's 1994 book *Green Mountain Ghosts, Ghouls, and Unsolved Mysteries* was the first book ever to document ghostly and other paranormal activity in Vermont. His *Vermont Monster Guide*, published in 2009, was named one of the Top 10 Cryptozoology Books of the Year by a fansite dedicated to this fantastic and spooky genre. Because Joe Citro thrives on research and loves to "show and tell," his presentations about Vermont's most peculiar legends are very much in demand, and not just for Halloween! (Photograph by the author.)

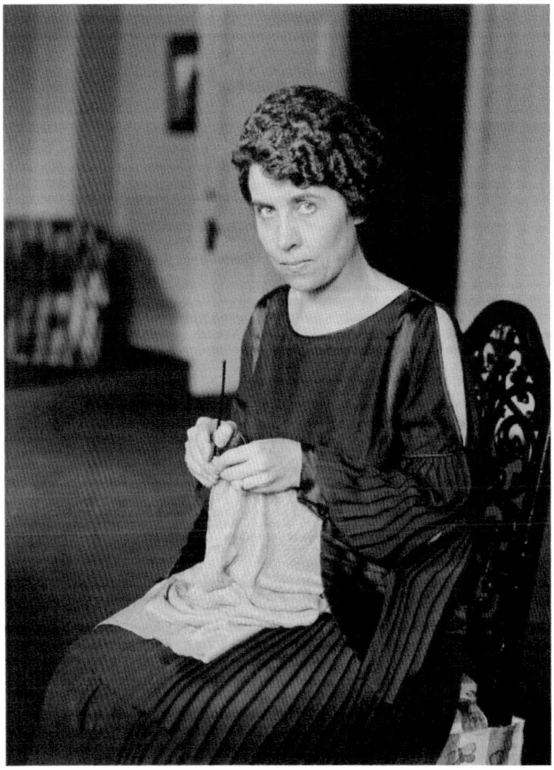

### Grace Coolidge

The house at 312 Maple Street was the childhood home of Grace Goodhue, a student at the University of Vermont and a founding member of Pi Beta Phi, the first national college fraternity for women. In 1905, Goodhue married Calvin Coolidge, then a young Massachusetts lawyer from Plymouth Notch, Vermont, in her parents' Burlington home. Grace and Calvin had met while she lived in Northampton, Massachusetts, after graduation, working as a teacher at the Clarke School for the Deaf. During and after her time as first lady, Grace Coolidge continued to be an advocate for education for the deaf and addressing the needs of the disabled. (Photograph by Herbert E. French.)

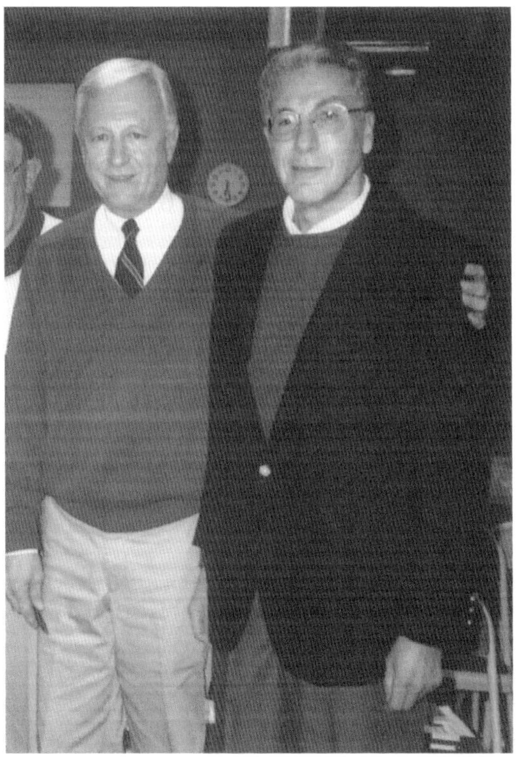

### Stump the Chumps

Herb Bloomenthal (1940–2000) loved Burlington. He was a sports fan, a rabid Little League coach, chairman of the Burlington School Board and his local neighborhood planning association, and the producer of *Stump the Chumps*, the most popular show ever on channel 17. The call-in program, hosted by Bloomenthal, featured local personalities and historians and focused on the history of and trivia about Burlington and surrounding towns. Here, Herb Bloomenthal (right) poses with his longtime friend and television cohort Al Bernadina. The Herb Bloomenthal Award for Community Activism honors "a volunteer whose leadership, tenacity, and dedication have somehow improved Burlington's neighborhoods." (Courtesy of Al Bernadina.)

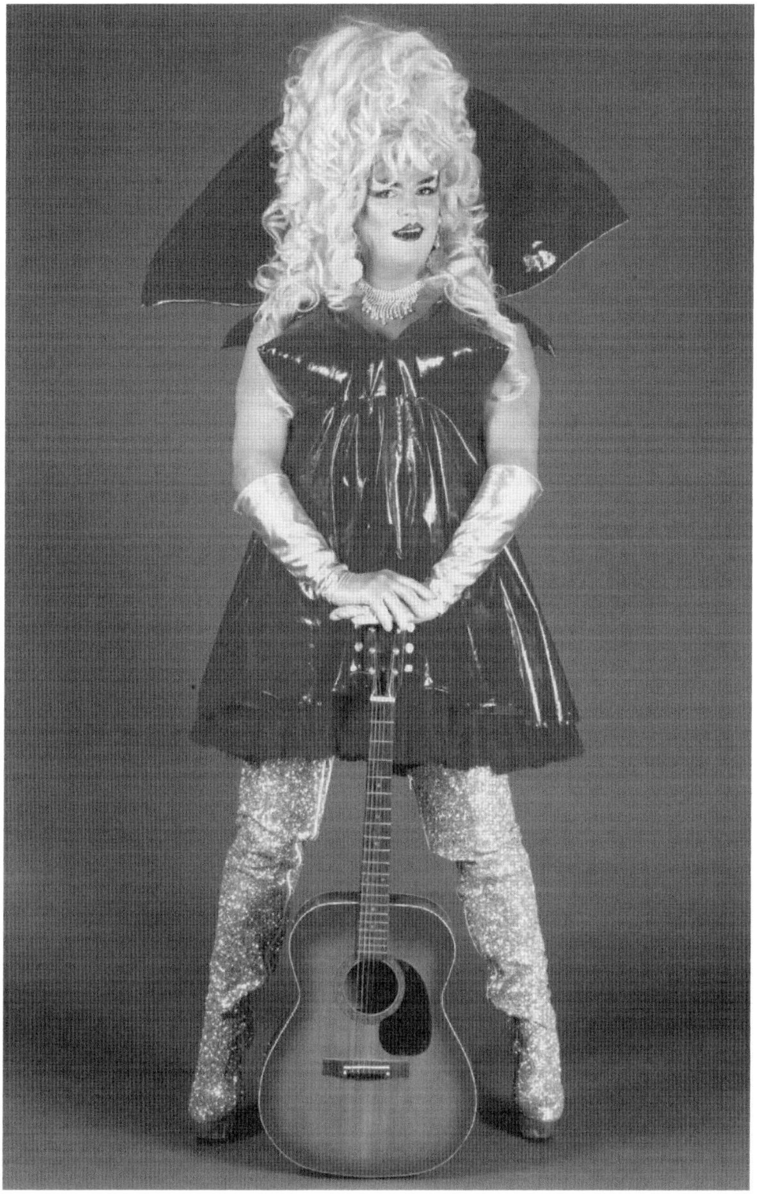

**Yolanda**

Rev. Roger Anthony "Yolanda" Mapes, a 2005 inductee into the GLBT Hall of Fame for "Activism, Art Excellence, and Community Awareness," moved to Burlington in 1995 from New York City. Inspired by Burlington's lively arts scene and by the wealth of local music, Mapes debuted Yolanda in a variety show with Cherie Tartt, another beloved local drag queen, and formed her own band, the Plastic Family, in 1996. Before moving back to New York in 2001, Yolanda was instrumental in envisioning and organizing Burlington's first "Winter is a Drag Ball," an annual fundraising event that opened doors for Vermont's queer and straight communities to socialize at a huge party. The ball has done much to create a visible trans community in Vermont. Yolanda's performances and the Drag Ball she helped to create remain legendary in the Burlington area, and the ball continues to be a successful and much-anticipated winter event. (Courtesy of Yolanda.)

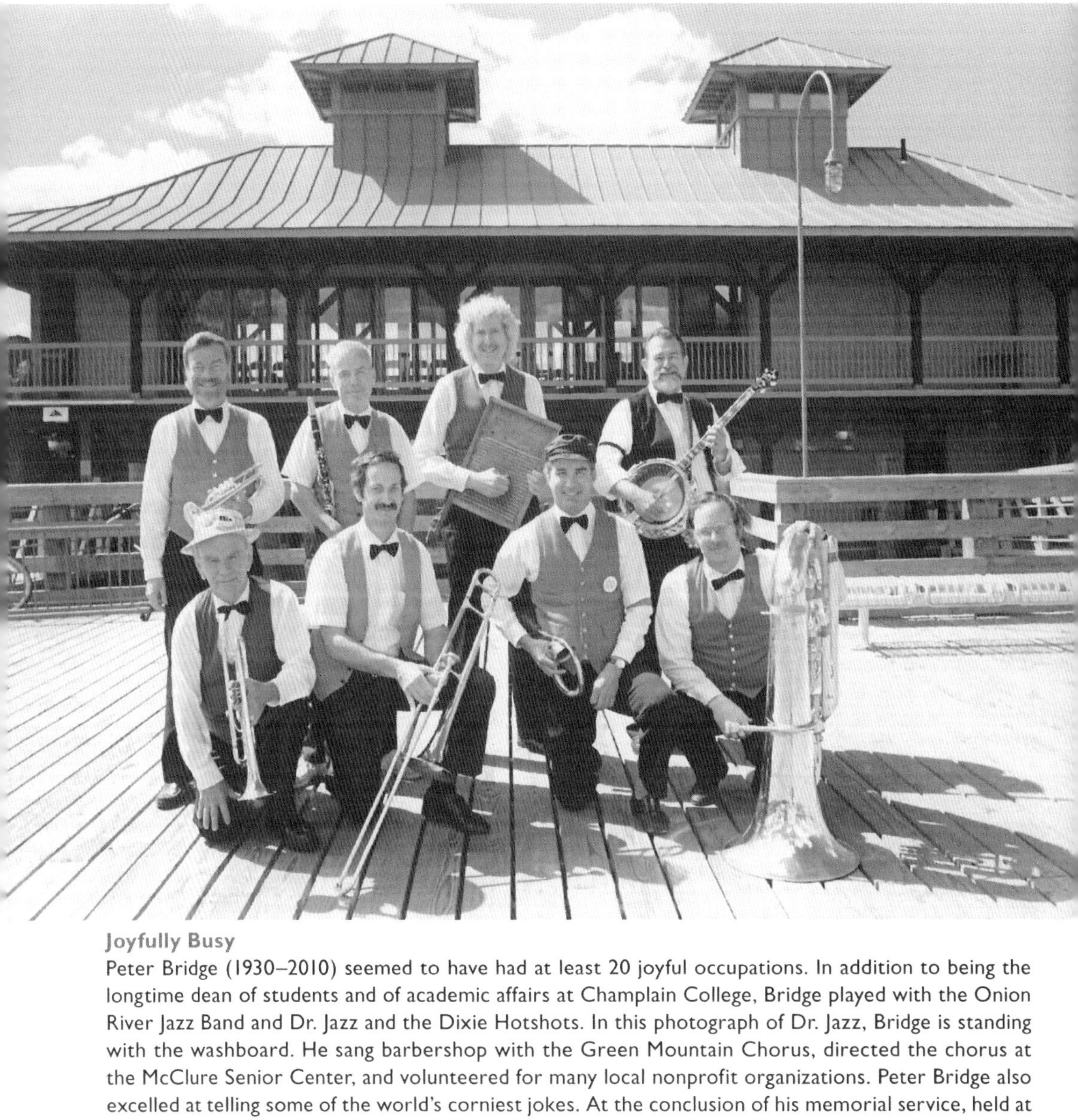

**Joyfully Busy**

Peter Bridge (1930–2010) seemed to have had at least 20 joyful occupations. In addition to being the longtime dean of students and of academic affairs at Champlain College, Bridge played with the Onion River Jazz Band and Dr. Jazz and the Dixie Hotshots. In this photograph of Dr. Jazz, Bridge is standing with the washboard. He sang barbershop with the Green Mountain Chorus, directed the chorus at the McClure Senior Center, and volunteered for many local nonprofit organizations. Peter Bridge also excelled at telling some of the world's corniest jokes. At the conclusion of his memorial service, held at St. Paul's Episcopal Church in Burlington, an impressive collection of local Dixieland jazz musicians, all of whom had played with Peter in one group or another, struck up "When the Saints Go Marching In," startling a flock of pigeons that had settled just outside the sanctuary's big picture window. The soaring music and the wall of panicky birds created a perfectly fitting and humorous musical tribute for Peter Bridge. (Courtesy of Bill Wicker.)

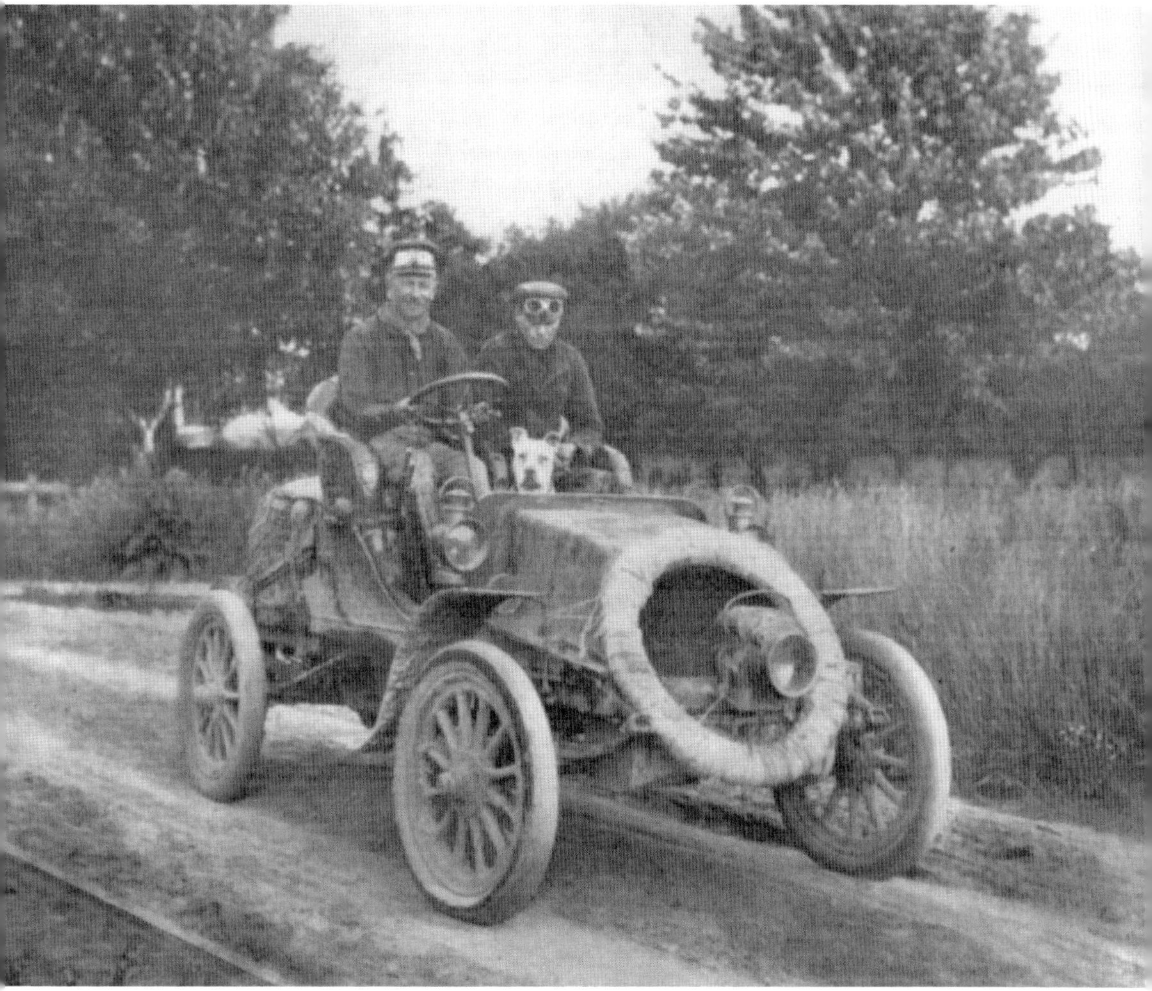

**Horatio Nelson Jackson**

In May 1903, H. Nelson Jackson (1872–1955), a wealthy Burlington physician and a fan of the newfangled automobile, made a $50 bet while visiting San Francisco that he could drive across the entire country. At the time of his bet, Jackson did not even own a car and had practically no experience driving one. Pictured above (driving), Jackson purchased a slightly used Winton automobile that he named "Vermont" and, accompanied by a young mechanic named Sewall Crocker, headed east. The intrepid travelers, accompanied by Bud, a pit bull terrier that they had picked up near Caldwell, Idaho, arrived in New York City 63 days later. The crew had faced many harrowing adventures, particularly west of the Mississippi, where there were few paved roads at the time. Jackson's journey is the subject of a documentary by filmmaker Ken Burns titled *Horatio's Drive*. (Courtesy of Special Collections, University of Vermont Libraries.)

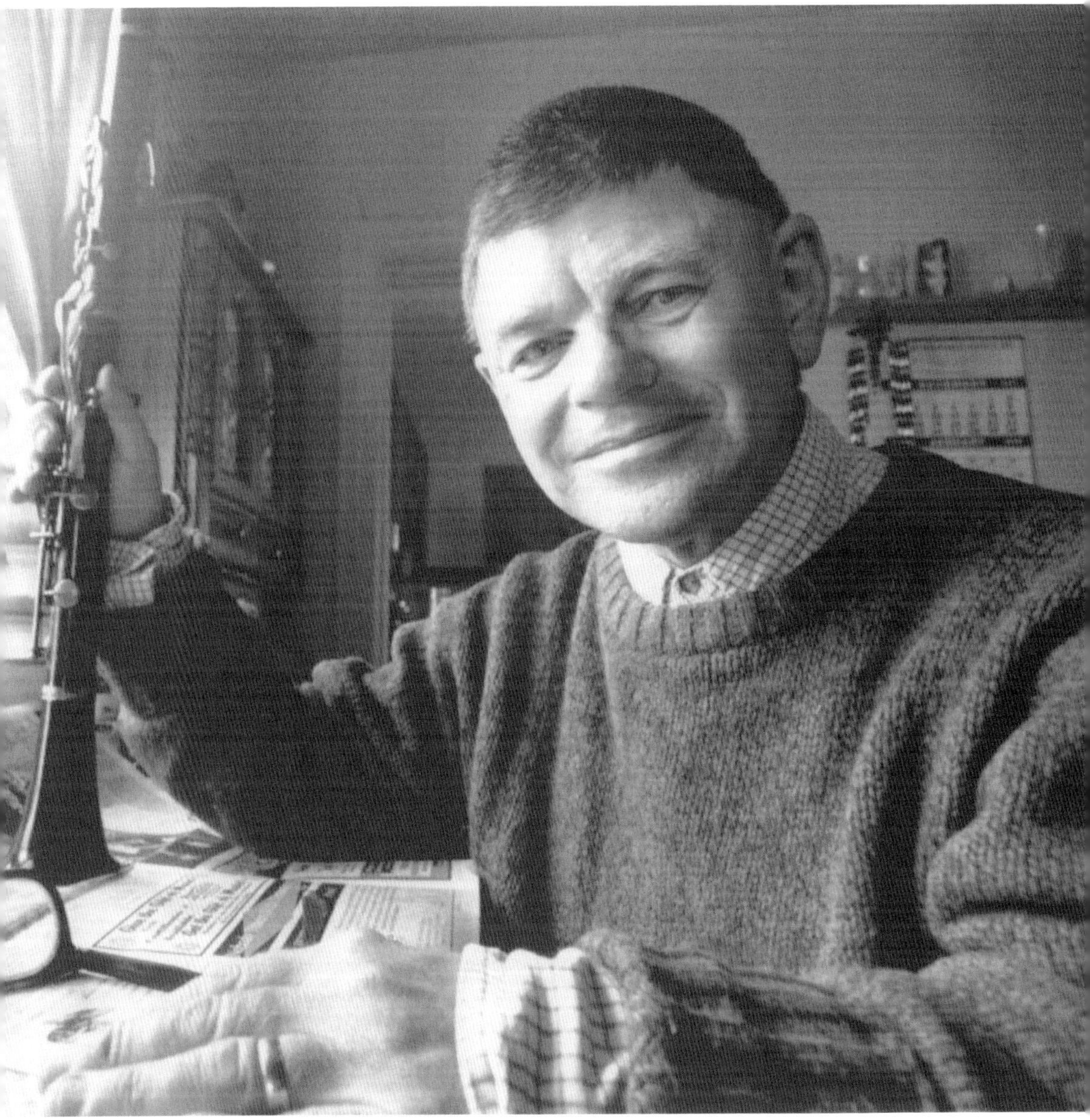

**The Clarinet Man**

Richard Haupt (1937–1997), also known as "The Clarinet Man," spent a good part of the 1980s and 1990s playing his clarinet for tips on Church Street, in all kinds of weather. Haupt had a limited repertoire, so he played the same tunes over and over again. This sometimes drove local merchants and downtown regulars to distraction, but for many, Haupt was a popular Burlington fixture. In May 1997, he moved to New Orleans to fulfill his lifetime dream of playing his clarinet in that fabled music town. He died of a massive heart attack two months later. Local author Philip Baruth may have described him best: "Richard Haupt was not afflicted with the disease of our time, the disease of professionalism. Richard was an amateur, and he played his clarinet for the love of it." (Courtesy of Matt Thorsen.)

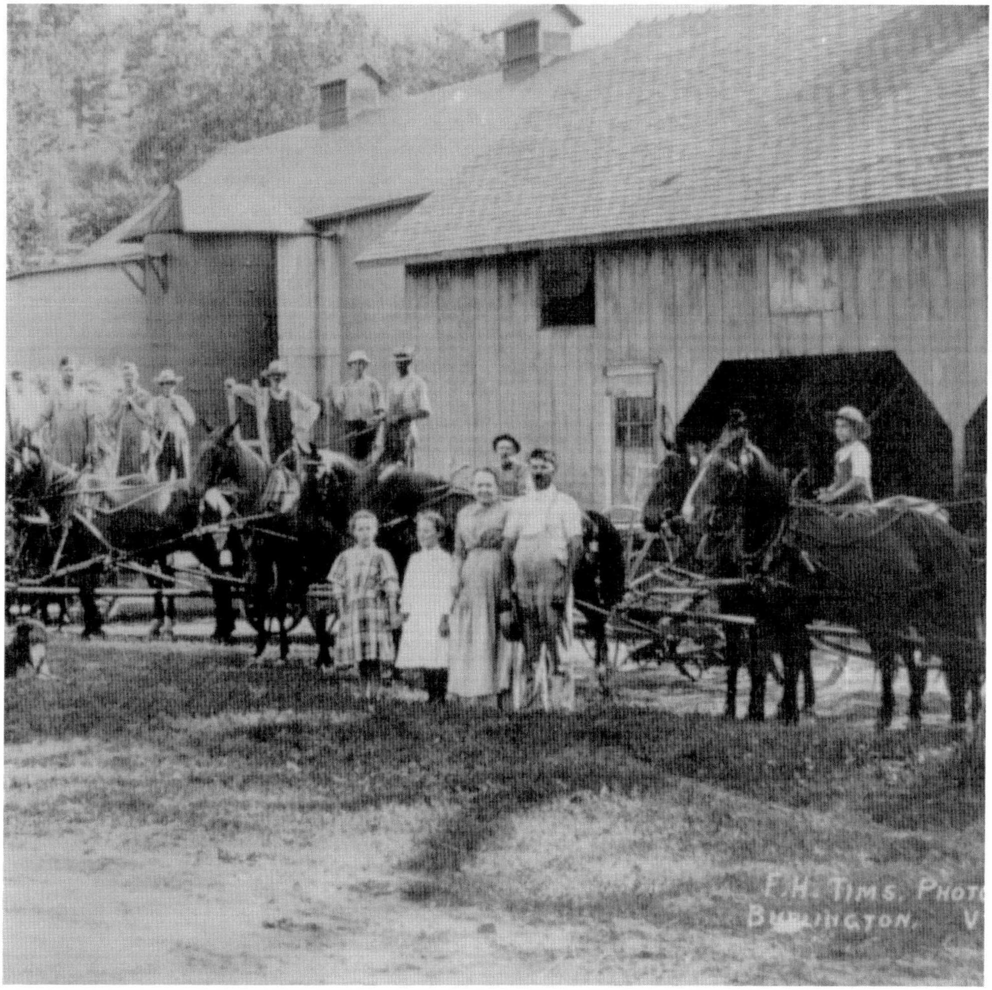


**Rena Calkins**

The life of Rena Calkins (1900–1996) was inextricably tied to Burlington's Intervale, a large tract of prime bottomland along the Burlington side of the Winooski River. Her family purchased land in the Intervale in 1904, and she operated the family farm for decades until she suffered a stroke at the age of 91. Anyone who spent time in the Intervale during the second half of the 20th century would sooner or later have encountered Calkins and her hired hands, driving her cows out to the far end of the cornfields in the morning and bringing them back in at milking time. Her death signified the end of an era—she had the last operating dairy farm in the City of Burlington.

Happily, farming was not gone forever from Burlington. In the last 20 years, the Intervale has undergone a slow renaissance thanks to an effort to restore the land to its agricultural roots by Will Raap (see page 66) and the Intervale Center, a foundation that launched the Farms Program to help small farmers. In 2012, the Intervale Center succeeded in raising $400,000 in order to rebuild the Calkins Dairy Barn in early 2013. The Rena Calkins Trail circles the Intervale Center and passes very close to the Winooski River, crossing land that Rena Calkins no doubt knew very well. She is pictured in the checked dress on her family farm in the Intervale around 1910. (Courtesy of Gardener's Supply.)

# INDEX